Blessings and Woes

*The Beatitudes and the Sermon on the Plain
in the Gospel of Luke*

Megan McKenna

ORBIS BOOKS

Maryknoll, New York 10545

Third printing, July 2001

The Catholic Foreign Mission Society of America (Maryknoll) recruits and trains people for overseas missionary service. Through Orbis Books, Maryknoll aims to foster the international dialogue that is essential to mission. The books published, however, reflect the opinions of their authors and are not meant to represent the official position of the society.

Published by Orbis Books, Maryknoll, NY 10545-0308
Manufactured in the United States of America

Scripture quotations are from the *Christian Community Bible*, 17th edition, (Claretian Publications, 1995).

Library of Congress Cataloging-in-Publication Data

McKenna, Megan.
    Blessings and woes : the Beatitudes and the Sermon on the plain in the gospel of Luke / Megan McKenna.
      p.   cm.
    Includes bibliographical references.
    ISBN 1-57075-221-4 (pbk.)
    1. Beatitudes. 2. Bible. N.T. Luke VI, 20-26—Criticism, interpretation, etc.   I. Title.
BT382.M386   1999
241.5′3—dc21   98-27151

I bless the Lord for the justice and mercy of your lives.
May your name be a blessing.

Rutillo Grande, S.J.
Ignacio Ellacuría, S.J.

Daniel Berrigan, S.J.
John Dear, S.J.
William Hart McNichols, S.J.

Phyllis J.

Contents

Introduction

*From age to age his mercy extends to those who
live in his presence. (Luke 1:50)*

In the course of writing this book I discovered a series of
stories by Daniel Rhodes, called the "Legends of Ahimsa."
The stories, which were photocopies someone had given me,
have haunted me and seeped into my understanding of the
beatitudes and woes, of the poor and those not as fortunate
who are wealthy and esteemed by the world.

This story is short and goes right to the heart of things.

✳ Once upon a time the Master returned from the market
where he had sold all but one of his pots. The day had
been a great success, and the left-over pot was discarded
and put under the table in the workroom. But the next
morning his students noticed that a new pot had been
added to the shelves where prized pieces were displayed.
These were pots and vases, bowls and plates that were literally priceless, first of show and one of a kind. The discarded pot now reigned with these exquisite pieces.

The students were puzzled. "Why, Master? Yesterday
it was the piece under the table in the workroom, the one
no one thought enough of to buy at the craft fair."

"Exactly," said the Master. "I want you to study it
carefully—its form, glaze, style, firing effects—and know
it intimately. It is now the new standard for all our work.
Contemplate it and enter its empty space and penetrate
its mystery."

It seems that even what is not immediately wanted or val-
ued can be worthwhile. The beatitudes and woes of Luke's
gospel begin with what is discarded and disdained by the
world but immediately searched out and discovered by our
God in Jesus. Obviously, there is something that is not immediately apparent to those of us whose gaze is not steeped in
grace and mercy, whose hearts are not tuned to compassion
and salvation. We who live on the surface of reality miss that
which is more elusive and more deeply seeded in some of the
people that the Maker of all things has touched. Being disciples of Jesus, the servant of Yahweh who carries the mark of
Isaiah in his flesh, must entail having the veil lifted from our
eyes and souls so that the glory hidden in unlikely places and
faces can be revealed to us.

Luke's blessings and lamentations never cease to catch us
off guard and unawares. They must have had the same effect
on those who heard Jesus' strong defense of the poor, those
suffering terribly and further humiliated by other human beings who considered them worthless, sinners, and despised
even by God. When he spoke with equally forceful words
about the wealthy and respected, the well-fed and well-
thought-of, and warned that they were really the unfortunate
ones in dire danger because of their situation, his hearers
must have gasped with disbelief and wondered about his san-
ity. And, of course, when they realized Jesus was both deadly
serious and intent on getting others to listen to him, when
they understood that he was speaking as a prophet and defending the covenant, they were equally intent on resisting
him with all the force of their position, power, and investment
in the society that he critiqued.

These words, both blessings and woes, are primarily about
conversion. They are about seeing as God sees, not through
rose-colored glasses but in the light of God's kingdom that
emerges in the world as a vibrant force to be reckoned with in
the person of Jesus, in his words and actions and prayers, and
in the community that takes his point of view to heart. The
words of blessing and woe are born of compassion. They are
the words of the healer Jesus, bent low over people in pain,
those broken in body and mind, the economically and socially

condemned and religiously scorned. This was his place, as servant, close to the ground. Here he could speak with the poor, humbly telling them that this is where God is, close to the ground and to their hearts that were mourning and hungry for love, for human dignity and liberation from the burdens that other humans had laid on them. And it was as servant that he would take his last stand, hung from the cross, nailed to the evil that we can do to one another when we resist truth and imprison ourselves in our own kingdoms based on selfishness, greed, insensitivity, and violence. If we are to follow this servant who suffers because the pain of others seeps into his own soul and marks his own flesh, then we must learn how to bless and how to lament, how to rejoice exceedingly with those in need of hope and how to confront those who are trampling the rights of others and breaking the backs of those already bent double. These statements of blessing and woe are about standing straight and giving praise and thanks to God for liberation and freedom; they are about standing up to the hard-heartedness of the world that spits in the face of those who are lowly or deemed unworthy of the fullness of life.

At their core, the blessings and woes are about mercy, about God's forgiveness and hope for us who are unfaithful, small-minded, selfish, and often evil. The prophet Isaiah sings of the goodness of God over and over again to a people who have forgotten. The songs are always about mercy and blessings, about Israel's experience with Yahweh and what they have ignored or cast off.

> I will sing in praise of Yahweh and recall his kindness, according to all that he has done for us, his great goodness to the family of Israel. He has granted us mercy in the abundance of his blessings.
>
> For he said: "Surely they are my people, sons who will not be disloyal." So he proved himself their Savior in all their trials.
>
> It was not a messenger or an angel but he himself who delivered them. Out of his love and mercy, he redeemed them, lifting them up and carrying them throughout the days of old.

Yet they rebelled, giving grief to his holy Spirit.
(Isaiah 63:7-10a)

This is the tradition, the memory, and the reality of God's relationship in covenant with his own people. God redeems them, yet their unfaithfulness, disobedience, and disregard of promises form a continual refrain. From the beginning, this God of ours both blesses and laments over us. The prophets return again and again to their cry for conversion, for remembrance of the poor in the land, for a turning to God in true worship that brings forth justice so that the people of God are a light to the nations. And promises of more blessings abound.

> When at last the spirit is poured on us from on high, then will the desert become a garden, and this garden will be free as a fallow land.
>
> Justice will dwell in the wilderness; and in the fertile land, righteousness. Justice will bring about peace; justice will produce calm and security forever.
>
> My people will live in comfort and bliss in a land of secure dwellings and undisturbed resting places. While the forest will be beaten down and the fortress laid waste.
>
> How blessed you will be, sowing by every stream, letting your work animals roam contented and free. (Isaiah 32:15-20)

And what follows is a chapter of woes! Announcements of blessing and denouncements of lamentation go hand in hand throughout the history of the people bound to God. As prophet and Word of God in flesh among us, Jesus picks up the same pattern. He connects the descriptions of justice and blessing to the kingdom of God that comes with his presence. The first to receive the good news and the invitation are the poor. But all are invited in, even those who resist. And God, now in Jesus, laments and warns, cajoles and threatens, beseeches and tells stories, all with the intention of breaking the hard hearts of those who will not hear or believe.

The message takes on intensity because no longer does the word of the Lord come from a prophet's mouth; the Word of the Lord is a person, poor, come as a servant who will suffer with all those who live in a world where the people of God choose death and not life, evil and not good, sin and not mercy or salvation. The prayers and hopes of the people, first found in the mouth of David the king, are now heard in the person of Jesus. Long had Israel and the faithful of Yahweh waited for the king of peace, "he who will do justice for the humble. The expectation of universal peace after so much obstinacy in murdering one another" as the introductory notes to Psalm 72 (71) read in the *Christian Community Bible*. We sing:

> O God, endow the king with your justice,
> the royal son with your righteousness.
> May he rule your people justly
> and defend the rights of the lowly.
>
> Let the mountains bring peace to the people,
> and the hills justice.
> He will defend the cause of the poor,
> deliver the children of the needy,
> and crush the oppressor....
>
> Justice will flower in his days,
> and peace abound till the moon be no more....
>
> He delivers the needy who call on him,
> the afflicted with no one to help them.
> His mercy is upon the weak and the poor,
> he saves the life of the poor.
> He rescues them from oppression and strife,
> for their life is precious to him....
>
> Praised be the Lord, God of Israel,
> who alone works so marvelously.
> Praised be his glorious name forever;
> may the whole earth be filled with his glory!

Amen. Amen.
This concludes the prayers
of David, son of Jesse.
   (Psalm 72:1-4, 7, 12-14, 18-20)

This too is the heart and soul of Jesus' message, especially as it is articulated in the blessings and woes that form the foundation of the Sermon on the Plain in Luke's gospel. In her marvelous book, *There Shall Be No Poor Among You: Essays in Lukan Theology* (Quezon City, Philippines: JMC Press, Inc., 1978), Maryknoll Sister Helen R. Graham speaks of the basic meaning of "poor":

> The word which Luke uses for poor (*ptochos*) trans-lates a Hebrew word (*'ani*) which, in its developed sense,... describes the abject poverty of one who is to-tally destitute.... the antonym for this particular He-brew word for poor (*'ani*) is not, as would be expect-ed, "rich," but rather "violent," thus giving an insight into its original derivation and meaning.... Here it is clear that in opposition to "the poor," "the needy" and "the weak" [are] "oppression" and "violence."
> (pp. 6-7)

Helen Graham goes on to cite references to the royal psalms: 2, 18, 20, 21, 72, 101, 110, 132, and 144, as well as refer-ences to the prophets: Isaiah 53:9 and Micah 6:12. Micah sim-ply puts it: "[Your] rich are full of violence." This is of crucial importance when reading the text of Luke and interpreting the meaning of Jesus' words for us today. In the introduction to her book Helen Graham writes :

> Notions like colonialism, multi-nationals, trilateral-ism, institutionalized structural violence, and the ide-ology of the national security state, etc. did not exist in Luke's day. But the biblical tradition is conscious of what we would today call "social sin" and records for us consistent strong prophetic denunciation of such situations which exist today in much more complex

forms. Luke, who saw Jesus in terms of the prophet promised in the book of Deuteronomy (Dt. 18:15), devotes much space in his gospel to Jesus' prophetic critique of riches which he regards as "money of injustice" (Lk. 16:9) and his predilection for the poor as those to whom the Good News of the Kingdom is proclaimed. (p. viii)

Helen Graham wrote more than two decades ago from Asia, responding to the call of the bishops to listen to the poor, to listen to the gospel through the lives of the poor, and to seek a way of proclaiming this as Good News. Twenty years later we stand in the United States, a dominant pinnacle of power, looking down on a good deal of the world that is poorer than it was then. Again in our times Jesus the prophet cries out from every plain in every country where the church finds itself close to the ground, tending to the victims of misery, violence, and injustice brought about by personal sin, collusion with evil, structural violence, and social sin. The words ring out the ancient promise of the mercy of our God and elicit either hope or resistance.

We stand too at the end of two thousand years of Christianity, on the edge of the third millennium, contemplating "a year of favor from the Lord" as a way to worship God publicly and be called once again to conversion, to discipleship in Jesus' kingdom of God. It is time for us to choose. May we choose, as did Luke's community, to stand together. Like Mary in the hills of Judah, may we commit ourselves to making Jesus' words come true. Perhaps if we say them enough, sing them often enough, they will take flesh in us and we will know in our own hearts the first beatitude, the first blessing of Luke's gospel: "Blessed are you who believed that the Lord's word would come true!" And Mary said:

My soul proclaims the greatness of the Lord,
my spirit exults in God my savior!
He has looked upon his servant in her lowliness,
and people forever will call me blessed.
The Mighty One has done great things for me,

Holy is his Name!
From age to age his mercy extends
to those who live in his presence.
He has acted with power and done wonders,
and scattered the proud with their plans.
He has put down the mighty from their thrones
and lifted up those who are downtrodden.
He has filled the hungry with good things
but has sent the rich away empty.
He held out his hand to Israel, his servant,
for he remembered his mercy,
even as he promised our fathers,
Abraham and his descendants forever.
  (Luke 1:46-55)

Our God holds out his hand to us, his servants, for he remembers his mercy. May we grasp hold of that hand and the hands of the poor stretched out to God and together bring blessing upon the earth like rain, like hope, like mercy that sings and sets us all free. Amen. Blessed be the Holy Mystery of God forever in those who believe in the Lord's word. Amen. Amen.

1

Blessings

A blessing is the visible, perceptible, effective proximity of God. A blessing demands to be passed on—it communicates itself to other people. To be blessed is to be oneself a blessing. (Dietrich Bonhoeffer)

In the musical *Fiddler on the Roof*, the Russian Jewish peasant Tevea sings of life—glorious, hard, demanding, ordinary life—using the image of the fiddler dancing and playing on the steep roof of a village house. He must remember to keep his balance, to keep playing and, of course, to remember the tune. It isn't easy, but sometimes the music carries and lifts him. He is something to behold, this fiddler on the roof, this Jew in the world. And in the course of the song, Tevea sings a blessing on his family, on his neighbors, even on the tsar—that the tsar be kept far away from the village! It is a moment of laughter in a serious presentation of life, a lighthearted prayer in the midst of beseeching the Holy One's blessings on the world, on the Jews, and on all that rubs shoulders with them, good and not-so-good. And his prayer too is a blessing: a blessing of God, a giving thanks for life and all that life entails, both what is easily grasped as worthwhile and what is harder to take hold of with gratitude.

Many of the ancient Jewish psalms begin with this image of blessing, of being blessed and of praising someone who is a blessing. Psalm 34 (33) begins with such exaltation:

I will bless the Lord all my days;
his praise will be ever on my lips.
My soul makes its boast in the Lord;
let the lowly hear and rejoice.

Oh, let us magnify the Lord,
together let us glorify his name!
I sought the Lord, and he answered me;
from all my fears he delivered me.

They who look to him are radiant with joy,
their faces never clouded with shame.
        (Psalm 34:1-6)

This psalm and so many others sing of relationship and of the intimate care and high expectations of one who is blessed by God and so blesses in return. The source of the blessings overflows and the one who receives gives back from the plenitude.

This sense of blessing extends into many cultures. The Celtic Isles are rich with blessings: for travelers, friends, the dead, guests, cows, the hearth, the coming of dawn and dusk, the stars, one's family, just about everything and everyone. Here is one that I have heard and received often on greeting cards and even had sung to me after a few pints in a pub:

An Irish Blessing

May you have many friends
And may they be as mature in taste and health
and color
and sought after
as the contents of this glass.

May you have warm words on a cold evening
A full moon on a dark night
And the road downhill all the way to your door.

May every hair on your head turn into a candle
To light your way to heaven,
And may God and his Holy Mother
Take the harm of the years away from you.

And may you have no frost on your spuds
no worms on your cabbage.
May your goat give plenty of milk
And if you should buy a donkey
Please, God, she be pregnant!

Again, the blessing mixes the frivolous and the near irreverent with the sublime and the pure, drawing heaven and earth close and magnifying the simple graces of life alongside the eternal hopes of hereafter. I have no goat, nor need of a donkey, pregnant or otherwise, but the sentiments are clear enough. May my life be amply rich and blessed with excess of what really makes for a life—a blessing.

A blessing: a beatitude, a prayer, a cry of joy, a description of reality present and to be fervently expected, an expression of life that at its fullest is a startling reminder of eternity, an acknowledgment of innate goodness and well-being, an affirmation that draws us into a charmed and intimate circle of people, the telling of a truth that honors our deepest realities. Even Jesus is blessed in such a manner. In the very first chapter of Mark we are told the story:

At that time Jesus came from Nazareth, a town of Galilee, and was baptized by John in the Jordan. And the moment he came up out of the water, Heaven opened before him and he saw the Spirit coming down on him like a dove. And these words were heard from Heaven, "You are my Son, the Beloved, the One I have chosen." (Mark 1:9-11)

Many other translations say: "This is my Beloved, on whom my favor rests." It is clear that this is a blessing, a testimony to love and to an existing relationship, an affirmation of belonging, the telling of a deep-seated truth that reveals the essence and meaning of who this person really is.

In the beginning of Luke's gospel this truth is told of Mary, the mother of the long-awaited one. She finds the Angel Gabriel's greeting and explanation a bit disconcerting, because she does not see herself in such a light. Luke writes of it this way:

> The angel came to her and said, "Rejoice, full of grace, the Lord is with you." Mary was troubled at these words, wondering what this greeting could mean.
> But the angel said, "Do not fear, Mary, for God has looked kindly on you." (Luke 1:28-30)

In other translations it reads "you have found favor with God." This blessing, this state of being, is conveyed by a glance from God. It gives favor, grace, and attention—singular attention from the Holy. It is a singling out, a pointing out of someone who hasn't been noticed or appreciated before. It seems too that people who receive such a blessing have been unaware of their favored status and position before God. In Mary's case, acknowledgment of the blessing takes the shape of a further acknowledgment: "I am the handmaid of the Lord, let it be done to me as you have said" (Lk 1:38). The blessing in words grows and becomes fruitful. In this case, it gives birth to a child who is a blessing, the long-awaited blessing of the nations.

Later in Luke's gospel, Joseph and Mary bring the newborn child to the temple to consecrate him to the Lord in accordance with the law. They are met by Simeon who rejoices at the sight of them in the temple. The time of the promise, of the blessing of God, is at hand. Simeon is described as "a very upright and devout man. . . . the Holy Spirit was in him. He looked forward to the time when the Lord would comfort Israel, and he had been assured by the Holy Spirit that he would not die before seeing the Messiah of the Lord" (Lk 2:25-26).

This blessing of God, this child, would be a comfort to Israel. In Simeon's words, blessing the goodness of God who keeps his promises, this child would be "a light you will reveal to the nations and the glory of your people Israel" (Lk 2:32).

This was the promise, the long foretold blessing to come:

Be comforted, my people,
be strengthened, says your God.
Speak to the heart of Jerusalem, proclaim to her
that her time of bondage is at an end,
that her guilt has been paid for,
that from the hand of Yahweh
she has received double punishment
for all her iniquity.
    (Isaiah 40:1-2)

These famous lines are quoted and sung during Advent and the season of Christmas: "Comfort ye, comfort ye, my people," we hear in Handel's *Messiah* and in numerous regional carols. A blessing, a beatitude, is a comfort. It may be long in coming, but it is promised and so it will become a reality. Those who believe stake their lives on the blessing and wrap their daily hopes and prayers around it. Because it is the Word of the Lord, it is reliable and it will come true, often in ways that are unexpected or startling.

The word blessing comes from the Latin root word *benedicere*, to speak well of, but this means more than just a compliment or a kind-hearted word. It points back to the source, to the ultimate goodness of the one who made us and keeps us all in existence, re-creating us moment to moment, keeping us in mind and heart. In our tradition, that takes us back to Genesis, to the stories of our beginnings and the meaning encapsulated in God's words repeated at the end of each day's work: "God saw all that he had made, and it was very good" (Gen 1:31). It is also expressed in the favor of God that Mary knew in the announcement of Gabriel and that Jesus heard from the mouth of God: "You are my Beloved, on you my favor rests." This is a blessing, a speaking well of, a delight in, a pronouncement of goodness.

Blessing is almost second nature to many of us. Every liturgy, many prayers, and times of departing from family and friends end with the simple, profound words "I bless you in the name of the Father, and of the Son and of the Holy Spirit." We trace or have had traced and etched upon us the sign of the cross, the marking of the presence and blessing of God upon our lives, our bodies, and our journeys. We pass on the blessing, and we carry with us the holiness and care of God, the love of others, and the remembrance of who we most truly are. The blessing tells the truth about us and we bend to it deep within. It is a gesture and prayer that respects our natures, our essences, and what we are to become as creations of the Holy One.

There is an Islamic story told of Hazrati Ali, a close friend and companion of Muhammad. He was a Sufi, one of the friends of God, intimate with the Beloved and with those who followed the path of ecstatic love of God. It is a custom among the Sufi to kiss the tea glass from which they drink and the hem of garments in which they dance, to show respect as often and as graciously as they can to all creation.

✱   Once upon a time Hazrati Ali's friend Muhammad was about to begin the prayers. He was anxiously looking about for his friend Ali, who hadn't yet come. It was very unlike his friend to be late, so devoted to the prayers as he was. Muhammad fidgeted about but then knew he must start.

Just then, the Angel Gabriel appeared and held him back, asking him to wait just a little bit longer—his friend would soon arrive. Ali, who had been hurrying to get to the mosque on time had fallen in behind an old Jewish man, moving very slowly, crippled and bent. Out of respect for the old man, Ali did not want to pass him up on the street. And Allah, the Most Compassionate One, did not want Ali to miss the first blessing and prostration of the day, so he sent the Archangel Gabriel to delay the beginning of the prayers.

This short story is full of blessings: Ali blessing the old man whom he followed in respect and humility, the first prayers and prostrations of the day, and the coming of the angel on behalf of another's soul, acknowledging that one blessing is rewarded by another, and another, and another. There are, it seems, no limits to blessings.

This is apparent in the psalms. The very first psalm begins with a blessing, a beatitude.

> Blessed is the one
> who does not go where the wicked gather,
> or stand in the way of sinners,
> or sit where the scoffers sit;
> instead, he finds delight in the law of the Lord
> and meditates day and night
> on his commandments.
> He is like a tree beside a brook
> producing its fruit in due season,
> its leaves never withering.
> Everything he does is a success.
> But it is different with the wicked.
> They are like chaff
> driven away by the wind.
> The wicked will not stand when judgment comes,
> nor the sinners when the righteous assemble.
> For the Lord knows the way of the righteous
> but cuts off the way of the wicked.
> (Psalm 1)

Psalm 1 is sometimes referred to as the "psalm of the two ways": the way of the righteous and the way of the sinner, the way of blessing and the way of woe, the way of beatitude and the way of evil and destruction. This theme is found throughout the earlier and older Testament. Moses brings the people to the edge of the promised land and confronts them with a choice. He describes the responsibilities and consequences of their choice, in word and deed, for themselves and for future generations.

> See, I set before you on this day life and good, evil and death. I command you to love Yahweh, your

God, and follow his ways. Observe his commandments, his norms and his laws, and you will live and
increase, and Yahweh will give you his blessing in the
land you are going to possess. But if your heart turns
away and does not listen, if you are drawn away and
bow before other gods to serve them, I declare on this
day that you shall perish. You shall not last in the
land you are going to occupy on the other side of the
Jordan.

Let the heavens and the earth listen, that they
may be witnesses against you. I have set before you
life and death, blessing and curse. Therefore, choose
life that you and your descendants may live, loving
Yahweh, listening to his voice, and being one with
him. In this is life for you and length of days in the
land which Yahweh swore to give your fathers, to
Abraham, Isaac and Jacob. (Deuteronomy 30:15-20)

And just a few chapters later, at the end of the book of
Deuteronomy, Moses declares to the people what life will be
like for them if they honor this choice. The terminology is the
same as that used by Jesus in the beatitudes:

Happy are you, O Israel! Who is like you, a people
saved by Yahweh? He is the shield that protects you,
the sword that gives you victory! Your enemies shall
flee from you, but you, you are outstanding in everything. (Deuteronomy 33:29)

Chapter 33 consists mainly of Moses' blessings of each of
the tribes of Israel, culminating in a litany of the blessings that
Yahweh has lavished on his chosen people. Yahweh will continue to bless his people if they continue to choose life as revealed in the law, another blessing that he has shared with
them. The same words will be in the mouth of the prophet Jeremiah generations later when Israel betrays its covenant with
God. This time the words will force the people to choose their
fate in the midst of battle and siege. Again it is clear. They
must choose.

And you will say to the people, "This is what Yahweh says: See, I place before you the way of life and the way of death. Whoever stays in the city will die either by the sword, famine or plague; those who go out and surrender to the Chaldeans who are besieging the city, will live and will be the only ones to be saved." (Jeremiah 21:8-9)

In the New Testament Jesus' words will echo these ancient ones.

Enter through the narrow gate; for wide is the gate and broad is the road that leads to destruction, and many go that way. How narrow is the gate that leads to life and how rough the road; few there are who find it. (Matthew 7:13-14)

In the early church, at the beginning of the baptismal rituals catechumens were asked to choose: life or death, the way of truth and salvation or the way of inequity and destruction. They first stood facing the west and listened with regret and horror to what their old way of life had looked like; they then turned toward the east and listened with hope and resolution to what their new way of life in Christ would now look like to others. They heard the proclamation of the last portion of Paul's letter to Galatians describing the way of the flesh and the way of the Spirit. Once they had made their choice, the ritual of baptism began.

The psalter's opening psalm, the psalm of the two ways, the first line of which is a beatitude ("Blessed is the one who does not go where the wicked gather, or stand in the way of sinners, or sit where the scoffers sit; instead, he finds delight in the law of the Lord and meditates day and night on his commandments" [Ps 1:1-2]), exhorts those who use the 149 psalms that follow to pray and to live in this attitude. And they will know the blessing of God, the promise of ever-lasting life, of growth and fruition, of wholeness in the presence of God; they will be like a fruitful tree whose leaves never wither. Those who do not meditate on the law of the Lord day and night, and who find no delight in the commandments of God will know the opposite: woe, a fleeting life, and failure, for in the end they will fall before the judgment of God. These are the two ways: the way of the righteous and the holy and the way of the wicked and the doomed, each by their own choice.

Psalms 112, 127, 128, 144 and others speak of God's blessings in specific terms: Psalm 112 describes the blessings of one who fears the Lord (its source is found in Sirach 25:7-11). This psalm contains themes that are picked up and expanded on in the New Testament.

> Alleluia!
> Blessed is the one who fears the Lord,
> who greatly delights in his commands.
> His children will be powerful on earth;
> the upright's offspring will be blessed.
>
> Wealth and riches are for his family,
> there his integrity will remain.
> He is for the righteous a light in darkness,
> he is kind, merciful and upright.
>
> It will be well with him who lends freely,
> who leads a life of justice and honesty.
> For the righteous will never be moved;
> he will be remembered and loved forever.
>
> He has no fear of evil news,
> for his heart is firm, trusting in the Lord.
> His heart is confident, he need not fear,
> he shall prevail over his foes at the end.
>
> He gives generously to the poor,
> his merits will last forever
> and his head will be raised in honor.
> The wicked will see and be furious:
> they will gnash their teeth in seething envy.
> The evil man's desires will fail.
>   (Psalm 112)

To read the psalms and selections from Sirach, Proverbs, and the prophets is to find myriad blessings that accompany the behavior of those who follow the way of the just. Their lives bless God in words and deeds and God, in turn, continues to bless them abundantly, and their children, and their children's children. The blessings are real and pragmatic; they are also promises of life beyond life in the generations to follow.

These blessings, like all religious blessings, including the beatitudes of Jesus, assert a religious truth about the proximity of God to specific people. They are a confrontational sort of truth-telling, asserting God's judgment on behavior. And they are congratulations, affirming certain people and their actions and style of life, encouraging them to hold fast in spite of the world and its reactions to them, and holding them up as examples to others. They seek to persuade the reader or listener or observer to do the same, to imitate them, and proclaim that these are values that a group or a community should adhere to and practice publicly.

The blessings also declare or hint at eventual judgment, at either blessedness or dire consequences that will follow from choices made now. They announce who is related to God and who is separated from God. As blessings, the beatitudes are an exhortation, shouting that the center of gravity in the world has shifted and that these people hold the key to the future, surprising as that may sound. For Jesus, the beatitudes are a forthright proclamation that his Father's kingdom is present in these people, available for all to see, and respect, and join—or else! For there is also a trace of judgment, and a warning about the consequences of not choosing. The beatitudes are different ways of shouting: Repent! They are about getting us to do something now.

The beatitudes have been variously translated as "blessed are they...happy are you...fortunate are you..." and so on. The word in Greek is *makarismos*, a noun that connotes being on the receiving end of divine action. And this divine action is prompted by a behavior and a condition of being as a people.

There are traditionally two kinds of beatitudes in the Bible. The first are the wisdom beatitudes that focus on the behavior and attitudes of a person or a group here and now. The second are apocalyptic in nature, focusing on behavior and attitudes that will be rewarded when God, in judgment and in justice, intervenes in the future of humankind's history.

One of the earliest of the apocalyptic beatitudes is found in the book of Daniel. Daniel is told to leave the future in the hands of God. He is told that the holy ones will be "purified, cleansed and proved. The impious will go on doing evil, [but] none of them will understand anything, only the learned will understand" (12:10). Then the message is stated boldly:

> Fortunate is the one who waits and reaches a thousand three hundred thirty-five days. And you, go your way until your end. You shall rest and then rise to receive your reward at the end of time. (Daniel 12:12-13)

The theme of "wickedness that will go on increasing" (Dan 12:4) is juxtaposed with promises of glorious vindication and hope, of righting the wrongs and balancing what is unjust in the presence of all peoples.

> Then all those whose names are written in the Book will be saved. Many of those who sleep in the Region of the Dust will awake, some to everlasting life but others to eternal horror and shame. Those who acquired knowledge will shine like the brilliance of the firmament; those who taught people to be just will shine like the stars for all eternity. (Daniel 12:1b-3)

Both kinds of beatitudes acknowledge as blessed, both now and in the times to come, the person or group who seeks to do the will of the Lord, obeys his commandments, and acts justly. This state of blessedness will be known in its fullness by all one day. There are at least forty-four New Testament beatitudes, most apocalyptic in some regard, like the clear one found in James 1:12: "Happy the one who patiently endures trials, because afterwards he will receive the crown of life which the Lord promised to those who love him."

The most famous beatitudes, of course, are the eight found in Matthew's Sermon on the Mount:

> Fortunate are those who have the spirit of the poor, for theirs is the kingdom of Heaven.
> Fortunate are those who mourn, they shall be comforted.
> Fortunate are the gentle, they shall possess the land.
> Fortunate are those who hunger and thirst for justice, for they shall be satisfied.
> Fortunate are the merciful, for they shall find mercy.
> Fortunate are those with a pure heart, for they shall see God.
> Fortunate are those who work for peace, they shall be called children of God.
> Fortunate are those who are persecuted for the cause of justice, for theirs is the kingdom of Heaven.
> Fortunate are you, when people insult you and persecute you and speak all kinds of evil against you because you are my followers. Be glad and joyful, for a great reward is kept for you in God. This is how this people persecuted the prophets who lived before you. (Matthew 5:3-12)

This is the version that is perhaps best known, though it is commonly agreed among theologians and exegetes that the blessings and woes found in Luke's Sermon on the Plain are an earlier version.

> Fortunate are you who are poor, the kingdom of God is yours.
> Fortunate are you who are hungry now, for you will be filled.
> Fortunate are you who weep now, for you will laugh.
> Fortunate are you when people hate you, when they reject you and insult you and number you among

> criminals, because of the Son of Man. Rejoice in
> that day and leap for joy, for a great reward is
> kept for you in Heaven. Remember that is how
> the fathers of this people treated the prophets.
> But alas for you who have wealth, for you have been
> comforted now.
> Alas for you who are full, for you will go hungry.
> Alas for you who laugh now, for you will mourn and
> weep.
> Alas for you when the people speak well of you, for
> that is how the fathers of these people treated the
> false prophets. (Luke 6:20b-26)

In this book we will focus on Luke's version of blessings
and woes as normative and on Matthew's version as exten-
sions of certain beatitudes. The blessings and woes have so
much depth and latitude, so many layers of meaning that are
unveiled throughout the gospel of Luke, especially in the
parables. Even the meaning of the word *beatitude* is rich and
complex when seen from different perspectives. In Elias Cha-
cour's book, written with Mary E. Jensen, called *We Belong to
the Land* (San Francisco: Harper, 1990) there is a marvelous
description of a beatitude that enhances our understanding
of what Jesus means when he says "blessed are you."

> Knowing Aramaic, the language of Jesus, has greatly
> enriched my understanding of Jesus' teaching. Be-
> cause the Bible as we know it is a translation of a
> translation, we sometimes get a wrong impression.
> For example, we are accustomed to hearing the Beati-
> tudes expressed passively:
> Blessed are those who hunger and thirst for jus-
> tice, for they shall be satisfied.
> Blessed are the merciful, for they shall obtain
> mercy.
> Blessed are the pure in heart, for they shall see
> God.
> Blessed are the peacemakers, for they shall be
> called children of God.

"Blessed" is the translation of the word *makarioi*, used in the Greek New Testament. However, when I look further back to Jesus' Aramaic, I find that the original word was *ashray*, from the verb *yashar*. *Ashray* does not have this passive quality to it at all. Instead, it means "to set yourself on the right way for the right goal; to turn around, repent; to become straight or righteous."

How could I go to a persecuted young man in a Palestinian refugee camp, for instance, and say, "Blessed are those who mourn, for they shall be comforted," or "Blessed are those who are persecuted for the sake of justice, for theirs is the kingdom of heaven"? That man would revile me, saying neither I nor my God understood his plight and he would be right.

When I understand Jesus' words in Aramaic, I translate like this: "Get up, go ahead, do something, move, you who are hungry and thirsty for justice, for you shall be satisfied. Get up, go ahead, do something, move, you peacemakers, for you shall be called children of God."

To me this reflects Jesus' words and teachings much more accurately. I can hear him saying: "Get your hands dirty to build a human society for human beings; otherwise, others will torture and murder the poor, the voiceless, and the powerless." Christianity is not passive but active, energetic, alive, going beyond despair.

"Get up, go ahead, do something, move," Jesus said to his disciples. (pp. 143-44)

In this sense the beatitudes mean deeper mercy for those who experience more divisive misery, deeper blessings for those whose hope is dimmest. They give an ultimate authority to certain people and their plight in the world. They signify not just a religious attitude, but a social attitude toward realities that should not exist among humans.

Jim Forest, who lives in Alkmaar, Holland, and is the secretary of the Orthodox Peace Fellowship, once asked biblical scholar Rabbi Steven Schwarzchild how to translate the word: *blessed.* His answer was: "There is no one word that will do. It is something like 'on the right path,' 'on the way the Creator wants us to go.' It is the opposite of the word for sin, which means 'losing your way' " (from "Climb the Ladder of the Beatitudes," by Jim Forest, *Salt of the Earth,* May/June 1997, p. 25).

In Spanish the translations read a bit differently. The sense of the word *blessed* is conveyed by the meaning "to have an advantage over others," so a beatitude would read something like "Blessed are you poor, for you have an advantage over those who are not poor." And the woes that are addressed to those in the opposite group, those who in Luke's gospel are told, "Woe to you," or "Alas for you," would read, "Woe to you who are at a disadvantage...."

In one of his columns in the *Prairie Messenger,* a Canadian diocesan newspaper, Ronald Rolheiser speaks of another way of looking at a blessing. He recounts the story from *Les Miserables* of Jean Valjean, an old man who goes searching for Marius, the young man who intends to marry Jean's beloved adopted daughter. Jean is curious about the young man, and protective of his daughter. Marius is at the barricades, trying to help the poor, accompanied by his idealistic young friends who are about to be attacked by government forces intent on destroying them and ruthlessly wiping them out. Jean Valjean finds young Marius exhausted. He bends over the sleeping young man and softly sings a blessing that is born of love and tenderness: "God on high hear my prayer, Look on this boy...he is young, he's afraid...tomorrow he might die, but Lord, let him live—let me die, let him live! Let him live!" Rolheiser writes:

> Those last lines are the prototype of deep blessing. They explain too why blessings work from the top down—from God to us, from old to young, from empowered to disempowered, from those who have full life to those who have not. They also show what is demanded in a deep blessing, namely, a giving away of life, a dying so that someone else might now have life. A blessing is not just simply an affirmation: "You are a

fine young man!" "You are a gifted young woman!" "I believe in you!" "I trust you!" These affirmations, good and life-giving as they are, are not enough. To bless someone deeply is to die for them in some real way, to really die, to give up some life for them.

Do you want to bless a young person? Give him or her your job! Give him or her some of your power. Step back and let him or her assume some of the leadership you have been exercising. Let his or her opinion overrule yours. Look at him or her, and like Jean Valjean, pray to God: "Let me die! Let him, her, live!"

Each way of translating this word *blessing* or *beatitude* adds to the richness of our understanding and moves us to act out that understanding in our own lives and toward others. Someone in Nicaragua once told me that the beatitudes are the new commandments and they, like the earlier commandments referred to in the first psalm, must be meditated upon night and day and taken to heart if one is to truly be a Christian. Somehow these blessings and woes reveal what is demanded and asked of us today when we are told: "Choose life!" and "Shun death!" We need to read the gospels, especially Luke, looking for and paying attention to the beatitudes hidden in the text and we need to do the same for the woes that are laced throughout the text. Later in this book we will look at some of these in detail.

Both the richness and power of blessing are illustrated in this ancient story from the Jewish tradition. Called "Saying Thank You," it contains a blessing that, I am told, is adapted from the *Talmud*.

✳ Once upon a time a young man, Natan, was traveling, on his way home to Beer-sheba. It had been a hard journey and he was still two days from home. But he'd been walking over the hills and through the valleys of Judea for three days and he was thirsty, hot, and weary. His water bottle had long been empty. Each step was harder, slower. The sun baked him mercilessly. He had eaten an orange early in the morning, but that seemed hours, even days before.

He was making for home, keeping to the back roads, sleeping in caves and staying out of sight of towns, for he had been a revolutionary, proud and defiant of the Romans. He had fought for freedom, for a future, for liberation. He and his friends had struggled long and hard against great odds and they had lost. Many had been killed and in the last battle they had been routed. Now they were scattered across the country, seeking their homes, rest, and time to regroup. They would struggle until they were free. Even though he was tired, hungry, and thirsty, he didn't dare approach anyone. He was on his own and wondered if he'd make it home or be captured like so many others and enslaved by the Romans, a fate worse than death itself.

He fell often, his tongue parched, his lips cracked and bleeding. He thought, "Have I come this far just to die in the sun?" At times he crawled on the ground to keep moving. If only there were some shade, a cave, an outcropping of rock, a tree. As he kept moving, he prayed, and suddenly he saw a tree in front of him. But was it really a tree? In the heat he could be seeing anything. As he drew nearer he could hardly believe it—it was an apple tree! He ran and stumbled and fell toward the cool, life-giving shade of the tree. He crawled under the branches and smelled the sweet blossoms and fell asleep exhausted, feeling safe at last.

Hours later he awoke, refreshed by the shade, and hungry. He reached up and grabbed an apple and ate it. Then another and another. The fruit tasted so good, luscious, fresh, sweet, and wet. It revived him. He knew he'd make it home. As he chewed the fruit he prayed aloud, giving thanks to God and then to the apple tree. But how could he show his gratitude to the tree? He really had nothing but the clothes on his back, and they were ragged and torn, dirty too. His pouch was empty, though he intended to fill it with the ripe juicy apples that would get him through the next two days on the way home. What could he give the tree? He must show his gratitude. The tree had literally saved his life, and probably saved him from the Romans as well.

He sat in the shade, savoring the coolness as night drew on. He said the psalms and prayers of his childhood, listening to the words anew, looking for an idea, a gift for the tree. And then he knew what to give! Of course, he could give a blessing! There were blessings for everything. He knew the one for daybreak, for food and wine, for children, for the Sabbath. He even knew Moses' and Aaron's blessing over his people from so long ago. He would have to make his own blessing for the tree. Long life—it already had that from the looks and the size of it.

He looked at the wide sweep of its branches and knew that its roots extended far. Fruit—he had already tasted of that and it was sweet and juicy and life-sustaining. Beauty—he realized he'd never seen a tree that wasn't beautiful. And then he smiled to himself. He knew the blessing. He stood to honor the tree and bowed his head, gathering his heart to put into the blessing. "May all the trees that are born of your seed grow as strong and true as you and be as richly giving and generous as you have been to me, a stranger who stumbled across your path and fell in your shade."

Natan spread his arms wide and called down heaven and earth, the stars and the rising moon to witness to his blessing, then knelt and put the palms of his hands on the ground beneath the tree. He arose and filled his pouch with apples that he would savor and space out over his journey. He would remember this tree that had saved his life, this tree that had been a blessing to him, and he knew then that he would make it home to his family. The tree had strong roots in Israel as he did. The tree served the Holy One as he did. He took one last look at this tree, so beloved now, and turned for home.

This is the ancient blessing that Natan knew from his own tradition. We use it often, on the feast of the Holy Family.

Then Yahweh spoke to Moses saying, "Speak to Aaron and his sons and say to them: This is how you shall bless the people of Israel; you shall say:

> May Yahweh bless you and keep you!
> May Yahweh let his face shine on you, and be
> gracious to you!
> May Yahweh look kindly on you, and give you
> his peace!
> In that way shall they put my name on the people
> of Israel and I will bless them." (Numbers 6:22-27)

We have been blessed, glanced upon by God, remembered, and given life. Even the name of our God is upon us, Emmanuel. It is Luke who tells the story of Gabriel coming to Zechariah in the temple with word of God's blessing on him and Elizabeth. Their child will be named John. He will bring joy and gladness to many who rejoice at his birth and what it signifies. When John is born, Zechariah, who has been mute since his encounter with Gabriel, can speak again. His first words are what we call the Benedictus, a canticle of praise.

> Blessed be the Lord God of Israel,
> for he has come and redeemed his people.
> He has raised up for us a victorious Savior
> in the house of David his servant,
> as he promised through his prophets of old,
> salvation from our enemies
> and from the hand of our foes.
> . . . This is the work of the mercy of our God,
> who comes from on high as a rising sun
> shining on those who live in darkness
> and in the shadow of death,
> and guiding our feet into the way of peace.
> (Luke 1:68-79)

This is the seedbed of the beatitudes, the long work of the mercy of our God that will come to fruition in the person of Jesus, the blessing of God, and in the presence of the kingdom that arrives with Jesus. The kingdom of God in Jesus set loose in the world is our blessing way. We enter it here.

2

The Reign of God:
Seedbed of the Beatitudes

"The kingdom of God is like...." So many of Jesus' stories start in this unassuming ritual way, and yet these are stories that can get you killed, and did get him killed. Jesus was a good Jew, and in his tradition—the tradition of the prophets— one is called to take apart and dismantle the old before announcing the new. He could just as easily have begun with the words: "God is like" or "Earth is heaven when" or "We are like God when," but Jesus used the more familiar: "What shall we say the kingdom of God is like? What parable shall we use to explain it?" (Mk 4:30).

Often people say that the parables are metaphors for life. This is partially true. There is a saying, "The one who masters the metaphor masters the world." And Jesus was a master: at words, at luring crowds to listen, at the audacious image, at the beguiling and bothering story, at telling the truth so that one had to hear. Metaphor has the capacity to talk about two or more realities at the same time. It can take us places we've never been before, even in our minds or imaginations. It is concerned with the unfamiliar, the mysterious, the heretofore unknown.

In Jesus' stories about the kingdom of God we are transported there! We are transported to a place that truly exists, to the world as it is seen and experienced in the presence of God, in the presence of Jesus here on earth. Buddhists would say that Jesus' parables of the kingdom are extraordinarily mindful, that they are tuned into the minds and hearts of his hearers, to their hopes and dreams, to their mourning and longing, and to their deepest aspirations and intuitions about religion and God. These descriptions and doorways into the kingdom are both entrance ways and mirrors. As mirrors, they are more like reflections found in clear still waters than hard substances. They are resilient, fluid, and transformative.

There are many stories of this elusive kingdom—elusive not because it's difficult to enter, but because you can stumble into it, upon it, just about anywhere. The reality of God's domain is not easy to grasp hold of or lay claim to. Jesus saw and expressed his Father's reign as "a hope, a goal, a beginning, a hidden force, a claim upon people's lives, a set of tasks, a boast, a gift. No wonder Jesus had trouble finding just the right image for it" (Frank O'Loughlin).

These stories teach us how to read and decipher the world from God's vantage point, from the point of view of a believer in Jesus, the beloved of God. And because they are of God, they have a certain shock value for human beings. They are shot through with the prophet's passion and are the healer's remedy for righting and repairing the world's deepest ills. They literally do in the realm of spirit what the healer does with the physical body. And just as a doctor often has to rebreak a bone in order to set it properly, the stories of the kingdom of God often break our hearts, break into our lives and minds, and shatter our old assumptions before drastically reconfiguring our structures of existence. Harold Fickett called them stories of "razing and restoration" not in theory but fact, in faith, in relationships. Parables, like Jesus, tend to remind us that "all the information I have about myself is from forged documents" (Vladimir Nabokov). They allow into our consciousness other possibilities about the universe, ourselves, and our image of God.

There are two marvelous parables that can perhaps startle us into a new awareness of the kingdom of God. The first is a Zen story by D. T. Suzuki, a version of which is found in *The Little Zen Companion*. It is specifically told in response to the question "What is Zen like?" and Suzuki's answer is cryptic and surprising: "It's like learning the art of burglary." But the tale fits the question "What is the kingdom of God like?" too!

✳ Once upon a time there was a family, well cared for by the father who was a burglar, a thief by profession. He was very good at what he did and the family wanted for nothing. The older children grew and went their ways. But one of the younger ones watched his father in fascination and in sorrow. For he saw his father aging and slowing down and no longer able to do the things he had done with such ease and grace. There were still younger children below him and he wondered who would care for them. Finally, after a good deal of thought, he decided it was he who was to follow in his father's footsteps and he respectfully requested that his father teach him the trade.

The father was delighted. Finally one of his children would follow him. And so one night he took his son out on a raid. Before leaving, the father explained the evening's work. He reviewed what they were going to do, the layout of the house and grounds, and the general plan for stealing the owners blind. Father and son were silent as they made their way stealthily onto the grounds of the estate, past fences, dogs, servants and into the great house. Once inside they crept upstairs and found huge chests and wardrobes full of clothes, kimonos, and jewels. After gesturing his son into one of the huge wardrobes and indicating that he was to choose only the best, the father proceeded to look elsewhere. The son dutifully obeyed. As soon as he was in the wardrobe, the father turned, closed the door, slid the bolt and locked his son inside!

Then the father slipped downstairs and out the front door and started loudly banging on the doors and windows, yelling "Thief!" "Thief!" "Thief!" Immediately bedlam broke loose. Everyone in the house was up and yelling, running around looking for the intruders. The father silently slipped away.

Inside the great wardrobe the poor young man sat sweating and thinking of his father. He had had no idea his father could be so cruel. He was a dangerous man. This was a side of his father he had never seen: the man was heartless to leave his son alone and put him in such jeopardy, to not only desert him but set him up to get caught. The son was near despair. Meanwhile, the residents of the house realized that the thieves had left; no trace of them could be found. In fact, there didn't even seem to be anything missing.

Inside the wardrobe, the young man was trying to figure how to get out and not get caught. He calmed his panic and made himself think carefully. Then an idea slid into his mind. He got up and made scurrying noises, like a trapped rat. A young woman heard the noise and carefully opened the bolt on the door. As soon as he heard it slide back, he pushed the door open and ran, remembering instinctively the way he and his father had come in, what seemed like hours before. He ran for his life, out of the house and through the grounds, but was spotted almost instantly, for the moon was near full. The servants were after him in a flash. Suddenly, while he was running, he remembered a large well, a cistern just off the path. He picked up a large stone and hurled it into the well and kept running. The pursuers heard the splash and thought he had fallen in. They all gathered around the well and peered down in the dark, looking for the burglar thrashing in the water or struggling to get out. Meanwhile, the young man continued running all the way back to the safety of his house. He ran in, slammed the door shut, and turned to see his father facing him, a broad grin on his face, arms wide open and waiting to embrace him. He was fuming at his father, blaming him for having deceived him, when he heard his father's words: "Congratulations! You have learned the art of burglary. You are truly worthy to follow in my footsteps!"

Sometimes this parable is called: "Ah, there you have learned the art!"

This is not what we expected, and if the parable is applied to God and to the kingdom of heaven and entrance into it, it is even more disquieting and arresting. But it holds true and has much to say about Jesus' kingdom and how one enters it, for it entails a process of learning, an initiation rite, a shifting of relationships and priorities, and even a new sense of who and what one is and how one lives on the fringes of society: in the world but not of it. The parable images work on many levels, beginning with the surprising thought that being a Christian, a follower of Jesus, is being a burglar! It is about stealing from others, about learning to work in the dark to enter others' homes and lives and wake them up, and about learning to live on one's toes, relying on insight and the power of the Spirit when one is in jeopardy.

On a deeper and more intimate level, the parable looks at the relationship between the father and his son who wishes to follow him and learn from him and so care for his family. The story throws the son into a quandary. It throws us into a quandary as well. Is this what God is like? Does God throw us back on our own resources, teaching us to rely on the spirit within us, leaving us alone in the lurch so that we can grow up and mature? This is not exactly what many of us have in mind when we consider a relationship with God or joining a group of people who believe in the kingdom.

Someone in a workshop once told me that telling these stories has the effect of throwing a hand grenade into a group of people. Initially there is silence, frozen paralysis, then panic and stampede, and afterwards no one remembers or can say whether or not the pin was released. The image is a bit violent, even threatening, but it does have some merit. Another comparison I use often is that of a sink hole that you discover in your front yard, except that the first time or two that you notice it you don't really know what it is and don't pay attention to it—until you have to! A sink hole is a geological phenomenon, often found in the southeastern part of the United States. A small hole appears out of nowhere and the ground around it begins to slide into it. First it is the size of a groundhog or a mole's burrow. Gradually you lose your front lawn; then your car slides in and your house lists and begins its descent and all along the street cars and houses and garages, and the street itself begin to disappear. A sink hole can be as large as a football field or two or three! The hole has always been there but it has needed a catalyst to open up. The catalyst can be something as simple as weather, a storm, too much watering of a lawn, a new house built on the block. Suddenly the whole thing lurches and the cave-in begins. It's a grand image for a parable, since the parable itself creeps up on you and begins to take over your whole life, insisting that you pay attention, repent, reform, and shift base, now!

There is an element of violence, for the kingdom "breaks in" to our personal lives, to society and structures. It points to those who have borne the brunt of our behaviors and especially actions that have been grounded in religious assumptions or laws, and it demands accountability. The stories are about injustice, inequality, and inhumanity, as well as about community, hope, God, and how those who believe in God are supposed to act. Jesus uses images of the kingdom coming "like a thief in the night," "like a master returning from a long journey away." He compares the kingdom to someone "reckoning the cost of going to battle" or "finishing a building project" that is bankrupting the owner because of lack of sufficient planning. The stories are cunningly disarming. They are about food, and money, and social structures that we all take for granted and accept because they have always been that way in our memory and experience. But these realities are not necessarily of God, and the parable reveals their falseness and the destructiveness of continuing to allow them to define and devalue life and people. A parable is God's Word interfering with and interrupting our settled existences, saying "No. This can't continue. Here's a new idea. Try this." And so, there is a sense of judgment and of God's power and its eventual effect on the world if we change our attitudes and behaviors in response to God's presence among us.

And Jesus himself is the parable of God, the presence of the kingdom of God, God's power let loose in the world just by his existence among us as a human being. He is unexpected, unplanned, and to all appearances illogical except in the logic of faith and God's grand love for us in the incarnation. Just as the parables are icons of the kingdom of God, Jesus is the icon, the doorway into the kingdom, into the presence of the Father close and nearby, within us and among us. The parables allow us a fleeting glimpse and experience of the kingdom here and now. With repentance, that experience can be extended into daily life and it can lay claim upon us and mark us out as dwellers in the presence of God, at home in God's kingdom.

Reactions to the stories, the felt experience of the kingdom are often: "You've got to be kidding!" Sometimes there is laughter, confusion, disorientation, a strong and vehement "No!" At other times there is a sense that one must decide NOW. Or there are blank stares of anger or statements like "No wonder they killed him—I'm surprised he lasted as long as he did."

Why did Jesus tell the parables? Some of the reasons could be to prepare us to be forgiven and welcomed, to inspire awe and humility in us once again; to move us to remorse, reconciliation, atonement, and the practice of virtue; maybe just to get us to wonder if perhaps we've been wrong, ignorant, using God and religion for our own ends rather than worshiping and honoring God in the world. Parables are grand for discussion, heavy, involved discussion. In Mark's parable of the seed growing by itself and the mustard seed, the stories end thus: "Jesus used many such stories or parables, to proclaim the word to them in a way they would be able to understand. He would not teach them without parables: but privately to his disciples he explained everything" (Mk 4:33-34).

These stories can go only so far in explaining what the kingdom of God is like. They can explain only up to a point. After that, my friend Frank O'Loughlin says, "There must be a living community in which experience is shared, sifted, explored, tested and celebrated. The experience of community finally dictates this or that image of the reign of God is to survive and be a living reality. Perhaps it may turn out that the really daring image is that of the community itself."

Jesus' parables are about just that: forming a community where the kingdom of God is a reality. It is a community of people who are initiated into the art of burglary, the profession of thieves who steal home, taking from the world what is not needed or is needed by others. It is a community of people who offer the world an alternative of grace and hope, of welcome and hospitality, while insisting that we all grow up and take responsibility for the power and insight of the Spirit within us, given to help us survive when we are locked in, left alone, and put in jeopardy. It reminds us that we are always a part of a family, a profession of faith that is an art, a way of living that is adventuresome and daring. It demands a long apprenticeship and there is always the risk of getting caught at doing justice, truth telling, and revealing to others what they would prefer to leave hidden. It involves the vigorous discipline of always learning to give more than we take, of living with awareness and drawing others into maturity, insisting that they take responsibility for their actions and for what happens in the world.

Here is another unfamiliar and very disconcerting parable that comes from the Gospel of Thomas (non-canonical scriptures from the early history of the Church). It is short and like a sword thrust.

* The kingdom of the Father is like a man who wished to kill an important lord. When at home, he took out his sword and pierced the wall. He wanted to know if his hand was sufficiently strong. Afterwards, he killed the important lord. (C.-H. Hunzinger, quoted in Leonardo Boff, *Jesus Christ Liberator, A Critical Christology for Our Time* [Maryknoll, N.Y.: Orbis Books, 1978], p. 87)

Whenever I've told that parable, people have winced visibly and reacted in rejection with a violence that mirrors the violence of the parable itself. C.-H. Hunzinger says:

What does Christ want to teach? Struck by the strangeness of his simile and left in sufficient doubt about its precise application, some biblical seekers have been teased into active thought to discover the meaning of the *mashal*: "When God begins some project he always concludes it, just as this assassin!" From this it follows immediately that as the Father brings the divine mission to a successful end so also does Jesus invariably, for the simple reason that his mission is simply identical with his Father's.

It is likely that the very unfamiliarity of the parable lends a certain persuasiveness to its suggested truth. Some of the familiar parables of Jesus too, for example: the Mustard Seed and the Sower, are pregnant with the same message. (p. 87)

Jesus is the thrust of God into the world, the double-edged sword of word and deed that is paradoxically nonviolent in its resistance to evil, yet in the end triumphs by the cross. The spear thrust deep into the side of Christ brings forth a new community where the kingdom will survive and thrive, continuing Jesus' own work of bringing his Father's reign to the world. And the kingdom will continue to creep in "inch by inch, row by row," as the song goes. The intrusion of the Word of God into the world creates a radical opening in history and brings about a global structural transformation. The new order can be described in the words of Isaiah the prophet:

> Here is my servant whom I uphold,
> my chosen one in whom I delight.
> I have put my spirit upon him,
> and he will bring justice to the nations.
>
> He does not shout or raise his voice,
> proclamations are not heard in the streets.
> A broken reed he will not crush,
> nor will he snuff out the light
> of the wavering wick.
> He will make justice appear in truth.
>
> He will not waver or be broken
> until he has established justice on earth;
> the islands are waiting for his law....
> I, Yahweh, have called you for the sake of justice;
> I will hold your hand to make you firm;
> I will make you as a covenant to the people,
> and as a light to the nations,
> to open the eyes that do not see,
> to free captives from prison,
> to bring out to light those who sit in darkness.
>   (Isaiah 42:1-4, 6-7)

This passage describes the suffering servant of Yahweh, the remnant of those faithful to Yahweh, Jesus and those who follow him, those who are the minority of the faithful and who struggle against the indifference of the majority to put into practice what they have heard from Jesus. Inauspicious beginnings, inconspicuous seeds, and unimportant, usually unnoticed people will usher forth the light of the nations and the work of the kingdom. Opening the eyes of the blind and freeing captives will be accomplished in spite of the history of violence and injustice in the world. Jesus' stories grip us with the notion of freedom and liberation, of a fidelity that costs nothing less than everything, and the conviction that this is the only way. The story will come true, shattering even the shackles of death and violence with the truth of resurrection, healing, and forgiveness. The kingdom of God is about sharing and passing on the passion of life, the presence of Jesus who himself was so alive that he gave hope and vision to all who could trust his words. And those words were about naming evil, discord, and the distortion of truth as well as outlining the foundations of an alternative social order that was life-giving and sustaining for all, especially those who had been excluded. The parables unveil evil and expose it starkly. They also uncover good and reveal it as attractive and freeing so that the power to transform society is loosed and those who believe can respond creatively to the needs of the world. The stories of the kingdom of God are spoken in the language of liberation, delight, and hope for the future. They are based on the present reality of conversion among us who listen and hear and take to heart. They are about fidelity to God, to one another, and to life.

The parables taken together are a charter for the kingdom of God, where the rich and the mighty must defer to the lowly and meek; where community and the common good, especially of the least, reign supreme; where solidarity and service—rather than competition and rivalry—are primary. Privilege gives way to compassion and violence is abhorred. All is done in memory of Jesus, the Crucified and Risen One who walks among us still in the poor and those most in need of hospitality, the embrace of tenderness, and the extended hope of liberation. Power sinks to the bottom, discernment is communal and subject to obedience to the common good. In the kingdom of God one needs to lose oneself in order to be found and to discover meaning, and denying oneself is a necessary starting place for learning. Truth and its telling are cherished and faithfulness is paramount. Community members are called "friends" and want to be "good servants." The corporal and spiritual needs of every person are given top priority: food, housing, clothing, shelter, medicine, education, work, dignity, freedom, and respect. One becomes a member of the community through obedience, forgiveness, praying unceasingly, being passionately devoted to justice, the practice of hope, the dispelling of fear and despair. Joy is an innate virtue and characteristic of members who share not only each other's resources but also each other's sorrows and sufferings. Community members live on the bread of the Word in scripture made flesh and blood in the bread and wine of eucharist. The community's only power is the power of the cross: hidden, surging up, disturbing, capable of unbelievable transformation. This community's so intolerant of unnecessary human misery that it is considered an honor to shoulder the burdens of those bowed down.

Those in the kingdom belong to a family bound not by marriage or nationality or race or gender. The only blood tie is the blood of Christ binding those who "hear the word of God and obey the will of God," those who side with the ones caught in the grip of injustice and evil, those who are tied to life-lines of the Spirit who teaches them to pray: "Abba, Father, may your kingdom come, your will be done, on earth, here and now among us, as it is in heaven. Give us today only our daily bread to be shared with all. Forgive us as we forgive those who are in need of forgiveness from us. Lead us into facing temptation and let us not at the end have to face what is evil alone. Blest be your Name. Amen."

The beatitudes are born of the kingdom, the result of belief in and the experience of initiation into this reign of God, this dwelling place of the Spirit of God. They are sourced in the Word of God as Jesus proclaims the Good News to the poor and all who are open to God's coming into the world.

The beatitudes come forth from the mouth of the One who is described in Isaiah 52.

> How beautiful on the mountain are the feet of those
> who bring good news,
> who herald peace and happiness,
> who proclaim salvation
> and announce to Zion: "Your God is king!"
> Together your watchmen
> raise their voices in praise and song;
> they see Yahweh face to face returning to Zion.
>
> Break into shouts of joy,
> O ruins of Jerusalem,
> for Yahweh consoles his people
> and redeems Jerusalem.
> Yahweh has bared his holy arm
> in the eyes of the nations;
> all the ends of the earth, in alarm,
> will witness God's salvation.
> Depart, depart from that nation, come out!
> Touch nothing unclean.
> Purify yourselves, you who bear
> all Yahweh's holy vessels.
> Yet not in escape, or in fright, will you come out,
> you will not leave in headlong flight;
> for ahead is Yahweh, your vanguard,
> and behind, the God of Israel, your rearguard.
>   (Isaiah 52:1-12)

This proclamation of the prophet is a rallying cry, a gathering song. It is an announcement of hope in a time that is at hand, at long last, resulting in joy at the nearness of God. There is an element of purification and preparation for this coming out: these people will now be at the center of all history, amazing as that might be.

And this remnant of authentic believers, those who clung to integrity in the face of suffering and persecution, will be the image of those who follow in the footsteps of the Word of God and become the dwelling place of God among people. Because of the incarnation, God is at home in all the world, but he is more at home, more easily recognizable and more clearly present in certain places, among certain people. This remnant is found in those described in the beatitudes.

The beatitudes are even more clearly expressed in the Isaian statement of choice, of vocation and relationship that Jesus uses to describe himself in Luke 4. Jesus' words are taken in part from Isaiah 61:

> The Spirit of the Lord Yahweh is upon me,
> because Yahweh has anointed me
> to bring good news to the poor.
> He has sent me to bind up broken hearts,
> to proclaim liberty to the captives,
> freedom to those languishing in prison;
> to announce the year of Yahweh's favor
> and the day of vengeance of our God;
> to give comfort to all who grieve;
> (to comfort those who mourn in Zion)
> and give them a garland instead of ashes,
> oil of gladness instead of mourning,
> and festal clothes instead of despair.
>
> They will be called oaks of integrity
> planted by Yahweh to show his glory.
> They will rebuild the ancient ruins
> and repair cities laid waste
> left desolate for many generations.
> (Isaiah 61:1-4)

And later in the same chapter, we find these verses:

> Since my people's shame has been twofold
> and disgrace has been their lot,
> they will possess a double portion
> of inheritance in their land.
> I will give them everlasting joy.
> For I, Yahweh, love justice,

I hate robbery and oppression;
I will give them their due reward
and make an everlasting covenant with them.
(Isaiah 61:7-8)

These lines of Isaiah formed and gave expression to the early church's understanding of the prophet/suffering servant Jesus, the beloved child of God who incarnated God's nearness in his flesh, in his stories and healings, and in his community that itself was a parable of the kingdom of God. This kingdom was made up of the poor, the mourning, the hungry, and those persecuted for his name's sake. And the same people who mirrored the kingdom so surely also revealed in sharp contrast those who are outside the kingdom and resistant to the presence of God: the rich, the content, those who laugh and are happy now, and those who are thought well of in the centers of the world's power and influence. The blessings and woes of Luke's gospel are prefigured in these passages of Isaiah that come from the mouth of Jesus at the beginning of his ministry. And after proclaiming these words aloud and appropriating them to himself, he announces that even now they are coming true because he is present in the world. He speaks the words with a few emphases that are worth noticing:

The Spirit of the Lord is upon me.
He has anointed me to bring good news to the poor,
to proclaim liberty to captives
and new sight to the blind;
to free the oppressed and announce
the Lord's year of mercy.
(Luke 4:18-19)

Then he goes on to preach to the people as a prophet, telling the stories of Elijah choosing a widow of Zarephath in the country of Sidon and not in Israel, and Elisha healing Naaman, the Syrian, and not someone of Israel. And when they hear this, they react bitterly and swiftly, seeking to destroy him. The seedbed of the blessings and woes, the separation of those who hear and heed and those who reject and resist, are apparent long before the blessings and woes are put so starkly into words in the Sermon on the Plain.

The immediate backdrop of the Sermon on the Plain (as it is often called to distinguish it from the Sermon on the Mount in Matthew's text) is very different from the background of Matthew's eight beatitudes. Look at Luke's setting carefully:

> Coming down the hill with them, Jesus stood on a level place. Many of his disciples were there and a large crowd of people who had come from all parts of Judea and Jerusalem and from the coastal cities of Tyre and Sidon. They gathered to hear him and be healed of their diseases; likewise people troubled by evil spirits were healed. All the crowd tried to touch him because of the power which went out from him and healed them all.
> Then lifting up his eyes to his disciples, Jesus said:...(Luke 6:17-20)

The text is so different from that of Matthew where Jesus, the new Moses, is the law-giver who goes up the mountain with his disciples around him, while the crowd remains. In Matthew Jesus teaches them from the mountain. In Luke, Jesus has just chosen his disciples after having spent the whole night in prayer in the hills. He comes down with them to a level place that is crowded with hordes of people from all parts of the region and beyond to the coastal cities: believers, unbelievers, outsiders, and probably many not welcome in religious society.

Before he teaches, he heals; or perhaps as he heals, he teaches. Those who have come to him are ill, diseased, troubled by evil spirits, despised by society. They are desperate, seeking to touch him, drawn as though by a magnet to his tangible power and presence. The scene is one of motion, reaching, grabbing, and we are told simply that "the power which went out from him healed them all." This power, his spirit and presence, is healing, comforting, soothing, calming, promising. But the most startling line of all is the last one: "Then lifting up his eyes to his disciples, Jesus said..." He lifts up his eyes: he is positioned below them, probably kneeling on the ground, tending to those in pain and suffering, attentive to the needs of those reaching for him. He is a servant, waiting on others, with more and more and more waiting for him and trying to get to him. He is in a position of vulnerability, of solidarity with the masses of people in need. From this position he speaks the beatitudes: the blessings and the woes, or lamentations as they are sometimes called. In Luke's gospel Jesus is more comfort-giver than teacher; more attentive than discursive; more tender than instructive; more embracing of the pain of others than distant as law-giver. And the words are addressed to his newly called disciples and then to all those healed and given heart by his presence and power among them.

These few lines of blessings and woes are followed by a staggering sermon that is often quoted with obvious cynicism, seemingly impossible to put into practice. There are exhortations to love your enemies and do good to those who persecute you and malign you, to turn the other cheek and go an extra mile. There are comparisons between sinners and "you" who are the disciples to whom he is speaking so intimately about the kingdom of his Father and his Father's love for all his children, and how we are to imitate that love in forgiveness and generosity "pressed down, full and running over" (Lk 6:38).

These exhortations are followed by examples: of the blind leading the blind and those attempting to extract a splinter from the eye of another while carrying a log in their own, and of trees and their fruit, and the goodness and evil in people's hearts and actions. And lastly the whole piece is made very concrete in the description of the person who listens and puts into practice what Jesus says. Such a person is like a builder who knows where and how to lay a foundation and build a house that lasts in the face of storms and rising rivers. The one who listens and does not put anything into practice is like one who builds without a foundation and sees disaster and ruin come upon him.

It seems that the blessings and woes and what follows from them in practical action form the foundation of the kingdom of God in the world. It is crucial to the whole endeavor of the coming of God's reign into our lives. These attitudes and behaviors cover all areas of human life: social, economic, religious. The words of Jesus empower and sustain those called to be responsible for the new public order and common good, the defense of the poor, the care of the despised and diseased. By living out the words of Jesus we express our belief in the God of Jesus, the Father who is described simply as "merciful." To do these things, to live this way, is to be "children of the Most High and our reward will be great" (Lk 6:35-36). All the beatitudes and woes and the sermon that follows are to be seen in the context of the mercy of God the Father, the mercy that is the person of Jesus in our midst. And when the words of Jesus are put into practice the kingdom comes. Thich Nhat Hanh has said: "The miracle is not to walk on water. The miracle is to walk on the green earth in the present moment, to appreciate the peace and beauty that are available now.... It is not a matter of faith; it is a matter of practice." We need to practice reading and hearing the beatitudes; we need to put them into practice.

In response to John the Baptizer's messengers sent to Jesus asking the question: "Are you the one we are to expect, or should we wait for another?" Luke writes:

> At that time Jesus healed many people of their sicknesses or diseases; he freed them from evil spirits and he gave sight to the blind. Then he answered the messengers, "Go back and tell John what you have seen and heard: the blind see again, the lame walk, lepers are made clean, the deaf hear, the dead are raised to life, and the poor are given good news. Now, listen: Fortunate are those who encounter me, but not for their downfall." (Luke 7:21-23)

Ah, another beatitude, so close on the heels of the originals! And it encompasses the sense of a woe as well. Meeting with Jesus, even in his words—let alone in his actions in the world—makes you blessed, but it can also set up your downfall. This short piece is the entire Sermon on the Plain in a nutshell: Choose! And then act upon that choice with others and tell what you have seen and heard. The messengers return to John who is in prison and tell him the Good News. Jesus goes on to praise John to the crowds, but ends by saying: "No one may be found greater than John among the sons of woman but, I tell you, the least in the Kingdom of God is greater than he" (Lk 7:28). Jesus declares the power of the kingdom and says that even the least in the kingdom is greater than John the prophet, the messenger who goes before the Word made flesh among us. Why? Those that come after are blessed, more powerful, more free, more intimate with this Word than John. A response to the beatitudes is a response to the person of Jesus. Jesus is the act of God that interrupts all of history and shatters all our illusions about the structure of the world. The beatitudes reveal how to restructure the world. They remind us of where God lives in history and where God acts most powerfully, more powerfully than through the prophets of old who spoke his word in the first person. Is this possible?

There is a marvelous Jewish story that asks just this in such a way that we have to live with it, have to decide. It appears in a written form in Martin Buber's *Early Masters*, part of a two-volume collection of the stories of the Hasidim. This story is found in the first volume.

✳ Once upon a time there was an unbeliever who was learned and articulate. He was the kind of unbeliever who sought to refute all statements of belief, especially intent on contradicting anyone who was dynamic in speech, truthful in practice and had an influence on others. He considered himself enlightened, and was secure in his certainty and lack of belief. He heard of a famous teacher, a zaddik, and was driven to accost him and dispute his words and preaching. And so he journeyed to the man's hometown and arranged an audience with him, as so many others did.

He entered the zaddik's room and watched disdainfully as the zaddik paced up and down, praying and lost in ecstatic thought and the presence of the Holy One. He had been studying the Torah and meditating on the words of the Blessed One. The zaddik, wrapped up as he

was in the power and presence of Another, absolutely ignored the man. Then all of a sudden, he stopped in his
walking and turned to look straight at his visitor. He
caught him off guard with the words: "Ah, but perhaps it
is true after all!"

The man was shaken to his core. His knees trembled
and his hands shook uncontrollably. His mind raced and
flew in every direction. His self-confidence and certainty
fled him and he could not take his eyes off the old zaddik
even though he tried with all his might. The sight of the
man's face was terrible to behold and beautiful beyond
rapture. The words kept sounding in the man's ears and
soul, thundering inside him and seeping into every piece
of his mind and body. The zaddik moved closer to him
and spoke in a soft voice, as though to an errant child
who was stubborn and willful. "My son, you have debat-
ed and argued with great scholars and teachers but they
wasted their words and time on you. You were always
sure of yourself and you laughed at them and their belief,
even at their struggles. They could not set God and his
kingdom on the table before you, and I won't try either.
But think! Think of this—what if it is true after all? What
if it is all true? Perhaps it is true, perhaps it is all true after
all!" The man tried to ignore the words, to erase the zaddik's face and eyes, but it was impossible. He couldn't
even reply. That terrible word: "perhaps." "Perhaps" beat
on his ears again and again, echoing in him, and broke
down his resistance.

Perhaps the beatitudes are true and the woes as well; perhaps it is all true and what each of us needs is someone who
fervently believes and confronts us to begin the process of
breaking down our resistance. Martin Heidegger said: "A person is neither a thing nor a process but an opening through
which the Absolute can manifest." God manifested himself
completely, surely, and incredibly in Jesus and now it is up to
us to let God manifest himself in us. Perhaps all the world
needs is enough of us to risk believing and putting the beatitudes into practice. Perhaps. . .

3

Blessed Are the Poor
for the Kingdom of God Is Theirs

Abundance is seeking the beggars and the poor,
just as beauty seeks a mirror.
Beggars, then, are the mirrors of God's abundance,
and they that are with God are
united with Absolute Abundance.
(Rumi)

"Blessed are you who are poor, the kingdom of God is yours." These words are staggering for modern North Americans and residents of many countries of the world. In many of the workshops and retreats that served as the foundation for this book, getting past this one line was nearly impossible. The reactions of revulsion, anger, and outright rejection were often overwhelming, and ended up short-circuiting any further look at the rest of the beatitudes. Sometimes the whole weekend retreat dealt with understanding the resistance this one sentence evoked. However, when this line is pronounced in poor areas of the countries I visit, the reaction is different. First there is disbelief. Then quickly, as awareness dawns, there is rejoicing and a sense of powerful hope based on God's closeness and involvement in human history and the affairs of the poor. In a sense, it almost makes being poor a bit easier to deal with, knowing and believing that God's kingdom is here now and that it can be grasped firmly in the situation of being poor, of being the *anawim*, as the poor are called in the scriptures.

This introduction to the beatitudes operates like a one-line parable, an upending of reality. It is like cold water in your face, or an oriental *koan* that must be pondered and struggled with before there can be any true understanding of experience.

Herman Hendrickx, in his superb book on the beatitudes, *The Sermon on the Mount: Studies in the Synoptic Gospels* (London: Geoffrey Chapman, 1984) puts the first beatitude in the context of the kingdom of God.

> The kingdom of God means, then, to be with and to identify with people, especially the threatened, the oppressed and the downtrodden; to give life to those who have none; to remove all oppressive relationships of one person over another, or one nation over another, to bring them to mutual solidarity; to liberate people from any kind of fear; not to condemn people, not to nail them to their sinful past or negative experiences, but to give them in all circumstances a new future, and hope that brings life; to love people without distinction, without selection, without limits; to oppose what is untrue, what is no longer relevant and has no future, a legalistic mentality which overlooks the actual person and promotes only uninspired conformity, and prayer that is not in spirit and truth but mere routine. In short, Jesus' words and deeds reveal the kingdom of God as God's rule concerned with the radical well-being and humaneness of man. (Introduction, pp. 2-3)

The beatitudes are indispensable to the faith of the Christian community and, at the same time, they are a sword thrust straight to our hearts. The words and concepts are so strange to our cultures and sensitivities and fears. No matter how many times we hear or read or meditate on these words, they leave us uneasy, for they reveal a God whose concerns do not mirror ours and a world that is out of sync with the Holy Mystery. They do not put our minds and souls at ease. However, they are linchpins for the kingdom of God, this kingdom that has been promised since the beginning of our religious history to one day become a vibrant reality that will transform the world. We believe that the kingdom arrived with the birth, life, and death of Jesus and that, since the resurrection, the kingdom is wherever Jesus is found. The Son of Justice lights the way of the kingdom as it spreads out across the earth like the rays of the sun. The kingdom is about internal attitudes (be-attitudes), but it is just as surely about economics, politics, and social relations. It is about history redeemed and it is found first in the poor of the earth, the poor who seem to be everywhere.

I don't often tell the following story because it is hard to tell. It is one of a few stories that I go "into character" for and tell in the first person. But it is so powerful that sometimes it is the only one that I can think of to get people off-guard and open to dealing with poverty, with what it means to beg for what you need, and the dignity of those who are poor. I usually wrap my head up in a dark serape and turn my back to people before I begin. Then I turn and start.

✳ Ah! Blessed be Allah, the most compassionate One! Welcome to the marketplace. I can see that you are staring at me and wondering already how you can avoid me, slip away perhaps, and hope that I do not catch sight of you. Ah, yes, I do know what you are feeling and thinking, by the grace of Allah I know.

You see, I am a beggar, but I like being a beggar! You find that surprising? Annoying? Well, believe me, I didn't always want to be a beggar. In the beginning I was furious with God for choosing me to beg, to make my way in the world dirty, smelling, ragged, and lacking everything that I needed. But eventually, after yelling and screaming at Allah, the most compassionate One, he gave me to see what was holy and good about my profession. And now I want to be a beggar. I like being a beggar. Why? Because

Allah in his mercy lets me see you just as you are, just as he sees you. Isn't that marvelous? You look a bit white and ashen, a bit grey. Why is that? Well, never mind, besides seeing you the way Allah sees you I also have a most important work to do. My path is to make you lighter, to help you part with what burdens you and holds you enslaved and bowed down—usually whether you want to or not! Ah, you look skeptical. Let me show you what I mean.

You see a beggar as you are walking down the street. What do you do? You quickly decide to casually cross over to the other side of the street—that's if you're attentive and can think of such a move before you're right up on the person. Or if you are engrossed in your own world and I come up to you without warning and catch you off-guard you frown and harden your face, or you clutch your purse and say something like "Uh, I don't have any change," or "Catch me on my way back." I see you as your back retreats down the street and I pray Allah in his mercy says to you in your need: "Uh, I'm in a hurry right now, I'll catch you when I'm coming back this way." I see you.

Or, say you've had a good day and you are coming down the street with a bounce in your step, feeling good about the world, and you see me with my hand out. You dip into your pocket and come out with a couple of coins and smile at me and go merrily on your way. As you go I pray Allah in his mercy will smile upon you and throw a few coins your way.

Or you are coming down the street and the world is heavy on your heart. You may even have come from the mosque or church and you are thinking about the prayers and how difficult it is to live in the world and be good and righteous and not contribute to the ills of society. Then you see me and you frown. But you stop and you dig into your wallet or purse and come up with a dollar or two. I smile gratefully and then you say: "Look, buddy, I don't want you spending this on booze or cigarettes. Get yourself a sandwich, go look for a job." Or you give me the money and quote scripture at me, something like, "Those who do not work should not be allowed to eat free." Off you go, feeling like you've made a statement while at the same time doing your charitable deed for the day. And I pray Allah in his mercy will give you enough for a sandwich, but I pray it comes with a lecture and a religious moral too—straight from the mouth of the Holy One.

Or you're coming down the street and you just clinched a big deal and you're on a roll. You see me coming and out comes (can I believe it?) a five dollar bill or a ten! You smile and drop it in my hand with a grin, and though you're only sharing your good fortune and don't care much about me, I pray Allah in his mercy will be gracious to you and share his goodness with you.

Or you come down the street and you see me, really see me, and you see what you've got: money, maybe the lunch you fixed this morning, an apple or a banana, and you stop and give it to me with graciousness. As you go, I thank Allah in his mercy that there are generous and good people in the world and I pray that he blesses you overflowingly, and I go more lightly on my way.

And then, sometimes, though it's very rare, one of you comes to me and gives to me before I can beg from you. You've been watching and you are moved to pity by my condition and you care, and then it's I who have to stop. I look hard at you and wonder who you are. Has God, the most compassionate One, come to visit his people again? Rarely does someone give to me before I have to beg for what I need just to make it through the next couple of hours. And then I pray Allah to visit you, to move on you and take over your life, and I give thanks that I have met someone truly holy and righteous.

So, you see, no matter what you do when you see me, I see you—really see you—the way Allah in his mercy sees you. And I'm here to make you lighter and freer, to open you up to the grace of God, to the Holy hiding anywhere in this world. You see, I'm a beggar, but I like being a beggar. I'm good at it and I'm going to lift a burden from you and make you poorer and freer, whether you

really want me to or not. You see, I do know you, and
God has blessed me in letting me share in his work of liberation and freedom. Well, I must be going now. [I turn
and then turn back with a bit of a smirk.] Oh, is there anything you'd like to part with now so that you can go more
lightly on your way? [Long silence.] No, I didn't think so,
but I thought I'd ask anyway.

Some day, one day, may it be soon, everyone will be
free and even in the marketplace all the beggars will be
gone! Yes, our path will be over. One day we will not be
necessary. On that day all of you will know your path.
Maybe one of you will even be called a beggar! You could
do lots worse, you know. If you want to be a beggar,
come, come with me and I'll sing with you and watch
people with you and praise Allah with you. Just remember: I know my path. Do you know yours? May Allah, the
most compassionate One, bless you all. So be it. Amen.
(original attributed to Ken Feit, IF)

The story devastates people (the teller too) but it brings
home to the heart and the mind what the very sight and
presence of the poor, of the homeless, of street people and of
beggars do to us instinctively and how they do it daily,
insistently.

This first beatitude and the last (the fourth in Luke) are
both in the present tense, while the others are in the future, the
not-yet-a-reality tense, and perhaps that is the real source of
the tension. The kingdom of God is present in a group of people, masses of human beings that are "stark reminder of our
failures. They are a model of faith for us. They call us to look
radically at our priorities. And they are vivid signs of the times
for us. Here are two questions for those who would be disciples of Jesus: Living as we do under the pervading and domi-
neering influence of our secular and materialistic societies, can
we still read such signs of the times? And if so, are we willing
to do something about them?" (Donald McQuade, M.M., in
"'Anawim'—Beloved of God," *America*, May 11, 1996.)

These people, the unnamed and faceless and forgotten of
the world, pose living questions to us, as they always have. In

Israel's history the poor, the *anawim,* were touchstones of faith. The quality of liturgy, faith, and life in the community was revealed in the way the poor, the widow, the orphan, the illegal alien, and the stranger were treated. When lack of care for these people reached a critical point then the prophets were sent to hound the people, to help them remember that the Holy One had led them out of bondage and slavery, giving them the law on Sinai so that no one in Israel would ever know indignity and suffering again. As God's people the Israelites were to reveal to the nations that God is a God of life and freedom and hope for all, especially those the world wishes to forget. All the prophets cried out against the basic inhumanity of people who ignored their neighbor's need or worse, made a profit off the suffering of others, all the while proclaiming to honor and worship God. Amos spoke to his people about the God who defends the rights of the poor because no one else will, but the words apply to every country and every generation of people.

> Hear this, you who trample on the needy to do away with the weak of the land. You who say, "When will the new moon or the sabbath feast be over that we may open the store and sell our grain? Let us lower the measure and raise the price; let us cheat and tamper with the scales, and even sell the refuse with the whole grain. We will buy up the poor for money and the needy for a pair of sandals."
> Yahweh, the pride of Jacob, has sworn by himself, "I shall never forget their deeds." (Amos 8:4-7)

Not only does God never forget the deeds of injustice, but God remembers the poor, those who have been cast aside and dishonored, as God and his law have been cast aside and dishonored. If God truly exists and is in relationship with human beings, then what transpires on earth has ramifications in heaven. We coexist both with God and with one another, and the two are inseparable. By the time the prophet speaks, God is thundering at our callousness and cruelty, our ability to ig-

nore and disdain the pain of others. God is a comfort and a security only to those who live with integrity; to use God as a
comfort when practicing injustice is an insolence and insult to
God. As Abraham Heschel (1907–1972) said: "God is a challenge, an incessant demand. God is compassion, not compro-
mise; justice though not inclemency. The prophet's predic-
tions can always be proven wrong by a change in man's
conduct, but never the certainty that God is full of compassion" (*The Prophets: An Introduction*, Vol. 1, New York: Harper
Collins, 1962).

The poor are all those without power, without influence,
without rights, those falling through the cracks in society. The
poor are welfare recipients and immigrants, all those who are
blamed for the economic problems of the day. They are the
victims and casualties of violence, those caught in political
cross-fires, made homeless, landless, nationless. Afterwards
they are caught in the web of economic injustices that result
from war, racial and ethnic hatreds, and religious conflict.
They are those who must rely on God's providence and care,
for *we* have abandoned them. They must trust God because
they know from experience that they cannot trust us, even
those of us who call ourselves faithful believers in God, the
God who became human and dwells among us in flesh and
blood. And the poor, those blessed in the scriptures, hardly
know that blessing consciously. More often they are completely unaware of being beloved of God.

I am always struck by a simple devastating memory
when I bless the food I am about to eat. One day a couple of
years ago when I was on vacation in southern Mexico near the
Chiapas border I had spent the morning with some young-
sters talking about the rebels and church, about Bishop Ruíz
and the gospel for the following Sunday. I bought lunch for a
half dozen of these street urchins, as most people would call
them, and one of them said grace. It was a direct hit: God is
great. God is good. God lives in this neighborhood. I have
never forgotten that experience, and when I eat in so many
places around the world, I wonder: does God live so clearly in
this neighborhood, in my neighborhood?

The early Christians, even in the midst of missionary travels and persecutions, always kept the poor close in mind and heart. In Galatians Paul writes:

> James, Peter and John acknowledged the graces God gave me. Those men who were regarded as the pillars of the Church stretched out their hand to me and Barnabas as a sign of fellowship; we would go to the pagans and they to the Jews. We should only keep in mind the poverty of our brothers in Jerusalem; I have taken care to do this. (Galatians 2:9-10)

This is not surprising, because from the beginnings of the church, care for the poor was a major characteristic of belief within the Christian community. Even outsiders noticed and commented upon this. We are told in the second chapter of Acts:

> They were faithful to the teaching of the apostles, the common life of sharing, the breaking of the bread and the prayers.
> A holy fear came upon all the people, for many wonders and miraculous signs were done by the apostles. Now all the believers lived together and shared their belongings. They would sell their property and all they had and distribute the proceeds to others according to their need. Each day they met together in the Temple area; they broke bread in their homes; they shared their food with great joy and simplicity of heart; they praised God and won the people's favor. And every day the Lord added to their number those who were being saved. (Acts 2:42-47)

The preaching of the gospel, prayer and the breaking of bread were always accompanied by transformation, by compassion for others in the body of Christ. It is interesting to note that all the accounts of the resurrection during the Easter season are accompanied by readings from the Acts of the

Apostles. The resurrection stories all emphasize that the body of Jesus was gone from the tomb. Long before anyone had caught a glimpse of the risen Lord they were all deeply concerned about what had happened to his body. It was gone and the women could not wrap it and prepare it decently for burial as was the custom. Those who went to the tomb were told, "He is not here, he goes before you into Galilee, into the world, and that is where you will find him." We hear those words and yet it takes a long long time to realize that the body of Christ, the risen Lord, is among us. The church is the body of Christ, and the poor especially are the body of Christ. What we wish to do for God, we can always do for the poor. And God takes personally what we do for them, as done for him. The experience of resurrection propels those who believe into care for the body of Christ in their midst. Just two chapters later in Acts we read:

> The whole community of believers were one in heart and mind. No one considered as his own what belonged to him; but rather they shared all things in common. With great power the apostles bore witness to the resurrection of the Lord Jesus, for they were living in a time of grace.
>
> There was no needy person among them, for those who owned land or houses sold them and brought the proceeds of the sale. And they laid it at the feet of the apostles who distributed it according to each one's need. (Acts 4:32-35)

By baptism we belong to Christ. In the words of the baptismal liturgy, we "live no longer for ourselves alone, but hidden with Christ in God," and so we belong to one another intimately. The memory of Jesus' love for the crowds, for the ragtag of the earth, for outcasts and sinners was embedded in the minds of the disciples and followers of Jesus. As care for the needy was essential to Jesus' ministry, so it is for those who follow him. In James's community it is put forth bluntly and unambiguously:

Brothers, what good is it to profess faith without showing works? Such faith has no power to save you. If a brother or sister is in need of clothes or food and one of you says, "May things go well for you; be warm and satisfied," without attending to their material needs, what good is that? So it is for faith without deeds; it is totally dead. (James 2:14-17)

Is our faith, our relationship with God, lifeless? Are we in a precarious position before God? Are we doing something about the state of the poor? Love of the poor, individually in the corporal works of mercy and corporately in the work of restructuring society, is one of the distinguishing marks of the church. To stray from this is to stray far from the heart of the gospel. There is a saying that one of the best kept secrets of the Catholic Church is its social justice teachings, expressed in such documents as *Justice in the World* (1971): "Action on behalf of justice and participation in the transformation of the world fully appear to us as a constitutive dimension of preaching the Gospel." We begin any action or work for justice with the practice of "keeping in mind and heart the poor and their needs" as Paul did, as the early church did, as Jesus did.

All of this theology is right and good, but why do the poor frighten us? Why are we so reluctant to draw near to them, afraid to let go of what we have, even what we don't need? Why do we admire people like Francis of Assisi and Clare and praise their love for Lady Poverty and even sing psalms that repeat the refrain: "And the Lord hears the cry of the poor, Blessed be the Lord," yet do not even think to practice the virtue of poverty? Perhaps more than anything else the poor remind us of things we want to ignore or forget, to not admit even to ourselves. In *The Jesuit Martyrs of El Salvador*, Dean Brackley, S.J. writes:

We suspect, deep down, that the world is a much crueler place than we dare admit; but we fear the encounter with the poor who bring us face to face with all this evil, and we expend enormous energy shut-

ting out this horror from our lives. If we let their stories break our hearts, however, the victims will invite
us to recognize that the world is also a much more
wondrous place than we dared to imagine. They will
reveal to us the revolution of love that God is bringing about in the world. "Where sin abounds, grace
does more abound." (p. xii)

The poor, the blessed who already have the kingdom, are
hard to describe. In a sense, those described in the first three
beatitudes of Luke—the poor, the mourning and the hungry
—are not three separate groups; they are the same people.
These are the people of the world who are so wretched and
miserable that they are forced to beg for their very survival
and so, of necessity, are always hungry and always lacking
and mourning their lot.

The beatitudes are about saving the world, about saving,
first, those who most need to be rescued from the calamities
of injustice and sin. The beatitudes are the rallying cry to believers who will not allow any human institution, government
or ideology to control and dominate the lives of others. Jesus
came to preach the Good News to the poor first, and the poor,
those in desperate need, are the first to really perceive what
this word of hope means to the world. They pass the Good
News on and witness to it by living in the midst of an unjust
society with dignity, with non-violence, and with community.

Elsa Tamez, in her book *Bible of the Oppressed* (Orbis
Books, 1982), speaks of the poor, the *anawim*, the afflicted, the
oppressed. They are called *hoi ptochoi*—those who beg, who
are dependent on others for support, and who are so oppressed that they are in special need of God's help. In Luke's
gospel many of the parables and stories that follow the beatitudes are about these poor folk, such as the widow who contributed all she had (Lk 21:3); Lazarus, the beggar at the gate
of the rich man (Lk 16:20); the rich landowner who is invited
to sell what he has, give it to the poor, and follow Jesus (Lk
18:18); the people to whom Zacchaeus gives half of his belongings (Lk 19:1-10); those who are the preferred banquet
guests at the kingdom's feast (Lk 14)—the ones who can't

repay their invitations. All these people are held up as models
for disciples to imitate and take notice of if they are going to
follow Jesus more closely and honestly.

Perhaps the shortest and most powerful story is that of
the widow and her gift to the treasury:

> Jesus looked up and saw rich people putting their
> gifts into the treasure box; he also saw a poor widow
> dropping in two small coins. And he said, "Truly, I
> tell you, this poor widow put in more than all of
> them. For all gave an offering from their plenty, but
> she, out of her poverty, gave all she had to live on."
> (Luke 21:1-4)

This short piece pointedly demonstrates that it is the poor
themselves who are the most generous, both to God and to
others. The poor widow has practically nothing to live on, yet,
like countless others who are poor, she can find something to
give away to God. Without access to resources, without security, with very little protection under the law and living on the
fringes of the community, she is a source of wonder and delight for God! Nothing in the universe is trivial. All of life is
full of possibilities, of miracles, of light and transformation.
This woman who had no security knew what freedom was.
She lived silently in the kingdom, in right relationship to
everything, unnoticed except by the Holy. Most of us come
from the other group of people: those who give an offering or
gift from our plenty, our excess—what won't really touch us
or bother us. We won't feel its pinch and pull and even then
we are often reluctant to give.

There is a Russian Jewish children's story called "As Big
as an Egg." A storybook version is retold by Rochel Sandman.
This is the way I tell it.

✳   Once upon a time Chaim was cold and tired from a long
day at work. He stood in line in front of the bakery and
fidgeted, stomping his feet and trying to stay warm. All
he wanted to do was go home, make some hot tea, say his
prayers, and go to bed. The line didn't seem to be moving

at all. This was Russia and it was a time of war and there was so little food to be had. But he had his card, his precious card that gave him the right to wait in line for a loaf of bread twice a week. And all he could think about was the bread and soaking it in tea and biting off little bits and pieces of it to make it last longer, stretching it out.

Finally his turn came and he turned to run home with his loaf of bread that was to last him the next four days. And who should he see making her way toward him but the old widow Hanna. His heart sank. No, he felt himself getting angry. This woman was always around when he got his bread. She had no family and nothing else to do but collect bread for others. He didn't want to give her any of his, but she was on him in a flash, with shining eyes in the cold night, smiling with all her teeth. "Bread?" she asked, opening her sack. When he looked in her bag he could see chunks and pieces of bread torn from other loaves. "Please," she begged. "There are so many who are old and crippled and sickly, and they can't wait in line in the cold. Just a piece or two, pulled off your loaf so that they can eat too." He didn't want to give to her. He didn't have enough to keep body and soul together for himself. He wished he'd seen her sooner and escaped. But he was trapped. So he pulled off a piece about the size of an egg, a small egg, and threw it in the sack with the other pieces. She smiled hugely and gave him a blessing and thanks: "May you live long and merit to do many more good deeds."

"Yeah, yeah," he mumbled as he hurried away.

At home he made his tea, hot and steaming, and ate his bread slowly, chewing each bite over and over again, wanting to hold onto the taste. There was never enough. He was still kicking himself for having run into Hanna and giving some of his bread away. "Next time," he decided, "I'll go to another bakery and then she won't bother me." He said his prayers and went to sleep, dreaming of food.

The next day he came home from work thinking only of his tea and bread. As he opened the door to his little room, he was dismayed to hear the scurry of a rat and catch the fleeting glimpse of a tail flying across the floor and into a hole! The tail was waving in the air, almost as though it was scolding him, shaking a wagging finger at him. "No!" he cried as he went for his bread. Sure enough, there was a piece missing—about the size of an egg. He would have to be more careful. But first he crawled around on his hands and knees and plugged up every hole he could find. Then, weary, he washed his hands, said the blessing, and slowly ate his bread. He was careful with the rest of that loaf.

The next time he got bread he picked another bakery and, sure enough, no Hanna with her wide-open sack and begging, making him feel guilty and angry.

Home he went and ate, savoring every bit. The next night he opened his door and oh, no! He caught sight of the rat, its tail shaking a finger at him as it disappeared into the floor. He grabbed his bread. Another piece was gone, about the size of an egg! After a hurried blessing, he ate. Then he carefully wrapped his loaf and put it on the highest shelf, arranging other things around it so nothing could get at it.

The next evening he came home and opened his door. NO! That rat scurried by him, tail waving, shaking a finger at him. His bread had a piece missing, about the size of an egg. This time he was determined. After praying and eating, he wrapped the loaf in paper and tied a string around it and hung it from the ceiling. It would be safe.

The next day home he came and opened his door. What? Not again! That rat, running across the floor, tail wagging its scolding finger at him. He pulled the bread from the ceiling and found another piece gone: about the size of an egg.

He sat and prayed the blessing and ate his bread in bits and pieces and thought about the bread. Something was wrong. What was it? Finally, he smiled ruefully and knew. All of his bread did not belong to him. Some of it belonged in Hanna's gaping sack; it belonged to those who couldn't wait on line. He should be grateful that he had a card and was guaranteed two loaves of bread a week. He slept deeply and next day stood on line for his bread. Hanna was there hovering about and as soon as he had his loaf he ran over to her and smiled warmly. She opened her sack and he tore off two pieces of bread, good-sized pieces, about the size of an egg, two large eggs. She smiled back and said the blessing, adding "May you live long and merit to do many more good deeds." She closed her mitzvah sack and scurried off.

Back home he went and opened his door to see the rat running across the floor again! But this time his tail seemed to be waving goodbye! He was not surprised that he never saw Hanna's little helper the rat after that, not surprised at all.

Do we give out of our poverty, our lack, our need, our longing for justice, our compassion for others? Are we like the lowly widow? No matter what our circumstances, do we have our hearts set on the coming of the kingdom, the coming of hope, the needs of others as well as our own? Is there room in our hearts for repentance, for generosity, for sharing? The widow in the gospel story is not just economically poor, or poor because she is a widow without the support of a family or a community, reduced to living on others' good will; she is poor in spirit. She belongs by her actions to that group of people that Luke describes in the first few chapters of his gospel, those who are poor in the Isaian sense. These are the ones who wait and are described as "upright in the eyes of God...[those who live] blamelessly in accordance with all the laws and commands of the Lord" (Lk 1:6). This is the description of Elizabeth and Zechariah who are old and childless, another form of poverty in the Jewish community. Others of this group are Anna and Simeon who are in the temple when Joseph and Mary bring the child to be dedicated to the Lord. And of course, Joseph and Mary themselves are lowly and meek servants, waiting on the will of God to come more surely into history. Mary herself in the song of the Magnificat sings: "My spirit exults in God my savior! He has looked upon his servant in her lowliness, and people forever will call me blessed. The Mighty One has done great things for me, Holy is his Name! From age to age his mercy extends to those who live in his presence" (Lk 1:47-50). Mary is, par excellence, one of the poor, blessed by God who dwells in the kingdom. And she knows it and exults in its gift and presence within her and around her in the world.

The other category that is identified as poor, as those who have the kingdom with them already, is children. Jesus blesses the children that gather around him and solemnly chides his disciples with the words: "Let the children come to me and don't stop them, for the kingdom of God belongs to such as these. Truly, I tell you, whoever does not receive the kingdom of God like a child will not enter it" (Lk 18:16-17). This little nugget of truth is wedged in between the parable of the Pharisee and the tax collector and the story of the rich landowner who cannot let go of his belongings to follow Jesus. Both stories are about resistance to the kingdom, to conversion, and to Jesus, and about what constitutes being a disciple of Jesus in the world: humility before God, a willingness to sell what you don't need or have kept unjustly and give it to the poor, leaving it behind to follow Jesus and join his company of disciples. Even the disciples are nervous about whether or not they are saved in this regard and feel the need to check their status with Jesus. Peter reminds Jesus that they have left everything to follow him and Jesus reassures him that anyone who leaves anything to follow him will "receive much more *in this present time* [my emphasis] and in the world to come...will have eternal life" (Lk 18:28-30). Letting go, giving away, sharing, and making the kingdom your most prized possession give you the kingdom now. These stories, along with the healing and giving of sight to the blind beggar near Jericho, are preludes to the story that culminates in Jesus' going to Jerusalem to die. His preaching and ministry have been set in motion. There is not much time left for him to throw the net of the kingdom over those who are open to it. The story that follows is that of the man in the sycamore tree, Zacchaeus.

Zacchaeus is sometimes referred to as the poor little rich man. Zacchaeus is rich, a tax collector, despised by his neighbors and the Romans alike. Tax collectors often made fortunes off their neighbors' misfortunes for, in addition to collecting the taxes for Rome, they frequently demanded extra money that often went into their own pockets. The tax collector Zacchaeus is small, not only in stature, but also in the eyes of his own society. But he's curious about Jesus, interested enough to climb a tree to get a better look at him.

And then it is Jesus' move, one that no one is expecting: certainly not Zacchaeus, who is thoroughly delighted, or the crowd, which is thoroughly put out and annoyed, or even the disciples, who later express their utter astonishment that even tax collectors are being converted (though Zacchaeus is the only one besides Matthew mentioned). Jesus invites himself to the known sinner's house for dinner. It's a comical situation, with Zacchaeus tumbling out of his tree. At the base of the tree Jesus announces his plans and everyone is aghast, because Zacchaeus is poor, too. He is a social outcast. Even though he has added to the economic misery and hardship of his own community, he is part of a despised group of people considered lost, rejected and cursed by God, unclean and proscribed and shunned, along with shepherds, prostitutes, and all public sinners. He is one of those who is known to be "habitually delinquent" in following the Law. Along with those who are plagued by physical infirmities, possessed by demons, or infertile, he is publicly judged as a social and religious outcast. Members of this group are never allowed to forget for a moment that they are worthless, scurrilous, and miserable wretches with no hope of salvation.

And that is the reaction of the people: How can Jesus eat with such a person, enter his house, and accept his hospitality? Why, it is well known that even God shunned them, as all good religious people do. And so the crowd murmurs against both Zacchaeus and Jesus. They are comrades in derision and insult now. But Zacchaeus has been touched by Jesus' kindness and attention. He holds his ground, stands up, and publicly witnesses to the effect that the presence of Jesus has already had on his life. For the kingdom is here in the person of Jesus and a sinner, Zacchaeus, is drawn and attracted to it like a nail to a magnet, unlike many of the more acceptable folk who can't see past their own assumptions and agendas.

Zacchaeus announces two remarkable projects. First, he will give half of his goods to the poor and then, if he has cheated anyone, he will pay them back four times the amount (Lk 19:8). This is no mean feat. The first action will drop him out of his economic caste and into another social group. The second action will definitely drop him into the category of the poor—those to whom he has just promised half of his belongings. He has jumped out of a tree and into the kingdom of God in one leap. And Jesus is delighted. In response he announces: "Salvation has come to this house today, for he is also a true son of Abraham. The Son of Man has come to seek and to save the lost" (vv. 9-10). Another lost soul has been reclaimed and brought into the kingdom of God. Allegiance with Jesus, repentance, public care of the poor, and restitution in the cause of justice make one blessed and immediately give one a home in the kingdom of God. The Word of the Lord is reliable and Zacchaeus is home free.

In one sense, Zacchaeus' actions are penance for sin and collusion with evil and injustice, a righting of the balance that he has been partially responsible for upsetting. Zacchaeus is repentant. But, in another sense, Zacchaeus is opting for solidarity with the poor, joining them by his actions and becoming one with them. Now he will live with them and be associated with them, even though he will still, it seems, be a tax collector. The outsider and outcast has become an insider by his choice to stand with Jesus and be worthy of having dinner with him (which represents, of course, the Eucharist).

How are we poor? How do we get into the kingdom? Nelsa Curbelo of Guayaquil, Ecuador, the general secretary of Servicio Paz y Justicia en America Latina, has said:

> When you choose an ideology,
> you can fool yourself.
> When you choose the poor
> and are one of them
> you can be sure you won't fool yourself...
>
> The reading of history depends
> on the place in which we locate ourselves...

And we locate ourselves in and with the poor,
with the cultures that are oppressed but alive,
like the yeast in the dough,
like the seeds that tolerate the hot sun
and the desert but are ready to germinate,
to flourish and to provide food with the first dew
and early rain that nourishes them.
(From a card sent to me from Salvador by a friend)

One of the ways into the kingdom is solidarity, being mindful of the poor, listening to them, speaking with them and reminding others of their existence. Albert Camus wrote in *The First Man*, "Rescue this poor family from the fate of the poor, which is to disappear from history without a trace." It is a requirement of this first beatitude that we give voice to those who have not been listened to with respect and care, that we speak their words and attend to their needs and agendas that are always more crushing and essential than ours. Our cry for justice must be first and foremost a cry for the poor, for their justice and life, for their survival and dignity and future.

Another way of being blessed and being poor is to begin to practice the virtue of poverty by making ourselves poor for the kingdom, poorer so that others might have life. This includes practicing the corporal works of mercy, simplifying our own lives and needs, restraining our greed and avarice, and making sure that what we let go of and give away goes to those who need it. We must make friends with the poor and know and visit and come to love people who just happen to be less secure financially than we are. We must begin to barter for goods and services, providing dignity and respect to those who do have something to give, but not necessarily in the market economy of capitalism and the mall. Goods that are cooperatively made, those manufactured by indigenous people and people struggling to recover from war and discrimination must be our first choices, while we boycott goods and services that are produced cheaply by slave labor of women and children. (Check the logo on your sneakers and be sure your running shoes are not beggaring those already poor.)

Politically we must be conscious of our government's choices and aware of the effects of our economic initiatives. To provide most favored nation status to China in the wake of human rights offenses and that country's destruction of Tibet is criminal. To profit from treaties with neighboring countries that give huge income boosts to a few while contributing to massive injustices, such as those experienced by the poor in Mexico, is to split a country into a nation of beggars and the privileged, with an ever-widening gap between the two. To allow welfare laws to be enforced selectively in states that destroy already poor families and push those on the edge already over the brink is mean-spirited and unjust. Our personal lifestyles and political and economic choices must be consistent with the call of the gospel to "deny ourselves, pick up our cross, and come after Jesus." We must remember that there is still one thing we lack. "Sell all you have and give the money to the poor, and you will have riches in God [treasures in heaven]. And then come and follow me" (Lk 18:22). The practice of detachment is essential and freeing. We are not allowed to acquire and collect for the sake of having more than what we need. Sharing is central to the practice of faith. There is an ancient Buddhist story of the saint Nagarjuna that makes this quite clear.

✳   Once upon a time Nagarjuna was traveling. As was his custom, he traveled only with a loincloth and, oddly enough, an exquisite golden begging bowl, etched and inlaid with detail and design. It had been a gift to him from a king who was one of his favorite disciples, and he treasured it because of the relationship and memories they had shared together.

One night he was about to settle down to sleep. Having sought out a suitable place so that he could pray and meditate when he awoke, he had found the ruins of an old monastery that had obviously been glorious in its day and now was empty and in disrepair. But as soon as he wrapped himself in some leaves, he noticed a figure lurking in the shadows. A thief, obviously. He sat up and beckoned the man over to him. "Here," he said, "take this," and he held out his begging bowl, the king's gift! "I need to sleep and then to pray and this way you won't disturb me later." The man couldn't believe his good fortune. He snatched it from Nagarjuna's hands and set off running before the crazy *fakir* might change his mind and come after him.

Nagarjuna slept and, refreshed, awoke to pray and meditate. He was just finishing in the morning when he saw the figure again, hiding in the shadows of the great trees. He gestured him forward and again the thief approached him. The thief stood before him and handed him his begging bowl. It was a while before he found the words he wanted to say and spoke: "When you gave me your begging bowl so freely last night, you made me feel suddenly so very poor. Will you, can you teach me this kind of light-hearted detachment that makes you so free? I want to be that free and I won't care if I'm poor or rich."

I want to be that free! One way to be that free is to be attached first to the kingdom of God, to the poor and to the Word that is the way, the truth, and the life that is given to be shared so that others too might have life ever more abundantly. There is a French proverb that says: "When you die, you carry in your clutched hands only that which you have given away." Once we dwell in the kingdom of God, we can give everything away with foolish freedom to all those who are afraid of being poor. To be poor and dwell in the kingdom of God is hard, but it is harder still not to be in that kingdom here and now. Blessed are the poor for the kingdom of God is theirs!

4

Blessed Are You Who Are Hungry Now
Blessed Are You Who Weep Now

One cannot weep for the entire world. It is beyond human strength. One must choose. (Jean Anouilh)

If you've not been fed, be bread. (Rumi)

These two beatitudes are made of food and tears, body and soul so intertwined as to be inseparable. The first three beatitudes are really three descriptions of the same group of people we often refer to as "the poor." The poor are those who find themselves hungry and weeping because of their position, their infirmities, and their lack of place in any community. They are the truly wretched and miserable of the earth, reduced to begging for bare survival in a world of plenty and wealth. They must depend on the kindness of others; they have no resources of their own and live in a state of constant insecurity.

The issues of bread and tears are very closely connected. Our insides hunger, first for food and drink, and then for love, acceptance, justice and dignity, hope, and a future. We weep when we have reached the end of our endurance, when we are weary, alone, without meaning or hope, overwhelmed by fear, or evil, or destruction. Hungering and mourning make us lose control, lead us to outwardly claw and crawl, and isolate us from others. And yet, Jesus' words ring with power and life: "Fortunate are you who are hungry now, for you will be filled. Fortunate are you who weep now, for you will laugh" (Lk 6:20-21).

Stories can uncover something of the meaning of this seeming contradiction. This old Persian story, from the area around present-day Iraq, is still told among immigrant families. It is called "The Sweetest Sound in All the World."

✳ Once upon a time there was a good king who sought to be just and attended to his people, listening to them and consulting with his advisors. Periodically he would throw a lavish dinner party and invite his trusted inner circle as well as newcomers and people who were musicians, poets, teachers, and strangers who were visiting in his domain. To make the evening more entertaining for his guests and instructive for himself, he would usually set a theme or a question for the evening that would constitute the conversation during dinner. It was always stimulating, informative, and helpful. On this particular night the question was put to them: "What is the sweetest sound in all the world?" And the conversations and stories, illustrations and opinions flew across the tables, and from group to group. It was a heady and emotional evening.

The guests were quick with their answers and intent on hearing the responses of others sharing their own beliefs and experiences. The question provoked passionate thoughts. There seemed to be no end to the answers. One man immediately spoke: "Why, of course, it is the sound of the lyre or harp, or any stringed instrument. It is haunting, lovely, capturing even the most hardened souls and reminding them of beauty, of what has been lost or what is larger than any small life. It carries you on the wind back to youth or away to unrealized dreams. It tugs at all the strings of your soul."

And another was quick to contradict: "No. It is the sound of the drum, the heartbeat of the universe that is echoed within everyone's body. It is the rhythm of life, primitive and demanding, binding us together, drawing us close in spite of ourselves. It is powerful, freeing, and evocative of all that is within us."

He had barely finished when another spoke. "No, no. It isn't a musical instrument, though each does have a unique sound. It's the song of the birds in the morning air. It is announcement, promise, genesis, and a fresh start. It is faithful, consistent. After all, what would life be if there were no birds to welcome each day?" And the discussion continued like this.

Soon an old woman spoke definitively: "You are all wrong. It is much more personal than anything you have mentioned. It is the cry of a newborn child torn from the womb and thrust into the world and the mystery that awaits the child's touch." There was silence, and thoughts went in other directions.

Someone else added, "It's the welcome greeting of someone who loves you when you return home after a long journey and you know this is what life is all about."

"Or," someone else chimed in, "it's the sound of words of forgiveness that heal and give you another chance." Well, the night sped by and afterwards they were all still talking about the question, each sure of their answer.

Now Akiba, one of the guests, was a member of the king's inner circle, a trusted advisor. Throughout the dinner he had listened attentively to the conversations and heated opinions; he had not spoken The king noticed this, but he knew his counselor, and he knew that when Akiba had something to say, he would speak.

Weeks passed and Akiba decided to throw a dinner party in honor of the king's goodness and in gratitude for all the many meals they had shared together. The guest list went out and all in the city were curious to know who had been invited. It promised to be a magical night.

The guests arrived to find the tables set most elegantly, the seating arrangements carefully selected, the decor truly magnificent. They were welcomed and the king was honored. Then the entertainment began: music, dancers, poetry, acrobatics, fireworks. One exceeded the other. And from the kitchen came the most incredible smells and sounds, aromas wafting through open doorways. The evening moved along and yet no food was served! They could hear the rattle and bang of pots and pans, the orders of the chief cook, even sounds of stirring, tasting, and "ahs" emanating from the official tasters as the evening wore on. But no food was served.

Initially the guests enjoyed the entertainment and the atmosphere but soon the talk and the undercurrent turned to food, the lack of food, and the rudeness of the host in being so tardy and unfeeling of his guests. What must the king be thinking, since he was the guest of honor and his plate was still empty, as was his glass! The hours dragged. They had been there forever. It was actually only three or four hours, but it seemed eternity. And then the guests began to slip away or grow more agitated, dropping louder and louder hints about their hunger. Many had not eaten all day—or even the day before—in anticipation of the food, for these banquets were noted for sublime servings and new versions of old favorites. But there was nothing.

Finally, at midnight, when they were faint, angry, and ill-tempered, there was the sound of clanging lids being uncovered, of knives being sharpened, and the cooks came out, laden with platters heaped high with food. Brandishing a knife and fork, the head chef rubbed them together and proclaimed: "Dinner is served." A cheer went up and the food was consumed. Nothing had ever tasted so good!

While they ate, and ate, the king looked at his advisor and waited for him to speak. Finally he did. "My king, at your last dinner party your question was intriguing: 'What is the sweetest sound?' I declare that the sweetest sound on earth is the sound of pots being uncovered, the clatter of knives and forks and empty plates being filled heard by the ears of hungry men, women, and children. You know how hungry you have grown this night. What if you were hungry all the time, as many in your kingdom find themselves? What if you were starving in the midst of plenty and excess? What would be the sweetest sound in your ears?"

The king listened and heard. From that night forth all his priorities changed: his laws, policies, and building projects. All served the growing of food, the harvesting and provision of adequate food for everyone in his kingdom. He became truly just and never enjoyed another meal without remembering the one that introduced him to the sweetest sound in all the world—the sound of expectation for hungers being met.

A marvelous story. Usually when I tell it, I pause halfway through, before the end of the first dinner party to ask those listening what they think is "the sweetest sound in all the world." Of the many times I have done this, only once did someone mention the drift of the story: hunger and the sound of food being served, eaten, and shared. That was from someone who had spent many years in Peru, learning from his own people how to share food and stretch what little they had so that everyone got some, and those most in need—children, the elderly, and the ill—received the best, first. Always the end of the story is sobering, for it reminds very full people of what is most often taken for granted: food.

"In the 1990's still 18 million people every year die from hunger and poverty-related causes, that is 1700 unnecessary deaths every hour—they are an insult to God our creator." These are the words of Julian Filochowski, director of CAFOD in the United Kingdom, giving his Oxford Address in July 1996 at the European Congress of Jesuit Alumni on the prospect of the celebration of the Jubilee in the year 2000 A.D.

And these are deaths by hunger. There is no mention of the millions more who are hungry every day, who are slowly dying of starvation and the related ills of disease and illiteracy and poverty and the added burdens brought on by local conflicts, devastation of natural resources, and war. The need is not only for food but also for aid in the time and place of crisis and developmental aid and monetary resources earmarked for social change for the long haul in all the major countries of the world. The issue has become, not the fact that we cannot solve this problem, but that we choose not to address the problem as primary in our agendas.

Julian continues in his speech:

> How can this be when our one world has supposedly become a global village? Globalisation is the word of the moment; information technology allows instant communication; globalised investment, instant financial transfer; globalised profit flows; [a] new GATT arrangement leading inexorably towards a single global market. Our one world seems smaller every day. But do not be deluded. In this one world the richest fifth of humanity, the richest one billion people on our planet, take for themselves every year 83% of the wealth produced; they leave for the poorest fifth, the poorest one billion on our planet, 14% of the world's income. The richest billion includes all of us in the North; the poorest billion are peoples of Bangladesh, India and sub-Saharan Africa. This means we take sixty times as much every year of the world's production as the poorest fifth. The U.N. tells us this and it is reconfirmed in the recent Human Development Report. Thirty years ago the richest fifth took only thirty times as much as the poorest fifth so we have to say that the gap, the inequality, is actually growing. With research and development in key technologies concentrated and controlled by the richest fifth that process is destined to continue.

That is the world view economically and politically, but oftentimes this concentration of wealth is hard to comprehend. It is even harder to imagine that 80 percent of the world cannot even dream of living in a manner the top 20 percent takes for granted. We talk much these days about the global village, with slogans like "Think Globally and Act Locally" even found on bumper stickers. If we were to reduce the population of the world to one hundred people, this is what the Human Global Village would look like:

57 Asians
21 Europeans
14 from the Western Hemisphere
8 Africans

51 Female/49 Male
70 Non-white/30 White
70 Non-Christian/30 Christian

50% of the entire world's wealth would be in the
    hands of 6 people and all 6 would be citizens of
    the United States
80 would live in substandard housing
70 would be unable to read
50 would suffer malnutrition
1 would have a college education

This was printed in 1996 on the back page of the *Catholic Agitator*, the Los Angeles Catholic Worker newspaper. Along with this information was the following closer-to-home glimpse of how the rich are getting richer and the poor are getting poorer in the U.S. This piece was reprinted from the *National Coalition for the Homeless Newsletter*, Aug./Sept. 1996.

The United States has the widest gap between rich and poor of any industrialized country. According to a recent Federal Reserve Board study, the top 1% of households control 30.4% of the nation's wealth. The next 9% control an additional 36.8% of the country's wealth. The bottom 90% of U.S. households account for the remaining 32.8% of wealth.

The legacy of the 104th Congress will be to have increased military spending by $32 billion, including nearly $18 billion beyond the increases requested by the Pentagon.

To put this last piece in a larger perspective of the world's military budgets:

U.S. military spending is 28 times as large as the combined budgets of the six "adversary" nations as defined by the U.S. military: North Korea, Iran, Cuba, Libya and Syria. (American Friends Service Committee)

The statistics are staggering. There are, it seems, more poor, more hungry, and more of those who weep and mourn than there are in the group of those not-so-blessed, to use the words of Jesus in the beatitudes. Jesus' singling out of the blessed began with his own inauguration of his ministry in the synagogue of his home town, Nazareth, with the ringing words of Isaiah that he "found" in the scriptures:

Jesus acted with the power of the Spirit, and on his return to Galilee the news about him spread throughout all that territory. He began teaching in the synagogues of the Jews and everyone praised him.

When Jesus came to Nazareth where he had been brought up, he entered the synagogue on the Sabbath as he usually did. He stood up to read and they handed him the book of the prophet Isaiah.

Jesus then unrolled the scroll and found the place where it is written: *The Spirit of the Lord is upon me. He has anointed me to bring good news to the poor, to proclaim liberty to captives and new sight to the blind; to free the oppressed and announce the Lord's year of mercy.*

Jesus then rolled up the scroll, gave it to the attendant and sat down, while the eyes of all in the synagogue were fixed on him. Then he said to them: "Today these prophetic words come true even as you listen." (Luke 4:14-21)

This is Jesus' definition of his mission and purpose, the reason for his coming into the world and the declarative statement of who he is: the anointed of God. He uses what is termed Jubilee language to express God's intentions for him in the world. He quotes selectively from Isaiah 61:1-2 and 58:6 to announce what has already happened in the world by his arrival "in the power of the Spirit." It has begun! God's work is coming into reality, a reality that must be faced, embraced, or rejected in the person of Jesus.

He announces in true prophetic style "the year of favor from the Lord" or "the Lord's year of mercy." Jesus picks and chooses from the Isaian texts to highlight what he is going to do. He drops the phrase "the day of vengeance of our God" (61:2b) and adds in "setting the oppressed free" (58:6). All of Isaiah 58 is often referred to as the Jubilee chapter and it describes clearly what God is looking for from his people. This passage is about atonement for evil and sin and about the favor and grace that God extends to his people and that must, in turn, be extended by the people to their neighbors. God will liberate his people but they must liberate one another. The phrase that Jesus inserts comes from the description of fasting that God wants from his own:

> See the fast that pleases me:
> breaking the fetters of injustice
> and unfastening the thongs of the yoke,
> setting the oppressed free
> and breaking every yoke.
> Fast by sharing your food with the hungry,
> bring to your house the homeless,
> clothe the man you see naked
> and do not turn away from your own kin.
> (Isaiah 58:6-7)

It really couldn't be said more clearly. Jesus' ministry is about jubilee, about celebration, about freedom and release, cast not only in religious terms for individuals, but also in practical economic and political terms for the people and nation. The word *jubilee* comes from the Hebrew *yobel* which signifies the ram's horn that is used to open the year: "Only when the ram's horn sounds may some of them go up to the mountain" (Ex 19:13). Israel had cast off the yoke of slavery and oppression when God's redeeming grace had led them forth from Egypt. Never again was anyone in Israel to suffer degradation and lack of human freedom, hunger for food, for dignity, for the opportunity to worship their God and to live on their land in peace. Leviticus 25 and 27 offer pragmatic and specific directions for celebrating this Jubilee year, the opportunity to begin again and to remember all that Yahweh has done for his people in setting them free from the burdens they have known for generations. It is to take place every seven years and then at the fiftieth year.

> Yahweh spoke to Moses on Mount Sinai: "Speak to the Israelites and tell them: When you enter the land I am giving you, let the land rest for Yahweh every seventh year. For six years you shall sow your field, prune your vineyard and harvest the produce, but in the seventh year the land shall have a rest, or sabbath, a sabbath for Yahweh. You shall not sow your field nor prune your vineyard; you shall not reap the aftergrowth of your harvest nor gather the grapes of your uncultivated vines.
>
> This shall be a year of rest for the land, but whatever it produces of itself will provide food for you, for your male and female slaves, for your hired servant and for the stranger who lives with you. . . .
>
> When seven sabbaths of years have passed, that is, seven times seven years, there shall be the time of the seven weeks of years, that is forty-nine years. Then on the tenth day of the seventh month sound the trumpet loudly. On this Day of Atonement sound the trumpet all through the land. Keep holy the fiftieth year and proclaim freedom for all the inhabitants of the land. It shall be a jubilation year for you when each one shall recover his property and go back to his family." (Leviticus 25:1-10)

> "I will make my Dwelling among you and I will not reject you. I will walk among you; I will be your God and you will be my people. I am Yahweh your God, who brought you out of Egypt to be their slaves no longer. I have broken the bars of your yoke letting you walk erect." (Leviticus 27:11-13)

The jubilee is about food, rejoicing, laughter and having one's fill—but it is about everyone in the land experiencing this as a recurring reality, a reality that can be fallen back upon every seven years, a hope that sustains in time of lack, hunger, oppression, and mourning. Isaiah proclaims this loudly in the lines that immediately follow the description of the fast that Yahweh wants, the line that Jesus quotes in his own reading of the scriptures:

> Then will your light break forth as the dawn
> and your healing come in a flash.
> Your righteousness will be your vanguard,
> the Glory of Yahweh your rear guard.
> Then you will call and Yahweh will answer,
> you will cry and he will say, I am here.
>   (Isaiah 58:8-9)

The four demands of the Jubilee year are: remission of debts, restoration of the land, Sabbath rest for the land and all persons, even slaves and strangers in Israel, and release from economic servitude. The demands touch on injustices that are rampant in the majority of nations today. And just as the jubilee prescriptions were incumbent on all Israelites and arrived periodically to right the imbalances that had developed, so too it is incumbent upon all of us to celebrate this Jubilee on a regular basis, starting, perhaps, with preparation for the coming millennium in the year 2000.

It is interesting to note that the world's debtor nations have issued the following demands to their creditor nations who require payment not only of their past debts but also exorbitant interest that has accrued over the years: (1) cancellation of their debts; (2) restitution of land and resources to their original owners; (3) cessation from pilfering natural resources and from polluting them; and (4) the termination of economic slavery by universally raising wages to a subsistence level. They echo the Jubilee demands precisely on a world-wide structural level. The Jubilee prescriptions provide a pragmatic blueprint for correcting existing economic injustices and for bridging the gap between those who have too much and those who do not have enough. It is interesting to note that the United Nations defines being "rich" as having more than what you need in order to survive. Jesus begins his public preaching with a rallying cry for the hungry and the poor, those who mourn their position in the world as the least, those without sustenance or hope for a better and more secure future.

What then is the cure? What can we do? The American poet Walt Whitman says:

> This is what you should do: love the earth and sun and animals, despise riches, give alms to everyone who asks, stand up for the stupid and the crazy, devote your income and labor to others, hate tyrants, argue not concerning God, have patience and indulgence towards the people, take your hat off to nothing known or unknown or to any... re-examine all you have been told at school or in any book, dismiss what insults your own soul, and your very flesh shall be a great poem.

Jesus tells a number of stories (on the Sabbath, of course) to reinforce what he is doing and saying. The first is told in the context of a dinner party that a leading Pharisee has thrown and to which he has been invited as a guest.

> One sabbath Jesus had gone to eat a meal in the house of a leading Pharisee, and he was carefully watched. In front of him was a man suffering from dropsy; so Jesus asked the teachers of the Law and the Pharisees, "Is it lawful to heal on the sabbath or not?" But no one answered. Jesus then took the man, healed him and sent him away. And he addressed them, "If your lamb or your ox falls into a well on a sabbath day, who among you doesn't hurry to pull him out?" And they could not answer. (Luke 14:1-6)

Dinner parties were public affairs. The invited guests were seated in an inner circle and waited upon by attendants. Those from the town who were spectators often stayed, listened, and watched and then went home with the leftovers. Jesus is watched, as it seems he often is in Luke's gospel. In the synagogue his listeners had been initially spellbound, though this quickly turned to rage and rejection. Now he is watched and it almost seems as if the poor man suffering from his ailment has been deliberately set before Jesus as one would set a plate of food before someone hungry to see if he will devour the food without blessing or pause for gratitude, or even civil manners. The man is bait for Jesus. Jesus rises to the occasion and turns the issue back on them with his question of sabbath law, jubilee law, and its underlying purpose. And no one will answer him. Even when he brings up the example of how they treat their property, their animals, with care, they still do not admit to their insensitivity and use of human beings so carelessly, as less than animals and beasts of burden. How low they have fallen! They have allowed so many in their own land to know again the humiliation of what they experienced as a nation in Egypt. But they are adamant in interpreting the Law for their own ends as justification for their behavior.

So Jesus tells them a parable that is directed at their own behavior at this dinner party:

> Jesus then told a parable to the guests, for he had noticed how they tried to take the places of honor. And he said, "When you are invited to a wedding party, do not choose the best seat. It may happen that someone more important than you has been invited, and your host, who invited both of you, will come and say to you: 'Please give him your place.' What shame is yours when you take the lowest seat!
>
> Whenever you are invited, go rather to the lowest seat, so that your host may come and say to you: 'Friend, you must come up higher.' And this will be a great honor for you in the presence of all the other guests. For everyone who makes much of himself will be humbled, and everyone who humbles himself will be esteemed." (Luke 14:7-11)

As in every culture, there was an order to the seating arrangements, an order of intimacy, of closeness to the host based on people's relationships and dealings with the host prior to the feast. Jesus' specific example of the wedding feast involves very specific and publicly acknowledged seats. The head table where the host would sit would have seats for the guests of honor: the bride and groom and those in the wedding party and the immediate family of the couple married. Even today in our culture no one would think of sitting in one of those seats if one were not in the family or wedding party unless, as a special honor, one were specifically brought forward.

Jesus is not speaking of false humility, of acting so that others will search for you and bring you publicly to a place that befits your position or role. Jesus' words have to be understood in context. He has just healed a person obviously not asked to be seated with the guests, but paraded before him like a piece of meat, something to be consumed or used like a knife and fork to make a stab at someone in public. In light of what he has just done, Jesus is speaking about root causes of injustice and inequality. Who we think we are and who we think is worth associating with and whose company we prefer and seek out reveal our values more clearly than the reciting of any creed. In our society we are intent on "upward mobility," on procuring a better place, a bigger house, a more influential position. We seek out more power and use our reputation and that of our friends to get ahead. People are either beneficial and useful or useless and of no account to us. But in Jesus' kingdom, the practice of "downward mobility" is virtue and truth. God became human and in doing so came down, down to an insignificant nation that not only had a history of being slaves but was presently oppressed and occupied by enemies. God became poor and then became poorer still through those with whom he chose to associate and the message that he preached: of liberty to captives and good news to the disenfranchised and hope for those enslaved, imprisoned, and despised by others. And then he was humiliated: he was rejected by his own people's leaders and tortured and executed by their enemies, suffering death on a cross. He was to know the reality of mourning, of suffering, of weeping. He was to know the disgrace of public betrayal by his own friends and followers, by those he had healed and helped, and by powerful strangers intent on making him an example to others, deliberately reducing him to "a worm and no man" in the words of Isaiah.

And then, to bring his story closer to home for his host and those who, like him, are invited guests at the table, he continues:

> "When you give a lunch or a dinner, don't invite your friends, or your brothers and relatives and wealthy neighbors. For surely they will also invite you in return and you will be repaid. When you give a feast, invite instead the poor, the crippled, the lame and the blind. Fortunate are you then, because they can't repay you; you will be repaid at the Resurrection of the upright." (Luke 14:12-14)

Ah! Another beatitude! And the response of one at the table, on hearing these words is: "Happy are those who eat at the banquet in the kingdom of God!" (Lk 14:15). Somebody heard the message! For this description is about God and how God works in the world, befriending the broken-hearted, the nation without power or prestige or influence in the world except for God's presence and choice of them as his own people. Again it is the prophet Isaiah who heartens his weary people with the wonders of God and what he does and will do for them:

> Come here, all you who are thirsty, come to the water!
> All who have no money, come!
> Yes, without money and at no cost, buy and drink wine and milk.
> Why spend money on what is not food and labor for what does not satisfy?
> Listen to me, and you will eat well; you will enjoy the richest of fare.
> Incline your ear and come to me; listen, that your soul may live. I will make with you an everlasting covenant. I will fulfill in you my promises to David. (Isaiah 55:1-3)

Joyous feasting is a loud sign, a sweet sign of the presence of God, of the reality of liberation in their midst. It is a sign of God releasing a judgment on the people and forgiving them their sin, just as Jesus' healing of the man brought to him at the table was a release, not just from physical ailment, but from the judgment of his neighbors. It was the removal of a curse, the lightening of a burden, and the breaking of a yoke that was tight and unyielding. Sometimes this is called "the preferential option for the poor," but Yahweh and the prophets and Jesus made the choice first and made it a fundamental imperative of believing in the God of life and compassion, Jesus' Father who hears the cry of the poor and glances upon all those who stand before him without pretense, knowing their need and knowing that God is their only hope.

Jesus goes on, reiterating the necessity of caring for those who cannot repay or reciprocate and of inviting them into our world.

> Jesus replied, "A man once gave a feast and invited many guests. When it was time for the feast he sent his servant to tell those he had invited to come, for everything was ready. But all alike began to make excuses. The first said: 'Please excuse me. I must go and sell the piece of land I have just bought.' Another said: 'I am sorry, but I am on my way to try out the five yoke of oxen I have just bought.' Still another said, 'How can I come when I have just married?'
>
> The servant returned alone and reported this to his master. Upon hearing the account, the master of the house flew into a rage and ordered his servant: 'Go out quickly into the streets and alleys of the town and bring in the poor, the crippled, the blind and the lame.'
>
> The servant reported after a while: 'Sir, your orders have been carried out, but there is still room.' The master said: 'Go out to the highways and country lanes and force people to come in, to make sure my house is full. I tell you, none of those invited will have a morsel of my feast.'" (Luke 14:16-24)

There is a vehemence in this parable and in the man who prepares the feast and invites his friends who refuse to come. Their excuses are economic and social and have to do with a betterment of their economic and social standings that would, in their minds, eliminate their "need" to attend the man's feast. These people are moving up in the world and changing their status according to their priorities; the man's feast no longer is high on their list, or on their ladder of ascent. Land, possessions, and relationships drastically alter who we align ourselves with and where we think we belong or choose to go.

The man responds quickly, decisively, and imperiously. He tells his servants to go out and compel the poor and those forgotten and destitute, those hiding in alleys, hedges, and abandoned houses, those falling through the cracks in society to come to the feast, to enter the kingdom of God. The invitation goes out to all, but first to these, the masses of people who have previously found no seat at the banquet table and have never known what it was like to be invited in, welcomed, seated, and waited upon. The notes of the *Christian Community Bible* put it well:

> Bring the poor... compel them to come to my church; force them also to fulfill the role fitting to them in society. God relies on the poor and the marginalized to maintain the aspirations toward peace and justice in the world, to awaken the consciences of those "good" people who are too comfortable. (p. 203)

We are summoned to work, to search out and encourage, to insist on the place of the poor at the table of the Lord, the table of plenty, the table of grace and freedom. Number 16 of the U.S. Bishops' Economic Pastoral *Economic Justice for All* says that this preferential option for the poor is also an economic principle of action. It is to "speak for the voiceless, to defend the defenseless, to assess lifestyles, policies and social institutions in terms of their impact on the poor and to strengthen the whole community by assisting those most vulnerable."

The kingdom of heaven is possessed by the poor and it is in the presence of the poor themselves that the kingdom is most accessible and most easily recognized and entered. Among the poor, the kingdom is there for the taking! Those who mourn will find comfort and the oil of gladness, for God delights in his people. Isaiah again offers consolation:

> No more will the sun give you light by day,
> nor the moon shine on you by night.
> For Yahweh will be your everlasting light
> and your God will be your glory.
> No more will your sun go down,
> never will your moon wane,
> For Yahweh will be your everlasting light,
> and your days of mourning will come to an end.
> Your people will be upright;
> forever they will possess the land—
> they the shoot of my planting,
> the work of my hand—
> in them I shall be glorified.
> The least of them will become a clan,
> the smallest a mighty nation.
> I, Yahweh, will do this,
> swiftly, in due time.
>   (Isaiah 60:19-22)

Consolation is an act of God, begun in the presence of Jesus among us and extended by all who believe in him, in their relationships and work with the poor and those who mourn, who do without and are in need. Simone Weil wrote: "Human beings are so made that the ones who do the crushing feel nothing; it is the person crushed who feels what is happening. Unless one has placed oneself on the side of the oppressed, to feel with them, one cannot understand." The suffering of the world is undeniable and religion is never to be a source of insulation from this suffering. In fact, true religion that ties and binds us all together in the presence of God makes us ever more aware of suffering and opens our hearts to the heart of the world. Real religion and faith, along with true worship and prayer, make us able to feel the world's suffering and other peoples' pain—even the pain of strangers and enemies—without being drowned by it or crushed by its power. Jesus taught us to see that being servants of the poor, the sick, those who mourn, those who are hungry makes us more human and holy and transforms us into the image of God. To live is to uncrucify, to alleviate others' sufferings, to bear one another's burdens, and to be a refuge for those who are in pain. Those who suffer because of injustice and others' sin and evil teach us what perhaps can be called prophetic mourning, in solidarity with them, raging against what is and should not be, was never meant to be. As Henri Nouwen wrote in the *New Oxford Review*, June 1992:

> Mourn, my people, mourn. Let your pain rise up in your heart and burst forth in you with sobs and cries. Mourn for the silence that exists between you and your spouse. Mourn for the way you were robbed of your innocence. Mourn for the absence of a soft embrace, an intimate friendship, a life-giving sexuality. Mourn for the abuse of your body, your mind, your heart. Mourn for the bitterness of your children, the indifference of your friends, your colleagues' hardness of heart. Mourn for those whose hunger for love brought them AIDS, whose desire for freedom brought them to refugee camps, whose hunger for justice brought them to prisons. Cry for the millions who die from lack of food, lack of care, lack of love. . . . Don't think of this as normal, something to be taken for granted, something to accept. . . . Think of it as the dark force of Evil that has penetrated every human heart, every family, every community, every nation, and keeps you imprisoned. Cry for freedom, for salvation, for redemption. Cry loudly and deeply, and trust that your tears will make your eyes see that the Kingdom is close at hand, yes, at your fingertips!

Our mourning, our prophetic rage must propel us into movement, into action on a personal level and as communities of believers. So much poverty, so much suffering, so much exploitation, so much evil and sin, personal and communal, cannot be abided. We, as Christians, have no choice but to revolt, to subvert any order that tolerates this situation, let alone encourages it or makes profit from it and increases it. What this prophetic mourning cries out is: the poor must come first. Those who suffer must be listened to first and attended to first. The priorities of the hungry, the sick, those dying because of violence, injustice, disasters brought on by economic exploitation and pollution of the earth and those caught in the vise of greed and avarice come first. Oscar Romero once preached on this option for the poor, this over-riding demand that the poor be listened to, now! He compared it to a fire in an apartment building. A crowd is watching. People are pointing at the people in the windows, talking and discussing, even asking if anyone has called the fire department and rescue squads and then someone yells: your sister is trapped in there! Or, your child is in there! And suddenly all theory and conversation ends abruptly. You move. You have to. It is imperative, even if all you can do is organize people into a water brigade, make telephone calls, or clear a space so that rescue workers can get through. The poor, the mourning, and the hungry come first. They are people who, like us, feel, hope, laugh and cry, dream and desire to live with their loved ones. There are prophets and martyrs who run into the building, searching for those trapped to rescue them, but all of us must put out the fire and root out the causes of the fires, the over-crowding in the buildings and the neglect and dismal conditions that create tinder-boxes that can be set off by a spark or even just too much sun. And we begin by listening to and watching the poor, and by being evangelized by them, opening ourselves to their ideas and dreams and coming to repentance through them and becoming their friends and servants, struggling with them.

There is a story about hunger that is fraught with mourning and yet brings tears that could be those of repentance and rejoicing at what human beings are capable of even in the face of misery and pain. It is about a photographer who watched the world through a camera lens yet never took the most arresting picture of his life.

✳   Once upon a time there was a photographer working on a book of black and white photographs of people caught in large world catastrophes and war, starvation, ethnic cleansing, and misery. He found himself in Ecuador in the late 1980s. The U.S. was pressuring the Latin American governments to pay their debts and to keep up their enormous interest payments while threatening to cut aid and investment. In response, and at the suggestion of the U.S., the government heavily taxed cooking and heating oil as a broad way to increase monies. This served to beggar an already struggling mass of people: the poor, the indigenous, and day laborers. Then the country was hit by a cholera epidemic of huge proportions. Then there were torrential rainfalls and land and mudslides that destroyed crops and brought devastation to whole villages and cities. The United Nations and Catholic Relief Services responded by bringing plane loads and truck loads of food into the devastated areas. They came with supplies of corn, soybean products, powdered milk, fruit, tortillas, rice and beans.

The photographer took up a position on a main street, crowded with refugees and people wandering about, lost, tired, injured, sick and hungry. They had lost their homes, their possessions, even, in some cases, relatives and entire families. He was struck by one young girl, about nine or ten, it was hard to tell. She was thin and scraggly, hair matted and clothes torn. She waited on line along with hundreds of others for food. The photographer noticed that while she waited patiently on line, she seemed to be looking out for three younger children huddled under a large bush that gave them some slight protection from the hot sun. Two boys, about five and seven, held between them a little girl of about three. Her attention was divided between watching them and keeping her place on the long line moving slowly toward the trucks of food.

He had been trained to see small details and developing situations. It was what made him a world-class photographer and what he noticed was dismaying: they were running out of food. The aid workers were becoming visibly distraught and anxious because the line was endless and the supplies were not. But the young girl hadn't noticed. She only watched her charges from a distance. The photographer's heart was pounding. His cameras were slung around his neck, at the ready.

After hours in the sun, the young girl finally got to the front of the line. All she was given was a banana. One banana. But her reaction stunned him and paralyzed him and brought him to tears. First her face lit up in a beautiful smile. She took the banana and bowed to the aid worker. Then she ran to the three children under the bushes and ever so carefully peeled the banana, split it evenly into three pieces and, almost reverently, put one piece into the palm of each child. Together they bowed their heads and said a blessing! They ate their pieces of banana, chewing slowly, while she sucked on the peel.

The photographer lost it altogether. First he wept uncontrollably, forgot all about his cameras and what he was there for. Then he began to question, not only himself and what he was doing and why, but also everything he took for granted and assumed the world was. He watched the girl and said later that in that moment he saw the face of God, shining. He had been given a glimpse of the kingdom of heaven in the face and actions of a poor street child rich in love, care for others, generosity, and such beauty in spite of poverty, hunger, international exploitation, the politics of greed and profit and human indifference. He never did take a picture of the young girl or her sister and brothers, if that is who they were, but her face and her smile are etched forever in his memory and his soul.

Rabbi Abraham Heschel once said: "It takes three things to attain a sense of significant being: God. A soul. A moment.

And the three are always there. Just to be is a blessing. Just to live is holy." And Rumi, the great Sufi mystic and poet, would tell his followers: "Look carefully around and recognize the luminosity of souls. Sit beside those who draw you to that." We are exhorted to sit beside the poor, to sit at table with them, to share our plenty, to walk with them and live with them and recognize the luminosity of their souls and to remember and make sure that for all peoples just to be is a blessing. Just to live is holy.

Jesus speaks only the truth: Fortunate are you who are hungry now, for you will be filled. Fortunate are you who weep now, for you will laugh. Alas, if we never see the truth in so many of the poor, the hungry, and those who weep around us. Alas, if we never realize that poverty, hunger, and mourning are the result of oppression. All of us are sinners, but there are some who are the sinned-against and their faces can be described as poor, as hungry, as weeping now, because they are the oppressed and captive of the land, those to whom we are blind in our injustice. The first three beatitudes in Luke proclaim Jubilee, a year of favor and God's mercy, and Jesus' words come true when we hear them and put them into practice. But it is God who is doing this marvelous work in Jesus, and until he comes again, in us. Blessed will we be if we accept the invitation to God's kingdom now.

5

Blessed Are You When You Are Persecuted: Rejoice!

When you die, you will be spoken of as those in the sky—like the stars. (Yurok)

We must embrace pain and burn it as fuel for our journey. (Kenji Migazawa)

This fourth and last beatitude in Luke is long, detailed, and explanatory in comparison with the other three, which are bare statements. The blessing is highlighted by repetition and put in the context of the history of the prophets in Israel, perhaps giving it more clout. It reads:

Fortunate are you when people hate you, when they reject you and insult you and number you among criminals, because of the Son of Man. Rejoice in that day and leap for joy, for a great reward is kept for you in Heaven. Remember that is how the fathers of this people treated the prophets. (Luke 6:22-23)

This is the beatitude that both Matthew and Luke use in the summation of Jesus' teaching on the kingdom. It is an end point and a beginning. It speaks of persecution in the broadest sense of the word: hate, rejection, insults, condemnation. It implies both psychological and physical violence and it can come from anywhere in the world, even from within the church community. Martyrdom is the supreme test of this beatitude and it is also the supreme identification with Jesus, the Son of Man, the ultimate beatitude of God. If one is true to the gospel, this beatitude is inevitable to one degree or another. It is a realistic statement, a sobering one that is paradoxically spoken with joy and exaltation. Segundo Galilea says in his book *The Beatitudes: To Evangelize as Jesus Did* (Maryknoll, N.Y.: Orbis Books, 1984):

> If you make an option for the poor, if you call in question the wealth of the rich and the power of the mighty, if you question all the false felicities, if you practice radical poverty of heart, if you are on fire for the justice of the kingdom, if your mercy refuses to discriminate and your pardon and reconciliation know no bounds, if you struggle with idols within and without, and if you respond to all the other demands of Luke and Matthew for following Jesus— sooner or later you will pay the price. And the price is persecution, all manner of persecution, which the disciples of Jesus must undergo to whatever extent his or her commitments and involvements go contrary to the interests of human beings and their unjust, sinful society. (p. 87)

There are going to be conflicts, estrangements, loneliness, isolation, humiliation: all sorts of problems in preaching the Word and in living it out. Later, in this same chapter on the beatitudes and woes, Jesus reminds his followers that "no disciple is above his master; if he lets himself be formed, he will be like his master" (Lk 6:40). This beatitude reminds all Christians that Jesus' invitation leads to the cross, to death as a prophet in Jerusalem, the city over which he would lament: "O Jerusalem, Jerusalem, you slay the prophets and stone your apostles! How often have I tried to bring together your children, as a bird gathers her young under her wings, but you refused. From now on your Temple will be left empty for you and you will no longer see me until the time when you will say: Blessed is he who comes in the name of the Lord" (Lk 13:34-35).

The preaching of Good News to the poor and the call to repent lead logically to Jesus' death. This last beatitude is a reality check against romanticizing any portion of the gospel and its demands. It anticipates the reaction of those who are heavily invested in what contradicts the truth and is the source and root of the conflict: sin, evil, and injustice committed and practiced by individuals, groups, societies, and structures. This long beatitude details what lies ahead both in the short run and the long haul. It acknowledges the existence of evil and depicts the ultimate nature of the struggle inherent in the reversal of what dominates the world. It is failure and hope bound together, the core of the gospel: from the suffering of the innocent issues forth life and resurrection, atonement and reconciliation. It is summed up in the cross, and its force and persistent power are not to be underestimated. Again, Galilea tells us starkly:

> The negative lesson of the cross is that evil is pervasive in history, that it will appear in ever new guises, that its stubborn persistence is a tragic fact of reality, that its opposition to the values of the kingdom of God is constant, and that, today as ever, it is capable of carrying the work of the church, together with the missionary effort of each of us, in any given instance (although not everywhere and always), down the road of failure.
>
> The cross teaches us that evangelization has a profound dimension of struggle against evil and sin, as concretely expressed today in the arms race, disrespect for life, the corruption of love, the exploitation of human beings by human beings, hunger, misery, materialism, and all manner of injustice. Evil is mighty, perduring, collective, and recurring. It can throttle evangelization. It can bring the cause of the kingdom to its apparent failure. (p. 89)

That last line is most crucial: "it can bring the cause of the kingdom to its apparent failure." Yet our faith teaches and we stake our lives, daily and ultimately, on the hope that even failure serves justice and love. Those who are followers of Jesus, members of his company, live by the power of his Spirit that resides in us. Paul, the apostle, in speaking of his own sufferings for the kingdom rejoices: "At present I rejoice when I suffer for you; I complete in my own flesh what is lacking in the sufferings of Christ for the sake of his body, which is the Church. For I am serving the Church since God entrusted to me the ministry of bringing into effect his design for you" (Col 1:24-25). We grasp hold of the words: "Christ is in you and you may hope God's Glory" (Col 1:27b).

In Romans Paul speaks of our redemption and of the transformation of all creation that has already been set in motion by the power of Jesus' death and resurrection:

> I consider that the suffering of our present life cannot be compared with the Glory that will be revealed and given to us. All creation is eagerly expecting the birth in glory of the children of God. For if now the created world was unable to attain its purpose, this did not come from itself, but from the one who subjected it. But it is not without hope; for even the created world will be freed from this fate of death and share the freedom and glory of the children of God. (Romans 8:18-21)

The suffering is there, but it will not have the last word. Although it can overwhelm us, discourage us, and destroy all we have worked for, even making inroads into our own communities and bodies, it is all part of the sufferings of Christ and part of the redemption of the world. This is what we stake our hopes on. That doesn't soften its bite or stop its pain, but it does help us to endure with gracefulness. And the command to rejoice puts God's great expectations before us and they are high expectations!

Eberhard Arnold, the founder of the Bruderhof movement in Germany, a movement that now has many communities around the world, struggled to keep his group together in the face of Nazi harassment, intimidation, persecution, and censorship. Arnold had founded an economic and residential community based upon the gospel and in response to Jesus' invitation to the rich ruler. He wrote in February 1935:

> Our experience of personal salvation has to go hand in hand with our expectation for the whole world. Otherwise we are not completely at one with God. And this will not happen until we are at one in the interests that the all-powerful, caring God has. Then we are truly at one.
>
> Who are the blessed? They are those who stand before God as beggars begging for His Spirit; who have become beggars in the material as well as the spiritual. They are those who are beggarly poor in goods and in grace. Only the beggarly poor know that to hunger and thirst means to agonize in this desire. Yet these are the truly blessed, who are plagued by this hunger and thirst for righteousness, who bear deep pain, who suffer the ultimate need, as Jesus suffered the ultimate need. Just as He suffered with the world's deepest suffering in the bitterest God-forsakenness, only those who are the blessed suffer to the verge of death, for the world and its need. They have pure, clear, radiant hearts, they are concentrated on God's cause with completely undivided hearts, they are at one with God's heart and live from their hearts just as God lives from His heart. So they are the ones who bring peace in the midst of an unpeaceful and corrupted world. (*God's Revolution: Justice, Community and the Coming Kingdom*, Plough Publishing House, Bruderhof Foundation, 1984, p. 97)

Any experience of this fourth beatitude comes from responding to Jesus' call to discipleship and this call is issued to anyone, to everyone. Early in Luke's gospel Jesus is clear about who he is and what that will mean for his mission and life. Immediately thereafter he lays out the demands of answering that call. He has been preaching of the kingdom of God, healing, sending his disciples out on mission and feeding the crowds . Then he pushes his own disciples to struggle with who he is; they use the words of others: a prophet, the Messiah of God. And then Jesus declares who he knows himself to be:

> "The Son of Man must suffer many things. He will be rejected by the elders and chief priests and teachers of the Law, and put to death. Then after three days he will be raised to life."
>
> Jesus also said to all the people: "If you wish to be a follower of mine, deny yourself and take up your cross each day, and follow me. For if you choose to save your life, you will lose it, and if you lose your life for my sake, you will save it. What does it profit you to gain the whole world while you destroy and lose yourself? If someone feels ashamed of me and of my words, the Son of Man will be ashamed of him when he comes in his Glory and in the Glory of his Father with his holy angels. Truly, I say to you, there are some here who will not experience death before they see the kingdom of God." (Luke 9:22-27)

These words of Jesus must have caused the disciples great dismay, consternation and confusion. He has upended all their grand designs and hopes for the messiah and their role in his coming kingdom. He is teaching them the inner core of his message and sharing his own values and orientation with them. "Deny yourself, take up your cross daily"; this is following Jesus' way, the way of life and truth and light. "Lose your life!"—not exactly what many of us have in mind for our immediate goal. But it's not as gloomy or pessimistic as it might initially sound to ears not tuned to Jesus' paradoxical way of speaking, his manner of hiding the treasures of his knowledge of God in kernels that are hard and rough. This way of losing life, of emptying oneself, of becoming single-hearted and single-minded is the process of freedom and individuation: of becoming truly who we are meant to be as human beings. In many eastern traditions and religions, it is the way of those seeking enlightenment. The way is twofold: through meditation that can empty and still our minds, and through enlightenment that can open us to the oneness of all existence and move us to compassion and mercy for all beings. The Master Hakuin told marvelous stories of how this happens and in the context of ordinary existence. His stories, though lighthearted, convey the wisdom of the maxim, "Deny yourself, pick up your cross."

Hakuin used to love to tell this story to his disciples. He would grin at them and begin:

❋   Once upon a time there was a student, a novice, full of enthusiasm and energy. He was very serious about enlightenment and what he had to do to reach it. His practice was meditation on emptiness so that he would be prepared at any moment to know the ultimate truth of all things. He meditated continually, no matter where he was, seeking to be recollected at all times. Of course, the young student was none other than Hakuin himself.

Once upon a time he went on a journey with two Buddhist monks who were older and more advanced in their studies and pursuit of wisdom than he. He was respectful of them and glad to travel in their company. They journeyed for a while and then one of them pleaded with Hakuin to carry his baggage because he was feeling faint from illness and very weak and tired. Hakuin gladly shouldered the monk's baggage along with his own. And they continued on their way.

After a while the other monk noticed that Hakuin was deeply absorbed in his meditation, despite carrying two loads of baggage. Nothing, it seemed, could deter him from his intensive meditation. He smiled to himself and thought to take advantage of the situation. Suddenly he wasn't feeling very well either and begged Hakuin to carry his baggage as well. Hakuin knew that along with meditation, service to those in need was crucial to his practice, so he picked up the other monk's baggage as well and continued on, though a bit more slowly now.

Still, he willed himself to keep at his meditation, to concentrate on being empty, on nothingness. It wasn't easy, and he wondered how long he could keep at it. Finally, when he was exhausted, he slipped back into counting his breaths and simply watching his erratic breathing.

Eventually they came to a stage in their journey where they could go no farther on foot. They had to take a ferry, which was waiting at the dock when they arrived. Hakuin was delighted and collapsed in a heap, falling soundly asleep with all the baggage around him. He was mindless, wiped out with exertion and grateful for the boat.

Later he awoke. At first he was disoriented and slow to wake from his deep sleep. As he stretched and breathed deeply, he immediately picked up an awful stench all around him. His eyes widened as he looked around at everyone in the boat. They all looked terrible. They were green and ashen and their clothes and the deck were covered with vomit. While he had slept, exhausted from carrying all the baggage, a storm had come up. Fierce winds and high waters had almost swamped the boat, pitching everyone to and fro and making everyone on the boat, except Hakuin, desperately sick. They had all spent the trip throwing up while he had slept peacefully. His compassion and his bearing of his fellow monks' burdens had been richly rewarded.

Hakuin would smile knowingly and give his students the punch line: "Hidden Virtue, Manifest Reward!"

This story teases out some of the meaning of the fourth beatitude that calls us to rejoice in the face of persecution and suffering that come to us from preaching the gospel, following Jesus, or working for the care of others. With discipline and devotion, and with the power of the Spirit and help from a community, we can rejoice even in painful situations. The Acts of the Apostles is rife with stories of persecution, jailings, beatings, exile, and all manner of hardship that the early church experienced because of its preaching about Jesus Christ. Peter and the others (we're not told exactly who) are

arrested at the instigation of the high priest and his support-
ers and the Sadducees and thrown into jail. But an angel
springs them overnight and the next morning they are back at
it, in the temple court. They are eventually re-arrested and
this time "whipped and ordered not to speak again of Jesus
Savior. Then they are set free." And the apostles' reaction is
reminiscent of the beatitude:

> The apostles went out from the Council rejoicing that
> they were considered worthy to suffer disgrace for
> the sake of the Name. Day after day, both in the Tem-
> ple and in people's homes, they continued to teach
> and to proclaim that Jesus was the Messiah. (Acts
> 5:41-42)

Later in Acts, as the Good News spreads out from Jerusalem and Paul and Barnabas begin their missionary journeys, Herod begins to persecute the church in Jerusalem. It is
reported matter-of-factly: "Herod decided to persecute some
members of the Church. He had James, the brother of John,
killed with the sword, and when he saw how it pleased the
Jews, he proceeded to arrest Peter also" (Acts 12:1-3). The experience of arrest, persecution and death becomes normative
for the church and is also the source of its growth. Dying
brings others to belief. "The blood of martyrs is the seed of
Christians" is literally true not only for the early church, but
also for many missionary endeavors and in many parts of the
church universal today.

Paul and Silas are imprisoned in Macedonia not for
specifically preaching the good news but for "being servants
of the Most High God" and for having expelled a spirit that
had given a woman powers of divination and fortune-telling.
Her owners were annoyed at the profits they lost and had
Paul and Silas arrested, dragged into the marketplace, and
flogged (Acts 16:16-24). Later in Acts, Paul has trouble again
because of the presence of the Way, as the church is now
called in Asia. The trouble is stirred up by a silversmith,
Demetrius, who makes silver models of Artemis, the goddess
of the temple. Demetrius realizes that Paul's preaching is cut-

ting into his business profit. He rallies the others of his trade and the people of the city to riot against Paul. Paul escapes, but in the end both Peter and Paul have died in Rome, one by upside-down crucifixion and the other by beheading. Both will pay the supreme price of faithfulness to their Lord, and their last statement of belief will have been the giving of their lives.

This fourth beatitude is linked to the following of Jesus as experienced by the early church. All the members of the church faced persecution from the Jews and from the Romans, and unfortunately there was division and dissension even within various factions in the church. Living with conflict was a daily struggle, and it was as effective as any preaching or ritual in forming the early Christians in their faith. Preaching leads to persecution as lived belief elicits reactions and stirs up conflict. The lifestyle of the missionaries and disciples was a source of contention, because much of what they did was based on prophetic strategy.

When Jesus sends out seventy-two disciples in the course of his mission, he gives them very specific directions on how to travel and what they are to do and to avoid.

> After this the Lord appointed seventy-two other disciples and sent them two by two ahead of him to every town and place, where he himself was to go. And he said to them, "The harvest is rich, but the workers are few. So you must ask the Lord of the harvest to send workers to his harvest. Courage! I am sending you like lambs among wolves. Set off without purse or bag or sandals; and do not stop at the homes of those you know.
>
> Whatever house you enter, first bless them saying: 'Peace to this house.' If a peaceful person lives there, the peace shall rest upon him. But if not, the blessing will return to you. Stay in that house eating and drinking at their table, for the worker deserves his wages. Do not move from house to house." (Luke 10:1-7)

This way of life is about hospitality, about setting up a new system of relationships that are mutual: the giving of food and shelter in exchange for preaching the kingdom of God. It is an itinerant lifestyle, gypsying from town to town, inviting oneself into people's lives and staying a while until they get the drift of the message and a sense of what living in the kingdom means. It involves the practice of holy poverty that Francis and his band will later espouse and make popular. This kind of poverty is not so much solidarity with the poor, but a dependence on others for shelter, food, and other necessities. These workers look a lot like holy fools for the kingdom, going two by two and using prophetic sign language to attract people's attention. They are saying with their presence that there is something new afoot in the land, something freeing, something dramatic that changes all our priorities and values, that reshapes our daily lives and will affect structures and governments and all of history. These people are the forerunners of a revolution, a gentle, nonviolent revolution, and they are well trained, another meaning for the word "gentle." They are respectful of others and offer greetings of peace before stepping over the threshold of a house. And yet this kind of behavior could evoke hostility as easily as hospitality and repentance.

Dennis Hamm, S. J., in his book *The Beatitudes in Context: What Luke and Matthew Meant* (Wilmington, Delaware: Michael Glazier, 1990) describes the ramifications of the radical behavior of Jesus' disciples sent on mission. They were to take no money, no bag, no extra tunic, no sandals, no staff, and no bread!

> And no one travelled the threatening rocky Palestinian roads without sandals and staff. Such behavior is not poverty but prophetic strategy. Indeed, after the sending of the Twelve, Luke narrates that this behavior generated the opinion that John the Baptist or one of the prophets of old was again at large (9:7-9). Such a way of travelling was a kind of prophetic sign-language, not the normal behavior of the needy but the counter-cultural style ("street theater" some might call it) of people with something very new to say. For

to travel without a staff left one without a means of defense against unfriendly persons or animals. And travelling without sandals meant one could not run from a threatening situation. It is the travel style of people taking a dramatically nonviolent posture toward the world. And travelling without money or bread left one utterly dependent upon whatever hospitality might be offered....

It has been noticed that rabbinical rules relating to the temple mount forbade the carrying of a staff, the wearing of sandals, or money carried in a bag or money belt, and that these surprising rules for mission may have meant that "the approach of the Kingdom makes the time a holy season, and the whole land a holy place." (pp. 48-49)

A close reading of these portions of Luke and the sections of Acts that describe the life of the first Christian communities suggests that there were basically two groups within the early church. The first group was a band of travelers, itinerants who went forth to preach the Good News, prophetic not only in their journeying and their words, but also in their practice of a radical hospitality that introduced people to the hospitality of God in the person of Jesus. The other was a more settled group of believers who did not live as spare a lifestyle but who contributed generously to the upkeep of the missionaries and to the other churches that might find themselves in need, like the Jerusalem community. They were the poor of Yahweh, intent on the coming of the kingdom of God into the world. And all suffered from persecution and hostile reactions to the gospel.

It's not surprising that the community of believers is told to "Rejoice in that day and leap for joy, for a great reward is kept for you in Heaven." These words echo the description of John the Baptist who leapt in the womb as Elizabeth heard Mary's greeting of peace (Lk 1:39-41). The prophet who will go before the face of the Lord to prepare his ways (Lk 1:76-77) recognizes in the voice of Mary the presence of the Word of God enfleshed in the world at last. And John will die for preaching repentance and preparation for the coming of the kingdom, and specifically for challenging the powers of his time regarding their personal sin and their injustice and their disobedience of God's law. John will do what so many of the prophets before him have done. The pattern will not change, but this time the outcome is declared: God now reigns and the kingdom will come in its fullness in God's good time.

Jesus is a truth-teller and those who come after him must follow him in this regard. The telling of the truth makes the fourth beatitude a reality. Many of Jesus' parables are imaginative ways of expressing religious truth, of calling people to self-examination so that they can confess their sin and do a complete turn-around in relation to God. But the opposite reaction is also possible: people can turn and attack the one who speaks so confrontationally. In the words of John K. Stoner,

> Speaking the truth is the most significant political action available to any of us—not voting, but speaking the truth. This view is based on the familiar biblical notion that the word is central. The word is the truth; the expression of the truth by human lips moves culture and history toward the government of God. There is no higher form of political action, nor is there one that can contribute more to the wholeness of the human community. (*Mennonite Life*, September 1996)

Jesus is the Word of God and his interpretation of the scriptures and his storytelling shocked and scandalized people. There was misunderstanding among his own disciples who saw their dreams shattered and their lives questioned by this man's teachings and actions. As Jesus approaches Jerusalem in Luke's gospel his stories become stronger and less oblique. The last story he tells before entering the city is that of the murderous tenants of the vineyard. The roots of this story are in Isaiah 5, and Jesus' listeners would have known the allusion and heard the story with sharpened ears. In Isaiah it is called the song of the vineyard.

> Let me sing for my beloved
> the love song of my beloved

about his vineyard.
My beloved had a vineyard
on a fertile hillside.
He dug it up, cleared the stones,
and planted the choicest vines.
He built there a watchtower
and hewed out a winepress as well.
Then he looked for a crop of good grapes,
but it yielded only wild grapes.
Now, inhabitants of Jerusalem and men of Judah,
judge between me and my vineyard.
What more was there to do
that I have not done for my vineyard?
Good grapes was the yield I expected,
why did it yield only sour grapes?

Now I will let you know
what I am going to do with my vineyard:
I will remove its hedge
and it will be burned;
I will break down its wall
and it will be trampled on.
I will make it a wasteland,
I will neither prune nor hoe it,
and briers and thorns will grow there.
I command the clouds, as well,
not to send rain on it.
The vineyard of Yahweh Sabaoth
is the people of Israel,
and the men of Judah
are his pleasant vine.
He looked for justice,
but found bloodshed;
He looked for righteousness but heard cries of distress.
    (Isaiah 5:1-7)

This is a lamentation, and what follows is a string of woes and threats of what will happen in the turbulent history of Israel. God plants his remnant of a small and insignificant group of tribes and attends to them with singular devotion only to have his choice ignored and his attention cast off. And so the love song turns into a cry of destruction because his love is not returned or honored. Their hearts are so recalcitrant and unyielding of anything human or good that it is as though he has been beating his head against a wall. Instead, his people are rife with injustice, violence, bloodshed and—what is worse—the victims are others of their own nation. This cannot be tolerated. It must be stopped.

The image of the vineyard is a favorite with the prophets. It is used again in Isaiah 27:6, when the prophet prays that the people will make peace with Yahweh so that they will know a season of blossoming and bearing fruit. And many of the prophets, including Jeremiah and Micah, Amos and Hosea, reproach the people for their ill treatment of those the covenant seeks to protect and for their disobedience and disdain for the God who has cared so faithfully for them. Listen to Hosea:

Hear the word of Yahweh, Israel! for Yahweh has an accusation to bring against the inhabitants of this land. There is neither truth nor goodness nor knowledge of God in the country; only perjury, lies, murder, theft and adultery, with continual bloodshed. (Hosea 4:1-2)

Such accusations against the people, especially their leaders and teachers, are the background for Jesus' story of the vineyard. This sets an ominous tone. And Jesus tells his story:

A man planted a vineyard and let it out to tenants before going abroad for a long time.

In due time he sent a servant to the tenants to get some fruit from the vineyard. But the tenants beat him and sent him back empty-handed. Again the man sent another servant; they beat him as well and treated him shamefully and finally sent him away empty-handed. The owner sent a third, but this one was wounded and thrown out.

> The owner then thought: "What shall I do? I will
> send my beloved son; surely they will respect him."
> The tenants, however, as soon as they had seen him,
> said to one another: "This is the one who will inherit
> the vineyard; let us kill him and the property will be
> ours." So they threw him out of the vineyard and
> killed him. Now, what will the owner of the vineyard
> do to them? He will come and destroy those tenants
> and give the vineyard to others. (Luke 20:9b-16)

The story is told to the people but it is told in the temple
just after Jesus has been subjected to an inquisition on why he
teaches and acts the way he does and who gives him the right
to do it. But Jesus refuses to answer their questions and instead
throws a question back to them on the nature of John's baptism: was it a work of God or merely something human? They
don't want to answer because they don't want to commit themselves. Jesus has trapped them with a question that demands
taking sides and they know it. If they answer "of God" then he
will ask them why they did not receive baptism from him. And
if they say "merely human," then they will lose face with the
people who might even stone them because John is regarded as
a prophet. So they feign ignorance and say "We don't know."
And Jesus retorts clearly: "Neither will I tell you what right I
have to act like this" (Lk 20:1-8). And then comes the story
where he is clearly saying that he is the beloved son of the
owner of the vineyard, and therefore beloved of God. All the
prophets of the Jews were referred to as the sons of God and
Jesus is claiming to be the one who is to inherit the vineyard.
But he knows their hearts and so he tells them he knows that
they intend to try to kill him, as those in the past have killed the
prophets who spoke the truth. The response is mixed:

> On hearing this, some of the rulers said, "May it not
> be so!" Then Jesus looked directly at them and said,
> "What does this text of the Scriptures mean: The stone
> which the builders rejected has become the keystone.
> Everyone who falls on that stone will be broken to
> pieces and anyone the stone falls on will be crushed?"

The teachers of the Law and the chief priests would have liked to arrest him right there, for they realized that Jesus meant this parable for them, but they were afraid of the crowd. So they left, looking for another opportunity. (Luke 20:16b-20)

This description of the teachers and priests scheming to get Jesus at another time brings to mind an earlier event in Jesus' life when, after having been unsuccessful in tempting Jesus in the desert, Satan, the Hinderer, leaves him. "When the devil had exhausted every way of tempting Jesus he left him, to return another time" (Lk 4:13). They will not quit until he is caught and Jesus will not allow their cold-blooded rejection and persecution to deter him from what he must do: preach the gospel of good news to the poor and proclaim the coming of his Father's kingdom, even if it means that his blood will seal the new covenant and promises of God.

And God still looks for grapes, not sour or wild ones, but a good vintage: one of justice and nonviolence. It is the fruit that belongs to him by right, since we belong to him and all that we have is given on loan to us. And this fruit belongs to the poor. It always has. In the parable, God is the accuser of the people, but the tradition is also clear that God is the advocate of those who have been despoiled and forgotten by the tenants of his vineyard. In an early chapter of Isaiah Yahweh speaks out for his people, those in his nation who have remained faithful in spite of what their countrymen have done to them, and of his special care for them.

The look on their faces denounces them: they do not hide their sin; instead, they parade it, like Sodom: Woe to them! they bring about their own downfall!

Say, "Fortunate are the righteous, they will eat of the fruit of their deeds." But woe to the wicked; the evil that their hands have done shall be done to them!

O my people, plundered by your rulers, enslaved by your creditors! O my people, your leaders deceive you and lead you astray.

Yahweh takes his place in court and stands to try his people. Yahweh calls to judgment the elders and the princes:

"You have devoured my vineyard. The spoil of the poor is in your houses. What right have you to crush the people and to grind down the poor?" declares Yahweh Sabaoth. (Isaiah 3:9-15)

In telling the story Jesus is both the prophet who denounces the elders and the wealthy and the advocate who lobbies on his people's behalf, concerned for their very survival. The church is called to do just that in the world, today and always. The promotion of human rights, advocacy on behalf of the poor, the defense of minorities, the landless, the immigrant and all those on the fringes of society are the concerns of the Church because they are required by the gospel. The Church needs to take the role of both denouncer of injustice and advocate for the poor and their rights in the world. When the Church in one part of the world speaks on behalf of the poor it calls all of us to conversion. The bishops of Asia in 1974 spoke clearly to the universal Church:

> ...opting to be with the poor involves risk: the risk of conflict with vested interests or "establishments," religious, economic, social, political. It also involves, for leaders of the Church especially, loss of security, and that not only material but spiritual....We cannot therefore assume that the Church in Southeast Asia will become the Church of the Poor simply as a matter of course. It can only be the result of an option, consciously and deliberately taken.... ("Reflections and Conclusions" of Bishops Institute for Social Action held in Novaliches, Philippines, March 1–15, 1974, #4 and #5)

And the Church must also speak out against government policies, philosophies, and programs that destroy the neediest. The bishops of Latin America did this in critiquing the history of development in their own countries:

If the Church were to recapitulate, in some way, the deeds of development... it would have to denounce that after ten years of "development," the results have been: hunger, more hunger and greater malnutrition; food more expensive and inaccessible to the poor; a decrease in the essential consumption of the people. ("Voice from Northeastern Brazil to III Conference of Bishops," an article distributed by MICC-PAX ROMANA/ International Movement of Catholic Intellectuals and Professionals, Mexico, Nov. 1977, reprinted in LADOC, May/June 1978, p. 5)

This emphasis on the poor in a chapter on being persecuted, rejected, scorned, shamed, and put to death is deliberate, for martyrs in this century have become nameless and numberless. In the words of Jon Sobrino: "to be poor means literally to be near to death." And the good news of Jesus Christ brought first to the poor demands that we take a risk in opting for a choice that will put us in conflict with the idols of the world. "What do we mean by idols? By idols I mean historical realities, things which exist which demand victims to survive. Archbishop Romero said an idol is the doctrine of national security, an idol is absolutized capitalism...." (Jon Sobrino, "Poverty Means Death to the Poor," *Cross Currents*, Fall 1986, p. 269). The poor in many places of the world die before their time and live threatened by assassination, violent sudden death, torture, disappearance; they die as refugees, on the road or living in camps, in war and through government policies, and they "die because they are poor; they are like the Servant of God" (p. 270). They die without dignity, without a face or a name or often even a burial. They die maligned by others, slandered, in a word, crucified. And Sobrino speaks of two basic affirmations of our faith as Christians:

It is obvious, I would think, that when we think about what the church should be and what the church should do, at least this much we know: We should try to stop death....

So Jürgen Moltmann talks about the crucified God; Luther also thinks along those lines. We should really understand, I think, that for us to grasp what it means that God may be crucified—these are human words which we do not understand exactly—but to grasp something about what that means—the best way is to look at the crucified people. And if we really believe that God has become a human being, that God has assumed this history of ours, then when we see this crucified people we might have a glimpse of what it means that God also is crucified—that the Son of God is crucified—because it is true.

A second point about the Salvadorean reality is the following: These people who are poor, for whom to live and survive is the basic task; these people who get up every day to struggle with life—these people have hope. Not all of them. I'm talking now about the Christians—Christians in basic communities, Christians in refugee camps. These people have hope—and that's a scandal. I mean we shouldn't take it for granted.

And their hope gives us hope. In this sense it is also true that these people are like the Servant of Yahweh. On the one hand they really take upon themselves and bear the sin of this world. They really tell us the truth about this world....

And hope for what?... for life. You might remember when Isaiah 65 describes the dream of God and begins by saying: "I will create a new earth and a new heaven." Then it goes on to say: "There will come a time in which people will build houses and will inhabit them, and they will work in the fields and eat the fruits they have produced. They will not build houses so that other people will live in them...."

Not only that. These people have hope because through their Christian faith they have changed themselves. The poor of El Salvador, at least many of them, at times use the language of St. Paul—without knowing it of course: "Before, we were nobody; we were

not a people. And now, we are a people." ...Before Father Rutilio Grande, before Oscar Romero...we were
poor without knowing what we were; without knowing our own possibilities. Now we know. Now we
come together. Now we have become a people....

These people have hope for very difficult things
like reconciliation. These people are ready to forgive
those who assassinate them...there is hope. (pp. 271-
72)

The role of the Church in the world is to fight for life, resist
death, humanize conflicts, defend victims and speak on their
behalf. It must listen to them, journey with them, pastor them
and learn from them how to hope, how to live in the face of
death, and sometimes die with them. The slave spiritual cries
out: "Were you there when they crucified my Lord?" Are we
there when millions are crucified today? Are we concerned
with human rights violations, with telling the truth and taking
risks to intervene in conflicts and defend those caught in the
middle? Do we have credibility with the poor? Do they know
us as friends of God and so as their friends? Sobrino's last re-
mark in his talk touches deeply on the last beatitude:

Once I asked somebody, a priest, what he was doing
with his community during a time of special turmoil,
and he said: "We pray and hope and wait for the resurrection; but in order to do that, we read the passion
of Jesus Christ."

...According to that, what should the church do?
Basically, be ready to become incarnate; be ready for
persecution if it comes; try to stop war, try to humanize the conflict; try to tell the truth; and try to main-
tain the hope of this suffering people. (p. 276)

This is where the Church, the believers in Jesus must
start: by reading the passion of Jesus Christ and telling the
truth. It isn't enough for a few prophets and poets to cry out
and try to put into words what is happening to a people; all
believers must do this. Philip Berrigan has said: "If enough

Christians follow the gospel, they can bring any state to its knees. Such Christians are a biblical remnant. In the providence of God, they are the ones who keep the human race from destroying itself" (from *Fighting the Lamb's War*).

In the garden of Gethsemane on Mount Olivet Jesus is in so much agony that he sweats blood seeking the strength to face what lies ahead of him: arrest, betrayal and abandonment by his own followers and friends, torture, beating, insults, a lying unjust court, a harrowing journey carrying his own instrument of execution, public humiliation, and hours struggling to breathe through hideous pain that reduces him to a state in which he is barely recognizable as a human being. Luke uses this as a continuation of the temptation story where Jesus bends and submits only to the will of God: Jesus will live and die humanly and gracefully in the face of hate.

> After this Jesus left to go as usual to Mount Olivet and the disciples followed him. When he came to the place, he told them, "Pray that you may not be put to the test."
>
> Then he went a little further, about a stone's throw, and kneeling down he prayed: "Father if it is your will, remove this cup from me; still not my will but yours be done." And an angel from heaven appeared to give him strength.
>
> As he was in agony, he prayed even more earnestly and great drops of blood formed like sweat and fell to the ground. When he rose from prayer, he went to his disciples but found them worn out with grief, and asleep. And he said to them, "Why do you sleep? Get up and pray, so that you may not be put to the test." (Luke 22:39-46)

The test: to submit and obey the will of God, even in the face of rejection, persecution, and death. And the struggle is internal, a soul-wrenching in the face of utter loneliness, discouragement, fear, terror of torture, betrayal, loss of one's friends, and death that is calculated and evil. And yet Jesus prays.

St. Thérèse of Lisieux, whose religious name was St. Thérèse of the Holy Face, based her spirituality on contemplation of the bruised, tortured, and suffering face of the crucified Christ. She wrote to her sister Pauline:

> One Sunday, looking at a picture of Our Lord on the Cross, I was struck by the blood flowing from one of his divine hands. I felt a pang of great sorrow when thinking that this blood was falling to the ground without anyone's hastening to gather it up. I was resolved to remain in spirit at the foot of the Cross and to receive its dew.
>
> . . . I don't want this precious blood to be lost. I shall spend my life gathering it up for the good of souls... for "to live from love is to dry Your Face— *vivre d'amour c'est essuyer ta Face.*" (*Last Conversations*)

St. Thérèse's spirituality provides a rich image for this beatitude and offers a reason for rejoicing in suffering and persecution. The work for justice—the works of mercy, advocating for the poor, working for just legislation and the transformation of unjust social structures—is bound intimately to prayer. Our public witnessing must be grounded at the foot of the cross. We must be willing to listen to, contemplate, and look hard at what is most unnerving to look at: the many of our brothers and sisters crucified today. And with Jesus in the garden we must warn each other and question one another as we face our tests: our moral choices and decisions about our priorities and lifestyles as believers. This is a lifelong task and we must return to it again and again when we find ourselves slipping back into carelessness and selfishness.

Don Eusebio, who was killed on the steps of the church in Guadalupe, El Salvador, in February 1983, wrote:

> At the beginning it filled me with hopes that those who came would perhaps help us, but in time I [have come to] know that we the poor and our misfortunes are written in thousands of books and notebooks, to be read and studied, perhaps offering ideas to im-

prove oneself. But it all just goes round and round and everything stays the same. Maybe those who write and understand our miseries find themselves in a world where it's worth more to be on the side of those who have. But if you're on the side of those who do not have, what you can expect is prison, persecution and death.

These are terrible words to write and to read, but they are necessary, required for memory and hopefully for conversion. The last beatitude is not so different from the others, except perhaps in depth and its extremity: unto death itself. This emphasis on the poor is a constant in all of the beatitudes.

A theology that views truth from the place of the poor is often called liberation theology. Gustavo Gutiérrez, often referred to as the "Father of Liberation Theology," says the following in an article "Option for the Poor: Review and Challenges" that appeared in *The Month*, January 1995.

People ask what impact liberation theology has had in Latin America. I always give the same answer: "What interests me is the impact of the Gospel and the presence of Christians in the liberation process of the Latin American people. Within that, a small part belongs to liberation theology." In saying this I am not trying elegantly to distance myself from this theology. I go on working at it, and I am convinced that it is a useful instrument for fostering concrete involvement in a Church which should be in ever greater solidarity with the poor. I think this theology definitely arises out of the contrast between a reality marked by poverty, which means death, and the need to proclaim the resurrection of Jesus Christ, which is the decisive victory over death, which is the death of death itself.

You recall the Old Testament text quoted by St. Paul, "O death, where is your victory?" (1 Cor. 15:55, freely quoting Is. 25:7 and Hos. 13:14). Every Christian celebration is a mockery of death, a claim that death does not have the final word in history. The final word of human existence is life, the gift of God. I believe that here is where you find the key to what is taking place in the Latin American Church. For this reason our theological reflection is of interest, because it is sustained by the life of a Church, of many Christian communities. Otherwise it would be of little significance, except perhaps in the intellectual world.

I conclude, rather unacademically, by asking you to pray for my continent and my Church. I am sure moreover, that, if you keep in mind the poor of the world, you are ready to find your place and your path in this preferential option for the poor. (pp. 5-10)

In our own lives we must learn the truth of the beatitude and in our churches we must together live as the true prophets and preachers of the gospel. We must learn to fearlessly and faithfully become the message from which we take heart. Learning how to do that is the process of conversion, a conversion. It is a process that takes place in community but can involve radical aloneness. First, an Asian story from the annals of Ahimsa (versions by Daniel Rhodes, in "A Potter's Companion").

✳ Once upon a time.... The Master seldom reminisced, but one day Boso asked him how he had acquired the ability to make pots so filled with energy and life. He replied by telling a story.

"When I was a young apprentice, I struggled at the wheel, like everyone else. I made good progress, but I was always dissatisfied, and sometimes discouraged. My pots seemed good to me while they were still on the wheel, moist, soft, and glistening. But later, when they began to dry—awful! And after the fire, worse still!

My master, knowing that I was discouraged, offered suggestions, advice and encouragement, but nothing seemed to help.

Finally, to my surprise, he ordered me to stand on the wheel head. He then began coiling thick ropes of clay around my feet. Then he coiled around my ankles, my legs, and then my body and my neck. I was covered with coils of clay! I stood on the wheel transformed. I was the space within the pot! Then he took a paddle, and as the wheel slowly turned he beat the coils against my legs and body, shouting, 'Foot! foot! (smack), belly! belly! (smack), shoulder! shoulder! (smack), neck! neck! (smack)!' After that day, my pots changed."

By discipline, spirituality, fasting, almsgiving, penance, honesty, solidarity, accompaniment, prophetic advocacy, and social justice, we change and know in some small measure persecution, ridicule, being branded criminal or stupid. We are rejected and unnoticed and alone and there is a basis for joy, for rejoicing and being one of those who are blessed.

And *Maryknoll* Magazine in its July/August 1997 issue printed a marvelous story that puts the beatitude in the larger context of history:

✳ An ancient Chinese text records that over 500 years before Christ, a man named Bian He found a large, intriguing stone. Bian He presented it as a gift to the emperor. Seeing nothing but a large rock, the emperor felt tricked and ordered Bian He's left foot to be chopped off.

Bian He sent the same present to the next emperor, who also rejected it and angrily ordered the donor's right foot to be chopped off.

When a third emperor came to the throne, Bian He held the stone in his arms at the gate of the emperor's palace and wept for three days and nights. The emperor sent someone to investigate, then ordered the stone to be polished. Only then did they discover it was priceless jade.

The commentary on the story continues: "Our faith resembles that jade. History has shown that Catholics in China will continue to witness to the Gospel in the spirit of Bian He. No matter the political climate, no matter the cost, we will

hold fast to our precious faith, persevering as Bian He did"
(as told by Bishop John Tong of Hong Kong, p. 11).

> May we all persevere and hold fast to our precious
> faith and know one day the truth of the fourth beati-
> tude: "Fortunate are you when people hate you,
> when they reject you and insult you and number you
> among criminals, because of the Son of Man. Rejoice
> in that day and leap for joy, for a great reward is kept
> for you in Heaven. Remember that is how the fathers
> of this people treated the prophets." Remember, and
> hold on for a truer life for all.

6

Woe to You Rich!

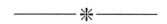

Sell your cleverness and buy bewilderment.
(Rumi)

If the beatitudes, the blessings, are a source of consternation, then the woes even more evoke distress and misunderstanding. The woes are not so much curses as lamentations, statements courageously announcing that some people are already dead, though they appear to be alive. Samuel Johnson once said: "When making your choice in life, don't forget to live." As human beings we often forget or ignore the obvious. A Chinese wise man, Fa-Yen, said it similarly: "The way is always with people, but people themselves chase after things." The woes, in their own way, Jesus' way, are ancient wisdom statements couched in language that is dismaying and bewildering for all of us. The *Christian Community Bible* notes couch the woes within this larger context of the beatitudes:

> In the words of Jesus, the beatitudes were a call and a hope, addressed to the forgotten of the world, beginning with the poor among his people, heirs of God's promise to the prophets.
> There are a thousand ways to present Jesus and his work. However, in order for such teaching to deserve the name evangelization (or communication of

the Good News), it must be received as Good News first by the poor. If other social groups feel more identified with the teaching, it means that something is lacking either in the content or in the way of proclaiming the message. Most probably, it has not been given in such a way as to do justice to the disinherited.

The lamentations in Luke recall those of Isaiah (65:13-14). These are lamentations for the dead, not maledictions, for the rich forget God and become impermeable to grace. The lamentations are a sign of the love of God for the rich, as are the beatitudes for the poor, for he loves them all, but in a different way. To the poor he affirms that he will destroy the structures of injustice, and to the rich he gives a warning: wealth brings death.

The beatitudes do not speak of the conversion of the rich, nor do they say that the poor are better, but they promise a reversal. The kingdom signifies a new society: God blesses the poor but not poverty. (p. 169)

Early in his gospel Luke puts a form of the beatitudes and woes in Mary's mouth as she sings the praises of God in her cry of liberation and freedom, the Magnificat. The reversals in her prayer specifically echo the first three beatitudes and woes:

> The Mighty One has done great things for me,
> Holy is his Name!
> From age to age his mercy extends
> to those who live in his presence.
> He has acted with power and done wonders,
> and scattered the proud with their plans.
> He has put down the mighty from their thrones
> and lifted up those who are downtrodden.
> He has filled the hungry with good things
> but he has sent the rich away empty.
>   (Luke 1:49-53)

All this work of God is couched in terms of the mercy of God who does this for his people, righting the imbalance and restoring creation to its original goodness. Many people have described God in terms of power and majesty and even wrath as well as displaying qualities of mercy, beneficence, beauty, intimacy, and compassion. And the first set of qualities is always seen as subservient to the latter qualities. Both destructiveness and compassion have their place. One of the sayings of Muhammad, known as *hadith qudsi*, reads: "Take refuge in My Mercy from My Wrath. Take refuge in Me from Me." There is always a balance and a sense of freedom and hope in the tension between the two qualities or contrasting ways of God. The poet Rumi said that mercy always takes precedence in God and that even wrath is a disguised form of mercy. A piece of poetry from Rumi's *Mathnawi* puts this insight in images that are rooted in the same foundation as the beatitudes and woes of Jesus:

> Lovingkindness is drawn to the saint,
> as medicine goes to the pain it must cure.
> When there is pain, the remedy follows:
> wherever the lowlands are, the water goes.
> If you want the water of mercy, make yourself low;
> then drink the wine of mercy and be drunk.
> Mercy upon mercy rises to your head like a flood.
> (*Mathnawi*, II, 1938-40)

As noted earlier, the woes and lamentations of Jesus' sermon in Luke are found originally in Isaiah 65. The prophet often refers to Israel as "a rebellious people who chose the evil way, following their own wishes"(Is. 65:2). They are described thus:

> But as for you who have forsaken Yahweh, you who have forgotten my holy mountain, you who spread a table for Fortune and fill the cups of mixed wine for Destiny, I have destined you to the sword. All of you will kneel for the slaughter.
> For I called and you did not answer;
> I spoke and you did not listen.

Instead, you did what was evil in my sight
and chose that in which I had no delight.
    (Isaiah 65:11-12)

The words are harsh, terrifying; they are the words of a God settling accounts and judging. We tend to see the judgment only in terms of punishment and destruction and thus often think of it as vengeance, but it is also a vindication and an undoing of evil, a righting of wrongs and a cleansing of land and memory. Jesus is utterly nonviolent. His message, his works, and his understanding of God as Father are not about calling down wrath. He is, however, threatening and warning of the new reality that has arrived with his own person on earth. The woes and lamentations are words of care—blunt, intense, provoking reactions, intent on catching the attention of a stubborn, lax and dishonest people who have betrayed their covenant with God and are afflicting their neighbors—with oppression, injustice, and violence. God cannot let this go unaddressed.

The situation is similar to that of the children of Israel in Egypt when God sends Moses to the Pharaoh with the command to set his people free. The Jewish Midrash tells a story of what happened between Moses and Aaron and the Pharaoh when Moses was trying to convince him to surrender to Yahweh and release the people. It is a hard story but, like the woes, it tells a hard truth that must be said.

✳   Once upon a time Moses and Aaron set out for the court of the Pharaoh, intent on delivering Yahweh's message and freeing the people Israel. They entered the bustling court and the room fell silent. Moses cried out: "Thus says the Lord God, the God of Israel: 'Let my people go!' " And Pharaoh retorted coldly: "And who is this god that intrudes in my kingdom? I've never heard of your god. What is his name? How many chariots and charioteers does he command?"

   And Moses answered him as one would teach a child: "The power of our God is not like your army or charioteers, or any other power on the face of the earth. Our God's power is seen in the heavens, in the creation of the earth and in those that he has made to worship him. He does not fight or need protection as the rulers of this world do." The answer infuriated and insulted Pharaoh and he spat back: "Your god's name, what did you say it was? I don't believe I caught it, or did you neglect to mention it?"

And Moses answered solemnly and reverently: "God revealed himself to me in a burning bush that was not consumed. He said, 'I AM WHO I AM.' Yahweh the God of our fathers, the God of Abraham, the God of Isaac, and the God of Jacob, has sent me. 'That will be my name forever, and by this name they shall call upon me for all generations to come'" (Ex 3:14-15).

"Oh!" said Pharaoh, "now we're getting somewhere. We have a name." And he ordered his wise men to bring the books that listed all the names of all the gods of the world. And they were commanded to search for the name of this "new and demanding" god. They searched through the books, histories, chronicles, prayers of their allies and even of their enemies' gods and could find no "Yahweh." "Well, that does it," said Pharaoh, "your 'Yahweh' doesn't exist. No one has ever heard of him before!" He was furious at Moses and derided him and his words.

Moses spoke again: "Any names that you could find in your books are dead gods. Only our God is the God of the living; the God who was, who is, and who will be for all time."

But Pharaoh was through playing word games and said: "Enough! I do not know your god. I have never heard of him and do not care to ever hear of him again. I refuse to obey a god I do not know. Be gone and do not return." But Moses eyed Pharaoh solemnly and warned him: "If you do not obey and let Yahweh's people go free, you will know him—in pain, in suffering, in punishment, and in his devastation and wrath upon Egypt." But Pharaoh dismissed him and the plagues began: frogs, gnats, boils, hail, locusts, darkness, blood, fear, and finally, the death of all the firstborn of man and beast in the land. Pharaoh came to know the God of the Israelites, the God of the living, in wrath and punishment.

The story is ancient, and was kept in the tradition of the Jewish people as an undercurrent to the hard-heartedness of Pharaoh and a reminder that they themselves were to honor God and so never come to know their God in wrath and punishment. But they, too, betrayed their God and turned from the covenant and from life. They suffered exile, the loss of the temple in Jerusalem, oppression, and occupation of their land by enemies. It wasn't so much that God did anything to them. Rather, God withdrew to a distance and they found themselves caught in a web of national allegiances, wars, political intrigues, lies and the brutality of a history that tries to use gods as instruments of power and control. The poor and those in need were their early warning system; the prophets a last hope of warning and repentance. And so Isaiah's words are forerunners to the beatitudes and woes:

> Therefore thus says the Lord Yahweh:
> Look, my servants will eat
> but you will go hungry;
> my servants will drink
> but you will be thirsty;
> my servants will rejoice
> but you will be disgraced;
> my servants will sing with gladness of heart,
> but you will cry with grief in your heart,
> and wail in anguish of spirit.
>   ... Whoever invokes a blessing in the land will receive the blessing from the God of truth; whoever takes an oath in the land will swear by the God of truth. For past troubles will be forgotten, and I will see them no more.
>   I now create new heavens and a new earth, and the former things will not be remembered, nor will they come to mind again. (Isaiah 65:13-14, 16-17)

The words of the prophets are dense with ancient formulas that reveal both God's dismay at what his people are doing and the judgment that will be reckoned as a warning to cease and to be converted. In comparison, the words of Jesus seem those of a mild and gentle, nonviolent prophet. Isaiah's words are scathing:

> Woe to you, O ravager
> who never have been ravaged,
> you O treacherous one
> who have not been betrayed!
> When your ravaging is over,
> you yourself will be ravaged;
> when your treacherous deals are ended,
> you yourself will be betrayed.
> O Yahweh, have mercy on us
> who put all our hope in you.
> Be our strength every morning,
> our salvation when trouble comes.
> Peoples flee when you thunder and threaten,
> nations scatter when you rise majestically.
>   (Isaiah 33:1-3)

Jeremiah himself cries out "Woe is me!" as he tries to preach to those who do not want to hear the Word of God. He is compelled to speak words when he would prefer to remain silent. He speaks because the Word is a fire within him:

> This is what Yahweh says,
>   "Cursed be the man who trusts in human beings and depends on a mortal for his life, while his heart turns away from Yahweh!
>   He is like a bunch of thistles in dry land, in parched desert places, in a salt land where no one lives and who never finds happiness....
>   Most deceitful is the heart. What is there within man, who can understand him? I, Yahweh, search the heart and penetrate the mind. I give to each one according to his ways and the fruit of his deeds.

Like a partridge hatching eggs it did not lay, is
the man who piles up unjust riches.

When his life is half over, his wealth deserts him,
and in the end he is nothing but a fool." (Jeremiah
17:5-6, 9-11)

Amos's book is full of woes, warnings, and dire threats.
He tries in vain to get the people to see the folly of their ways
and the inevitable coming of the day of judgment. But they
are heedless:

Woe to those whose decrees are bitterness, not justice,
who trample on the rights!

You hate him who reproves in court; you despise
him who speaks the truth.

Because you have trampled on the poor and ex-
torted levies on their grain, though you have built
mansions of hewn stones you will not dwell in them;
though you have planted choice grapevines, you shall
not drink of their wine.

For I know the number of your crimes and how
grievous are your sins; persecuting the just, taking
bribes, turning away the needy at the gates. See, how
the prudent keep silent at this time, for it is an evil
time. (Amos 5:7-13)

And lest we think that these dire words are addressed
only to men and to structures, Amos also singles out women
as wicked oppressors as well.

Listen to this word, you cows of Bashan, you women
who live on the hills of Samaria, who oppress the
weak and abuse the needy, who order your husbands,
"Bring us something to drink quickly!" (Amos 4:1)

And Micah continues the lamentation, reminding the people of their responsibilities and God's rights in the covenant.
God expects the people to fulfill their covenant responsibilities to their neighbors and the poor in the land.

Woe to those who plot wickedness and plan evil even on their beds! When morning comes they do it, as soon as it is within their reach.

If they covet fields, they seize them. Do they like houses? They take them. They seize the owner and his household, both the man and his property.

This is why Yahweh speaks, "I am plotting evil against this whole brood, from which your necks cannot escape. No more shall you walk with head held high for it will be an evil time." (Micah 2:1-3)

All of the warnings of the prophets are in the language of woes and lamentations for a people already dead. This is the denouncement of evil and injustice, of a people gone astray, but it is always balanced by the announcement of possibility, of hope, if only the people change, repent, and restore the rights that have been trampled upon. Jesus' teaching of care for the least is not new in Israel. It is old, found in the original law and in reminders that no one is to ever know the shame that the nation knew in Egypt. God's nation, land, and people were to be an alternative of hope, especially for the poor, the widow, the orphan, the stranger and the alien, those most vulnerable. This tradition of care for the dispossessed and those on the fringes of society is shared by all three of the nomadic religious faiths: Judaism, Islam and Christianity. There is a Muslim story told of Jesus that is so close to the heart of the matter as to be uncanny in its pointedness.

✳   Once upon a time Jesus was walking along the edge of a graveyard. He stopped and prayed for those in the tombs and with great desire prayed to his Father: "Please, O God, in your goodness, raise one soul from the dead and give that soul life again, for the love that you bear me." With that a stone rolled away and a man sat up in the grave!

Jesus blessed him in the name of God and asked his name. The man answered.

"When did you die?" Jesus asked.

He answered, "One thousand four hundred years ago."

Jesus was stunned that his soul should still be so tied to this earth. He looked at the man and asked him further, "What is it like to be dead?"

"Bitter, terrible, empty, and there is a sour taste of ashes and dirt in my mouth."

"What did you ever do," Jesus asked, "to have such a strong and lasting taste of death in your mouth?"

The man spoke immediately, "I don't know why there was such a fuss over it. It wasn't that much. I took a portion of what belonged to a widow and her children unjustly and God will never let me forget it."

Jesus looked at him and asked, "Are you done with making restitution and repairing the breach in their lives?"

"No," the man sighed.

And Jesus looked hard at him, pointed his finger at him, and the man lay back down in his tomb, still dead.

This is a story of a woe come to pass. The first three woes in Luke, like the beatitudes, are really three ways of describing one group of people, highlighting different aspects and characteristics of their values and behavior. "But alas for you who have wealth, for you have been comforted now." In the next two woes, the first is extended to include more specifics: "Alas for you who are full, for you will go hungry" and "Alas for you who laugh now, for you will mourn and weep" (Lk 6:24-25). But the first deals specifically with wealth, riches, money, an idol that is worshiped instead of, or alongside of, our God. And Luke's gospel is packed with Jesus' stories about greed, possessions, money and those who are so caught in the pursuit of wealth that they destroy their own souls—and those of others—in the process. Who are these rich, these who worship money?

In the gospel of Luke there are five individuals who are called "rich." Three are found in the parables: the rich fool (Lk 12:16), the master of the crafty servant (Lk 16:1), and the rich man at whose gate the beggar Lazarus lies (Lk 16:19). There are three generic references to the rich: the rich neighbors whom Jesus advises against inviting to dinner parties in his parable of the feast (Lk 14:12), the rich person who will find it harder to enter the kingdom than a camel trying to pass through the eye of a needle (Lk 18:25), and the rich who give out of their surplus to the temple and with whom Jesus contrasts the poor widow (Lk 21:4). Rich has to do with money and possessions but it has also to do with what we worship, what we wrap our lives around. It is most often revealed in the way we deal with economic matters and our own security. Let us look at some of Jesus' stories to better understand the warnings to the rich, the lamentations on the deadness that shrouds them.

Luke recounts the story of someone trying to use Jesus to get what he wants from one of his relatives in regard to an inheritance.

> Someone in the crowd spoke to Jesus, "Master, tell my brother to share with me the property of our father." He replied: "My friend, who has appointed me as your judge or your attorney?" Then Jesus said to the people: "Be on your guard and avoid every kind of greed, for even though you have many possessions, it is not that which gives you life." (Luke 12:13-15)

This is the heart of the matter: what is it that gives us life? It is not possessions, not anything that can be grasped, bought and sold, marketed and bargained for, nor is it anything that is external to us. There is a marvelous Zen poem entitled "Mountain Falling Flowers" that I have been carrying around with me for a long time. It reads:

> We accept the graceful falling
> Of mountain cherry blossoms,
> But it is much harder for us
> To fall away from our own
> Attachment to the world.
> (Rengetsu)

To speak about the core of life, of what is of ultimate concern, is much harder than to speak about commerce, politics, economics, and inheritance. Our life is precious and its quality is not defined by our lifestyles and bank accounts, our securities and living accommodations, not even by the work we do or what we desire. Jesus is turning his listeners' hearts to what is essential, and he continues by telling them a story:

> There was a rich man and his land had produced a good harvest. He thought: "What shall I do? For I am short of room to store my harvest." So this is what he planned: "I will pull down my barns and build bigger ones to store all this grain, which is my wealth. Then I may say to myself: My friend, you have a lot of good things put by for many years. Rest, eat, drink and enjoy yourself." But God said to him: "You have made a mistake! This very night your life will be taken; tell me who shall get all you have put aside?" This is the lot of those who pile up riches instead of becoming rich before God. (Luke 12:16-21)

Jesus' words are sharp: "This very night your life will be taken!" All else is seen in relation to that reality. The rich man has made a terrible mistake, a miscalculation in his plans. Who will get all that he has put aside for his own pleasure? And that is the bridge between this life and the next: who we share our wealth with in this life, now. The only thing that matters in the long run is what we have shared with others, how we have helped those who vitally need what we do not use. The story also has a hidden meaning suggested by Jesus' admonition in the last line, which in Greek reads more like "Beware of ruthless greed or unlawful gain!" There is a sense that this man has acquired his profit unjustly and that he is turning away from the effects his actions have on others.

The prophets and the psalms warn about this kind of selfish living: "Incline my heart to follow your will and not my own selfish desire" (Ps 119:36), and in Jeremiah, "But your eyes and heart are set on gain and the shedding of innocent blood, on the practice of extortion" (Jer 22:17). If the man has made his profit in this way then he is even more at risk this night. Jesus often told stories that were connected to the "year of favor from the Lord." In the Jubilee year the wealthy were exhorted not to hoard. If this man has been building barns for himself while ignoring others' basic needs he is in fact evil and a traitor to the community, much like someone who, devoid of any feeling for others, hoards food and blankets in the midst of a disaster, or sells relief supplies on the black market, again for selfish gain.

Death is the leveler, the glitch in all our plans, our collecting, and our storing up. It is usually unexpected, and we spend a great deal of time ignoring its reality, assuming it will not touch us anytime soon. A friend sent me an excerpt from a book, *As William James Said* (Elizabeth Aldrich, ed., Vanguard Press, 1942), that speaks about this shadow that can shift our priorities and reorient us to look at our lives in a different way.

> It comes strangely over me in bidding you good-by how a life is but a day and expresses mainly but a single note. It is so much like the act of bidding an ordinary good night. "Good night, my sacred old Father! If I don't see you again—Farewell! a blessed farewell!"
>
> The Pathos of death is this, that when the days of one's life are ended, those days that were so crowded with business and felt so heavy in their passing, what remains of one in memory should usually be so slight a thing. It is as if the whole of a person's significance had now shrunk into the phantom of an attitude, into a mere musical note or phrase suggestive of his singularity—happy are those whose singularity gives a note so clear as to be victorious over the inevitable pity of such a diminution and abridgment. (pp. 183-84)

What is that singular note so clear and victorious? Jesus goes on in Luke's chapter 12 to clearly define that note from his vantage point. He reminds his disciples not to be fearful and especially not to be overly concerned about what to eat, or what to wear. He instructs them to learn from crows and wildflowers how all the earth is so richly cared for by God. And if these millions of crows and fields of wildflowers do so well, why should we, whom Jesus calls "people of little faith," worry about God's care for us? The exhortation as to how to live is simple:

> Do not set your heart on what you are to eat and drink; stop worrying. Let all the nations of the world run after these things; your Father knows that you need them. Seek rather the Kingdom and these things will be given to you as well.
>
> Do not be afraid, little flock, for it has pleased your Father to give you the kingdom. Sell what you have and give alms. Get yourselves purses that do not wear out, and make safe investments with God, where no thief comes and no moth destroys. For where your investments are, there will your heart be also. (Luke 12:29-34)

It is disarmingly simple: singlehearted sight and remembrance of God and God's kingdom and actions that publicly reveal that priority in our lives. Our investments of money, time, and concern in society and in religion must be pure, all of a piece, whole. The kingdom comes first, for the kingdom is the life of Jesus with his Father shared intimately with all of us, his beloved children. One of the distinguishing marks of Jesus' company is that, in contrast to the nations of the world, Jesus' disciples do not make the accumulation of wealth or accommodation to business and dominant values of greed, materialism, and the pursuit of security their life's goal and work. The *Houston Catholic Worker* paper quoted theologian Father Michael Baxter, C.S.C., in this regard, pointing out that, unfortunately, we are not unlike the nations of the world.

> Catholic ethical discourse is under the hegemonic sway of nationalist and capitalist ideology, thus rendering Catholic theorists incapable of mounting a serious critique of the American cultural and social

order. The so-called arrival of Catholicism in the United States should be narrated not so much as a success but as a failure, inasmuch as Catholicism's entry into the U.S. mainstream has been an occasion of accommodation to unchristian elements of the existing political and cultural order.

This is a contemporary indictment of our unchristian lifestyles. It is also an indictment of the more selfish and debilitating aspect of the American dream, the belief that we can have everything we want and as much of it as we can get while selfishly creating laws and structures that defend the wealthy and penalize those struggling on survival levels. This is not a new phenomenon, but one now espoused by Christians as much as anyone else. Over a hundred and thirty years ago the people of this country were warned: "Corporations have been enthroned. An era of corruption in high places will follow, and the money power will endeavor to prolong its reign by working on the prejudice of the people until wealth is aggregated in a few hands and the public is destroyed" (a quote from Abraham Lincoln cited in *Green Cross*, Summer 1996). When they hear these words, people are surprised, not only because of who spoke them, but also because of how they fit today's economic reality. The remedy? To borrow from another tradition that puts it succinctly: "Abandoning things is superior, pursuing them is inferior." Yen T'ou Or, in a story pertaining to our own tradition, puts it just as simply.

✳ Once upon a time one of the monks, Serapion, sold his book of the gospels and gave the money to the poor and hungry, saying, "I have sold the book that tells us to sell all that we have and give to the poor."

A more irreverent description of the situation in which we find ourselves comes from comedian Lenny Bruce:

✳ Christ and Moses stand in the back of St. Patrick's, looking around. Christ is confused at the grandeur of the interior, the baroque interior, the rococo baroque interior. He is confused because his route has brought him through Spanish Harlem, and he is wondering what fifty Puerto Ricans are doing living in one room when that stained-glass window is worth ten Gs a square foot!

The point is not so much that churches and places of worship shouldn't be built; rather, it is about remembering that God is worshiped primarily in the Body of Christ, in human beings and not in buildings. The state of people's well-being is more an indication of true worship than any monument or cathedral. In the kingdom of God, the best investments of are people: children, the elderly, those in exile and caught on the wrong side of borders, and those who are victims of inflation, monetary markets, and unjust economic structures. Better distribution of the existing riches of the world is a place to begin to ease the burdens of the poor and to lighten our own hearts and free up our own lives. To concentrate on our own comfort as primary is to fall into the category of those to be pitied and lamented as rich, insensitive and without compassion for others.

In Luke's gospel the Pharisees are often portrayed as a group that betrays the covenant and exhibits behavior that Christians are to avoid. Later in Luke Jesus tells the parable of the crafty steward who has been fraudulent in the use of his master's resources and who knows that he has been found out. It is audit time and he is frantic and concerned about one thing only: his own hide. And so he uses his imagination and already existing good graces with his master's clients to ingratiate himself further and so secure a future for himself. He meets with them and alters their bills, always in their favor, compounding his own dishonesty and deceit, defrauding his master even more, but making sure that he will have friends to fall back on. Some people think that he has already juggled the books to skim the accounts for himself and now he is just setting them more to rights, easing the debt he will owe to his own master and treating the clients more justly. The man is interested only in himself, not in his master or his clients. Any situation is to be used for his own benefit, at whatever cost to others. And the reader senses that if the master employs him again, he will, once again, change the bills again and work out the situation to his own best advantage.

The amounts that are owed to the master are substantial, indicating that these are wealthy clients. Thus, the story also describes a system that breeds injustice and self-interest, a system based on indebtedness, bribes, and financial manipulations. One doesn't get the sense that the servant has repented or changed his ways. Rather, he has only momentarily realized he needs a community, since he is too proud to beg and too weak to dig ditches and fears "falling from grace" into poverty. The parable ends with a lot unsaid and left hanging. Will the servant return to his master's employ and revert back to his old ways, or will he continue to relate to his newly made friends, friends he discovered by doing what was right, even though it was for the wrong reason, that of self-interest? At the end of the story, Jesus puts his point across to his disciples and to the Pharisees who are listening:

> The master commended the dishonest steward for his astuteness. For the people of this world are more astute in dealing with their own kind than are the people of light. And so I tell you: use money, tainted though it be, to make friends for yourselves, so that when it fails, these people may welcome you into the eternal homes. (Lk 16:1-9)

We are to learn astuteness, to be crafty in the ways of light. And we are to use money, tainted and problematic as it is, to make friends for ourselves! But the crux is: What kind of friends? Where? We are to "push our privilege," not for our own ends but for those in need, for the people of light, making friends in the kingdom who will take us in where it matters, not only here but in the eternal kingdom. We are to invest in people, in communities, in those who are struggling and who cannot fend for themselves. Oftentimes when I am in Latin America or among the poor in my own country I come close to despair and I wonder if I'll make it into the kingdom as a member of the dominant culture, for I have access to so much: wealth, gifts, education, knowledge, money, security. I will never be poor and in dire straits like so many of my friends. I know how to work the system a bit and know others who do and my education gives me an advantage over so many. But my poor friends laugh at me and tell me not to worry. They say "Even if you don't make it into the kingdom on the first draft, slip around back. We'll unlatch the door so you can get in, and if we can't do that, we'll throw a rope over the wall. Don't worry, we'll get you in at the end." It is a comfort, for I know they mean it, one way or the other! It is this, I think, that Jesus is advocating and encouraging with this parable: to make friends with the poor and to be honest in our dealings with money, which he describes as a "slight matter" (Lk 16:10), so that we may merit being honored with a great matter, the true wealth of the kingdom of God. We are reminded, "And if you have not been trustworthy with things which are not really yours, who will give you the wealth which is your own?" (Lk 16:12). Money, along with our other possessions, is never really ours. These things are loaned to us. What is really ours is only this: our very self, our lives.

But all of this has led up to what Jesus is trying to get those resistant to him and his message to hear: "No servant can serve two masters. Either he does not like the one and is fond of the other, or he regards one highly and the other with contempt. You cannot give yourself both to God and to Money" (Lk 16:13). There it is in a nutshell: the reality of divided hearts, of the worship of idols alongside the God we claim is the one true God, and the impossibility of having both riches and comfort now, often at the expense of others' need, and an honest relationship with God. We live torn, pulled in opposite directions and waffling between what must be avoided and shunned and what is to be embraced and cherished—our idol or our God.

The reaction of the Pharisees is strong and accusing: "The Pharisees, who loved money, heard all this and sneered at Jesus. He said to them, 'You do your best to be considered righteous men by people. But God knows the heart, and what is highest among humans is loathed by God' " (v. 14).

It is a scathing indictment, a truth-telling that will cost Jesus dearly. The Pharisees are described as sneering at Jesus, ridiculing his words and being disdainful of his message. Those described in the woes as "the rich" are those who are resistant to the message and person of Jesus, those who will not repent or acknowledge their wrong-doing, their deceitfulness, and their divided hearts. Their gods are comfort, security, money, power, and reputation. They are selfish, greedy, and dishonest, and they reveal by their choices and lives that they have no faith in God. This passage sums up all the woes: those who are rich, those who are full, those who laugh at others' needs, scorning the truth and those who speak it, and those who are concerned that others speak well of them, knowing that it is false admiration.

Jesus follows his accusation with the story of the rich man and Lazarus, a story about lack of compassion and the refusal to listen to God's words and repent. We will look at this story in greater detail in the next chapter because it speaks of feasting and hungering, of judgment, and of living as though death does not reverse the fortunes of the world and reveal what is everlasting and true.

How does one divest oneself of riches and care for others' needs? How does one learn not to be obsessed with material possessions, wealth and one's own comfort? How does one learn to trust God for survival with gracefulness and to share one's true wealth with those who need it most? How does one come back to life after having been long dead? The practical aspects are simple: almsgiving, generosity, hospitality, sharing resources, wealth, and access to the structures of survival, working for just systems that provide for the rights and needs of the many. What is more difficult is learning to let go. Perhaps a story will help us see that what is asked of us is not so unnerving and awful and that we are not putting ourselves in terrible jeopardy or jumping into the deep end of a pool without water.

Last year while I was in Japan I was told the most engaging story called "The Farmer and the Poor God." Just the title grabbed me. In Japan there are many gods, gods of good fortune, gods of places, gods who care for the unborn and children, and so on. This is a folktale from the northern part of

Japan. I will share it with you as I was told it, though there is also a written version in the children's book called *The Peasant and the Poor God*, retold by Ruth Wells.

✳   Once upon a time there was a poor farmer. He worked hard, struggling with the land to feed his many children. It seemed that the harder he worked, the poorer he became and the less he had to show for all his struggle and toil. And his children—there were so many of them, they seemed countless. There were so many mouths to feed, and there was never enough to go around.

Well, actually, it wasn't exactly like this. The farmer did only what he had to in order to get by. It wasn't that he was lazy. It was just that he wasn't all that interested in working hard and, in fact, he had only four children. It just seemed like he had a lot more. They were terrible: yelling, screaming, fighting constantly, pulling each other's hair—awful children.

One day it was unusually terrible and his wife complained to him, "Our lives are so awful. We must have a poor god." And that was true. They did have a poor god. He lived quietly in a far corner of their attic crawlspace, with the cobwebs and dust. He liked living there, especially at night when the house finally quieted down and they all went to sleep. He would listen to their breathing and watch over them.

"Well," the farmer said, "you're right. That's why we're in the state we're in. We've got a poor god. Now, how can we get rid of him?"

The wife quickly suggested, "We could run away and hide from him. I could pack up everything we've got—it won't take long and we could get up early while it's still dark and leave, just slip away, and we won't have to worry about him ever again. We could start over somewhere else." So it was decided. Quickly they packed and went to bed early so they could get an early start while it was still dark.

But the farmer couldn't sleep. He was dreaming of his new life, of being rich and having servants to take care of him and order around, of having more than he needed and being esteemed in the land as a wealthy man. How grand it would be! Finally he got up and stepped over his wife and children as they slept soundly. He walked out on the porch in the moonlight. There, sitting on his porch, was a stranger making sandals out of straw. "Who are you?" the farmer demanded. "This is my porch."

"Why, I'm your poor god from the attic. I'm making sandals for our journey tomorrow. Traveling is hard on your feet and we'll all need them."

The farmer cried and wailed, woke up his wife and wept on her shoulder. "He knows. The poor god knows we are trying to run away from him. Now we'll never get away. We're doomed. You know what it's like when a poor god gets hold of you. Poor gods never let go. We'll never be rich." And finally, forlorn, he went back to bed.

Next morning the poor god sat on the front porch and continued making sandals. It was a good thing to do and he found he was very good at it. He took strands of sand-colored and yellow straw and wove them together into thick sturdy sandals. The husband and wife walked around moaning and bewailing their fate and the children fought and pushed each other, but the poor god kept making sandals. The children went out on the porch to watch him and he gave each of them a pair to wear. He made a dozen and then some more, stringing them from the rafters of the porch. This went on for days, with the poor god working away and learning as he went, even experimenting with some blue straw that he had found.

One day a man passed by the house on the way home from the village and admired the sandals. He complimented the poor god on his work and remarked on how lovely the sandals were. The poor god was touched. No one had ever cared about anything he'd done. In fact, no one had ever much cared about him. Everyone had always wanted to get rid of him and maligned his presence and company. He was delighted and gave away a pair, and then another for the man's wife and more for his children.

The next day a neighbor came by and said he'd heard about the sandals and had admired his friend's new pair. He went home with pairs for everyone in his family. The word spread and the poor god kept giving the sandals away until the wife noticed and grabbed her husband, instructing him to stop the poor god from doing this. She said to her husband, "Tell him that he should charge a bag of rice for each pair. That way at least we'll have something to eat."

The next day they had two sacks of rice and some lentils. The farmer thought about all those sandals hanging from the porch ceiling. "Tomorrow," he decided, "I'll take them into town."

He did, and he returned with three sacks of rice, a new hoe, a chicken, a cooking pot and some sweets for the children. Then he sat down beside the poor god on the porch. "Keep working, poor god," he said. "There are a lot of things we need."

"I will gladly," said the poor god, "but I'll need some help in harvesting and bringing in the straw and mixing some dye."

So they all went to work. The children brought in the straw, the wife mixed dyes of red, blue, saffron, and brown, and the farmer himself learned how to make sandals with different patterns and designs.

Time passed and changes started happening, unnoticeable at first, but eventually it seemed as though everything had changed. The children didn't fight so much; the yelling and hair pulling stopped. They were happy. In fact, they even sang sometimes and they laughed out loud. Even the poor god changed. He started getting chubby. His clothes were tighter and, though they were still ragged, they were now fixed and sewn and kept laundered. Even his attic had been swept clean of cobwebs and old junk. And—most surprising of all—the family seemed to enjoy his company. The year passed quickly.

Soon, New Year approached. This was the most solemn and important feast of the year—Shogatsu. They cleaned the house and then cleaned it again. They brought out new rice and prepared for Fukuno Kami, the god of good fortune, to visit them. This year the farmer was sure that they were going to be rich at long last. All the signs looked good. And the poor god gathered his few belongings to get ready to leave his family and let them meet the rich god who would care for them in the new year.

It is the custom in Japan to celebrate New Year's Eve by opening the front doors of the house as the temple priests ring the bells to welcome the new gods. They ring the bells 108 times and families gather to welcome the new gods into their homes.

That night, the farmer's door was flung open and the pealing of the bells echoed across the cold air of the valley. And the poor god with his few belongings made for the front door. Then bedlam broke loose. "Where are you going?" cried the children. The wife wept. The children started yelling and screaming again, their arms wrapped around the poor god's legs. "You can't leave us, we love you," they said.

"But I have to go," said the poor god, "or else the rich god can't come in. See—here he is at the door already, waiting for me to leave and make room for him."

And sure enough, there was the rich god, wrapped in his elegant kimono, and his jewels, standing fat and proud and imposing in the doorway. The rich god announced, "Yes, time for the poor god to go. You are my family now. You belong to me. Out, out! This is my house now. They're mine." There was a terrible din and in the background the bells were tolling.

Then the farmer yelled for everyone to be quiet. In the stillness, he said, "I made a mistake. I thought I wanted to be rich, but I was wrong. I am rich. My wife laughs and sings. My children do not fight any more and we all work together. In fact, I love making sandals and people think they are works of art—they hang them on the wall, like Buddha's sandals, as a reminder to walk with compassion and eyes wide open. I am rich. You have to stay, poor god. We need you." And with that, he shoved the rich god out the door and slammed it shut, just as the last bell sounded. Ah, they were safe. They cheered and hugged the poor god and each other and celebrated their good fortune.

And so they all lived together in happiness. The children grew up and married and settled down close by. They continued to work and make sandals for their neighbors and to sell in the marketplace. And every New Year's Eve when the bells tolled they would keep the door firmly locked and tell the story of how the poor god had saved them. The farmer would end the story with the words, "Thank heavens for the poor god. Lord knows where we'd be now if it hadn't been for our poor god." And so it was.

Well, the poor god had always been shy and retiring, and after that they didn't hear much from him any more. And he'd always loved his quiet and solitude up in the attic, and after that they didn't see him much. It wasn't that he'd gone away or disappeared. It was just that now he wasn't there the way he had been once before. It's a bit like the song of a rare bird that you hear once. It is lovely, stilling, haunting, and it takes you away to a place of hope and sheer delight. You're never the same afterwards and you listen to every bird, hoping it might be that songbird. The song is in your mind and heart but you never hear it again. After a while you wonder if you ever did hear it or if it was just something you made up, or wanted very badly. You miss it so that you live your life listening for it and hoping it will return. That's the way it is with a poor god. Once he gets hold of you he never lets go, even when you don't see him or hear him much any more. You might even begin to wonder if you ever did, but the memory lingers and you keep hoping and you live on that. . . .

That's the way it is with our Poor God, the servant of Yahweh, the beloved child of the Father, Jesus, who cares for the poor and brings them the Good News that God is loose in the land. Our Poor God cares for all his children, but some of them need to change in order to be able to even hear or see him. They have trouble recognizing him when he's around and spend a lot of time running from him, hiding from him, and collecting idols in their insecurity and fear. Our Poor God has visited us and pitched his tent among us. He walks with us and would love for us to make sandals that would make it easier for all to walk with him. Those who have met the Poor God or visited his friends know the song of blessing and they live in hope of hearing it again. Even if they never do hear it again, the memory is strong and his friends are many and life is so rich, such a delight. Truly it is a blessing just to live and to have been visited by the Poor God. Alas for you who have wealth, for you have been comforted now, but you have never known the kingdom of God so close at hand, the presence of God so near and intimate.

7

Woe to You Who Are Full
Woe to You Who Laugh Now

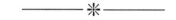

Prefer vegetable soup to duck broth. (Basho)

The man who has forgotten self may be said to have entered heaven. (Chang-tzu)

The second and third woes extend the description of those with wealth, those who attend to their own comfort and needs first, amassing riches while others go without. They read: "Alas for you who are full, for you will go hungry" and "Alas for you who laugh now, for you will mourn and weep." Again they are sharply drawn alternatives to existing wisdom, to the hopes of the dominant cultures and the way of the world.

The woes operate like mini-parables or *koans* that need to be meditated upon and taken to heart, taken personally and delved into with an open mind that does not resist but is receptive to a kernel of truth buried like a lodestone within it.

Jesus is teaching in the manner of a prophet of old, like Elijah, referred to in the book of Kings as that "disturber, that troubler of Israel" whose presence and appearance boded ill for those grown smug, content, and lax in their faithfulness to the covenant. There are many stories told of the prophet Elijah coming back throughout the centuries to teach the people. He appears in disguise, as a beggar or an itinerant, to see if the people are ready for the coming of the Messiah. The answer is found in the response to him as a poor beggar. But Elijah also is a teacher, discussing with the rabbis points of law and defending the rights of the poor and the honor of God. One such story is very simple, yet it goes right to the heart of what the woes are all about, especially the first three woes that speak about those who are wealthy, full, content, unaware of anyone's condition but their own.

✳   Once upon a time Elijah was walking along with one of the rabbis, delving into the Law and speaking of the wonders of God as they walked. On the road they passed a dead dog that had been hit by a wagon. The dog had been there for days with the birds picking at it and other wild creatures chewing on it. The rabbi immediately held his nose as he caught a whiff of the rotting stench. They passed it by and continued with their discussion, barely missing a beat.

About a mile down the road they passed a respectable couple out walking, dressed in their finery, proud and haughty, taking up the better part of the road. And this time it was Elijah who held his nose!

The prophet always discerns the truth of who someone is. And Jesus is no different: he sees straight into the heart of those in his audience and those who are curious about him. When the messengers return to John the Baptist in prison with a message from Jesus, Jesus turns to the crowds and praises John as "a prophet... and more than a prophet. For John is the one foretold in Scripture in these words: I am sending my messenger ahead of you to prepare your ways" (Lk 7:27). But he doesn't stop there. He continues with a comment directed at the Pharisees and teachers of the Law, a comment that summarizes what he knows about them as a prophet.

All the people listening to him, even the tax collectors, had acknowledged the will of God in receiving the baptism of John, whereas the Pharisees and the teachers of the Law, in not letting themselves be baptized by him, ignored the will of God. (Luke 7:29-30)

This is Jesus' evaluation of those who trail along listening to him but have no intention of letting his words touch their hearts. They are hardened in their positions and feel they have no need to repent or change their minds or ways. They ignore the will of God, intent on their own will and ego. They live falsely before the community and before God and they are seen through. Their conscience detects nothing amiss in their own lives, but they are often sure of others' failings and sins, and quick to judge whether another is worthy of them or not. Jesus knows them and he continues with a description that no one would find flattering:

"What comparison can I use for this people? What are they like? They are like children sitting in the marketplace, about whom their companions complain: 'We piped you a tune and you wouldn't dance; we sang funeral songs and you wouldn't cry.'
Remember John: he didn't eat bread or drink wine, and you said: 'He has an evil spirit.' Next came the Son of Man, eating and drinking, and you say: 'Look, a glutton for food and wine, a friend of tax collectors and sinners.' But the children of Wisdom always recognize her work." (Luke 7:31-35)

John practiced austerity, fasting and preaching a baptism for repentant people that they might obtain forgiveness of their sins. He cried out to all the people: "You brood of vipers! How will you escape when divine punishment comes? Produce now the fruits of a true change of heart, and do not deceive yourselves by saying: 'We are sons of Abraham.' For I tell you, God can make sons of Abraham from these stones. The axe is already laid to the root of the tree and every tree that fails to produce good fruit will be cut down and thrown into the fire" (Lk 3:7-9). And when the people ask sincerely what to do, John gives pragmatic directions: "If you have two coats, give one to the person who has none; and if you have food, do the same." To tax collectors he said: "Collect no more than your fixed rate." And to soldiers: "Don't take anything by force or threaten the people by denouncing them falsely. Be content with your pay" (Lk 3:10-14). Each is given sage advice for his particular vocation while all are told to give alms, to care for those who need food, clothing, and shelter. Repentance impinges on all areas of life, but especially the areas that are highlighted by one's work and vocation.

The Pharisees and teachers of the Law did not allow themselves to be baptized. They explained away John's message and even his popularity with the people by saying he was possessed. And now Jesus comes, with the power of the Spirit of God, healing, forgiving, and speaking the truth about the covenant and its call to faithfulness, not just in outward appearances, but with heartfelt submission to the will of God. But they write him off as a drunkard, a glutton who hangs around with public sinners and is not worth taking seriously.

No matter how God comes to some people, they will refuse him entrance because they keep the door well locked and guarded against any interference or change. They act like whining children, squatting in the marketplace, out of touch with everything around them. Jesus is very open about how he sees many who are there to hear what he has to say but do not let anything penetrate their souls. These are the people who not only set the standards for goodness, but also judge whether others are living up to those standards. They are careful not to let themselves become tainted or unclean by associating with anyone who is known to be a sinner, or lax in keeping to the letter of the Law. The soul of the Law is never acknowledged or honored.

Jesus' last line is aimed directly at those who most resist him when he says, "But the children of Wisdom always recognize her work." They, of course, are not the children of Wisdom, for the very first verse of the book of Wisdom is a command:

Love justice, you who rule over the world. Think rightly of God, seek him with simplicity of heart, for he reveals himself to those who do not challenge him and is found by those who do not distrust him.

Crooked thinking distances you from God, and his Omnipotence, put to the test, confounds the foolish....

For God's spirit has filled the whole world and he who holds together all things, knows each word that is spoken. So whoever speaks unjustly will not escape; the irrefutable sentence will reach him. The intentions of the unholy will be examined; what he has said will reach the Lord and his wickedness will be confounded. (Wisdom 1:1-3, 7-9)

And later, in that same chapter:

Let us oppress the upright man who is poor, and have no thought for the widow, or respect for the white hair of old age.

Let our strength be our right, since it is proved that weakness is useless. Let us set a trap for the righteous, for he annoys us and opposes our way of life; he reproaches us for our breaches of the Law and accuses us of being false to our upbringing.

He claims knowledge of God and calls himself son of the Lord. He has become a reproach to our way of thinking; even to meet him is burdensome to us. He does not live like others and behaves strangely.

According to him we have low standards, so he keeps aloof from us as if we were unclean. He emphasizes the happy end of the righteous and boasts of having God as father. (Wisdom 1:10-16)

There could not be a clearer description of Jesus' behavior and attitudes and preaching. The teachers and Pharisees know what he was alluding to in calling those who follow him and heed his preaching the children of Wisdom. And it was around this time, when Jesus healed on the Sabbath, that those who were resistant to his clear-eyed questioning of their intentions and obedience to the heart of the Law became "furious and began to discuss with one another how they could deal with Jesus" (Lk 6:11).

They are too full of themselves, of self-assuredness that never questions, of self-righteousness and power, ease and place in the community. They have compromised their beliefs in order to secure a well-ordered life and they strive to protect that life at all costs. They realize that Jesus' estimation of them is low and on target. Jesus often warns the people about being shallow and deceitful, and many of these confrontations and accusations fly at dinner parties and revolve around the issues of food, cleanliness and the dinner company.

In addition to the four woes found in the Sermon on the Plain, there is another set of woes, longer and more detailed, found in Luke 11:32-53. Jesus had been invited by a Pharisee to a dinner party at his house. Jesus entered and took his place at the table. Noticing that Jesus had not washed his hands before sitting down to dinner, the Pharisee wondered about Jesus' sense of propriety. Jesus immediately turned on him with the words of a firebrand prophet:

> But the Lord said to him, "So then, you Pharisees, you clean the outside of the cup and the dish, but inside yourselves you are full of greed and evil. Fools! He who made the outside, also made the inside. But according to you, by the mere giving of alms everything is made clean.
>
> A curse is on you, Pharisees; for the Temple you give a tenth of all, including mint and rue and the other herbs, but you neglect justice and the love of God. This ought to be practiced, without neglecting the other. A curse is on you, Pharisees, for you love the best seats in the synagogues and to be greeted in the marketplace. A curse is on you for you are like tombstones of the dead which can hardly be seen; people don't notice them and make themselves unclean by stepping on them." (Luke 11:39-44)

What Jesus says is awful. It is not an insult but rather the plain truth that no one has dared to say aloud. The Pharisees obey certain regulations and neglect justice and the love of God, which are at the core of any religious practice. Without justice and love of God and neighbor, which are the spirit and the heart of the Law, there is only hypocrisy, lack of integrity, and real evil. The Pharisees care only for external purification rites and neglect their own souls. Their hearts are growing rancid and are in need of cleansing. They are appalled by external impurity, fastidiously shrinking from it, but unaware that they carry it around within themselves. Jesus tells them they are dead and buried, tombstones to trample on. He adds that others become unclean without even noticing that it is their presence that is causing it to happen. Again, the woes are lamentations, strongly worded images and powerful statements, but lamentations nonetheless, mourning what is dead and needs to be brought to life again.

Jesus is furious at the disobedience and the dishonesty involved in what they are doing and its effect on the people. They are intent on taking what they want. They demand that others tithe while excusing and "atoning" for their own behavior with almsgiving that publicly makes them look good. There is an old Italian folktale about a holy and obedient Franciscan, Brother Martin. Since he was the newest novice, Martin would be sent out into the towns and villages to beg for the community.

✳   He loved this work and soon got to know just about everyone. No matter what he was given, he returned a kind word, a gracious bow, a word of prayer for the giver, or praise of God. He would follow the same route daily and some people would give him the same food or offering daily: bread, a bunch of vegetables, a few pennies, sometimes a fish or a few eggs. Everyone in town knew when he would appear and they would wait for him.

But one house Brother Martin avoided. Everyone noticed this, including the house's owner, who was a lawyer and landowner. He owned a lot of the town, including the rundown houses and shacks that the poor lived in. He did nothing to fix these places and charged exorbitant rents

and had no qualms about evicting people at the moment
they were late paying.

One day the man went to the monastery and complained bitterly and loudly to the superior. He was being
insulted publicly and didn't appreciate being excluded
from Brother Martin's daily begging rounds. After all, he
was a generous and upright man in the community and
he wanted to help the church out. In fact, he could be very
generous, giving the needed stone and wood for repairs,
tallow for candles, money (of course) for expenses and ex-
tras for the other brothers. But he wanted Brother Martin
to treat him with the same respect and care that he did
everyone else in the village and not shun him. The superi-
or assured him there had been an oversight and Brother
Martin would come to his house the very next day in
mid-morning when everyone was out and about. The
man was satisfied. Brother Martin was instructed to go to
the landowner's house with sacks and beg from him as
well as from others in the town. Martin bowed his head
and nodded his assent.

The next morning he went on his usual rounds and
then stopped at the landowner's house and knocked on
his front door. Martin was made to wait before the man
appeared with two of his servants who filled both sacks.
While they did that, he assured Brother Martin that there
was more where that had come from and that he was a
God-fearing and good believer who wanted to do his part
to help the church. Brother Martin stood before him
silently and respectfully and bowed his head. Then he
shouldered the sacks and left for home. They were heavy
and his step was slow and labored. And as he walked he
left a trail of blood! The sacks dripped in the late morning
heat. The people watched and turned to each other smiling and said, "Oh, the brothers will eat well tonight and
for a few more days, by the looks of those bulging sacks."

Brother Martin went straight home. When he entered
the courtyard his superior and the other brothers were delighted to see the blood-stained sacks and the trail he'd
left behind him all the way. They rejoiced and exclaimed

over the gift of meat, freshly butchered: such a marvelous gift and so rare in these days of hardship. Such generosity on the part of the donor.

The sacks were put on the table in the kitchen and Brother Martin disappeared. When the brothers slit open the sacks, however, they found no meat, only money. They were confused: Where had all the blood come from?

Brother Martin was summoned. He stood before the superior and spoke truthfully: "Anything that man gives is blood money. He has bled it out of the poor and those who struggle just to work and eat and sleep. He cares nothing for his neighbors or the poor. He is a thief."

They were stunned into silence and shame, that somehow they would reap the benefit of others' suffering. Brother Martin never returned to that house to beg and everyone in town noticed.

This is what Jesus is saying: their almsgiving is blood money. And there are others who are listening and who know that they too are included in the condemnation because immediately someone tries to stop him with a rebuke.

> Then a teacher of the Law spoke up and said, "Master, when you speak like this, you insult us, too." And Jesus answered, "A curse is on you also, teachers of the Law. For you prepare unbearable burdens and load them on the people, while you yourselves don't move a finger to help them....
>
> A curse is on you, teachers of the Law, for you have taken the key of knowledge. You yourselves have not entered, and you prevented others from entering." (Luke 11:45-46, 52)

There is no escaping the Word of the Lord, the finger of God pointed at them. Jesus is ruthless, like a surgeon trying to cut away dead tissue and cauterize an infected wound that can kill if it is not cleaned out. It is not surprising that their reaction is that they begin to "harass him, asking him endless questions, setting traps to catch him in something he might say" (Lk 11:54). The die is cast and they are standing their ground, adamant in their own self-righteousness, seeing Jesus only as a trouble maker and someone who must be eliminated and silenced. They will resist with every ounce of their strength and resources.

Jesus' lamentations, curses, and woes spring from his compassion and concern for the poor, the widow and orphan, those already burdened by humiliating conditions and poverty. These people find no hope of relief from those who have the ability to ease their lives and lift their spirits. Instead they are brutally treated and more is unfairly demanded of them. The teachers of the Law and Pharisees have no compassion, no feeling for their neighbors, those with whom they share the covenant. God is trying to break their hearts, to soften them and make them feel another's pain.

In Japan there are many stories of the Master Hakuin who was enlightened and considered a great teacher, able to bring others to the wisdom and insight known as *satori*.

✳   Once upon a time a great landowner came to visit Master Hakuin. He was already one of the Master's disciples and came on a regular basis for private instruction. The landowner often gave goodly sums of money to Hakuin for his temple repair, journeys, and projects. This day he sat with the Master, listening attentively. Before the session was finished, as they were sitting down to tea, Hakuin was visited by a woman from the local village. She brought her gift to the monastery and humbly offered it to Hakuin. It was a gift of millet cakes, carefully and individually wrapped. They were graciously and gratefully accepted. As the woman left, Hakuin ate one and offered one to his guest.

But the landowner was wealthy and had never eaten bare millet cakes before. He was used to much better food and, though he took one of the cakes, he could not bring himself to eat it. It sat on his plate. This was observed by the Master. He looked at him sternly, then commanded him: "Force yourself to eat the millet cake. First, because it was a gift. Second—and more important—it can teach you of the misery of the poor and the hard burden and food of the common folk. You see, my teaching is nothing but this. And you have learned nothing so far."

The teachers of the Law, the Pharisees, and many of us are very interested in the key to knowledge, whether it is self-knowledge, knowledge of mysticism, tradition, the Law, even the scriptures, but we are not at all interested in conversion of heart, or change of lifestyle, the practice of compassion, and the easing of the burdens on the poor and the oppressed. And by our refusal to change and our indulgence and use of religion we often keep others from experiencing true religion and the knowledge of what is holy and of God. We forget what true Wisdom consists of:

> If we desire riches in life, what is richer than Wisdom who is the active cause of everything? If the intellect shows itself in action, still more does she who fashions everything. If you love righteousness, every virtue is the fruit of her labor, for she teaches temperance, prudence, justice, fortitude—all that is most valuable in life. (Wisdom 8:5-7)

The second and third woes are about the denial of others' need and the lack of compassion that follows upon the gaining of riches. In the future there will be a reversal: consolation and fullness will be denied to those who idolized riches in this life. Perhaps the story in Luke that illustrates this most poignantly is the parable of the rich man and the beggar, Lazarus, at his gate. It begins with the simple words, "Once there was a rich man," which echo the parable of the rich fool whose life would be required of him when, after a good harvest, he made no provision for sharing it with his community.

There is a radical critique of riches in many of Jesus' stories. It is a critique based on the covenant demands for equality and dignity within the Israelite community as well as on the prophets' declarations that riches are the result of injustice, oppression, and exploitation of others. Joachim Jeremias says, "Riches come from injustice. Unless one person has lost, another cannot find. Therefore I believe that the popular proverb is very true: 'The rich person is either an unjust person or the heir of one' " (*The Parables of Jesus*, London: SCM Press, 1963, p. 46). The parable is directed to the rich and most probably to unjust and dishonest men such as tax-collectors, landowners, and so on. It appears only in Luke's gospel.

> Once there was a rich man who dressed in purple and fine linen and feasted every day. At his gate lay Lazarus, a poor man covered with sores, who longed to eat just the scraps falling from the rich man's table. Even dogs used to come and lick his sores. It happened that the poor man died and angels carried him to take his place with Abraham. The rich man also died and was buried. From hell where he was in torment, he looked up and saw Abraham afar off, and with him Lazarus at rest. (Luke 16:19-23)

The set-up is classic. It reads like many folktales that set up a reversal of fortunes, except that this one takes place in the hereafter and is forever! The rich man, who is not named, is described by two facts: his clothing is of fine purple linen, which means that he is inordinately wealthy, and he feasts every day. He is a glutton in a culture that considered this a terrible sin because of mass hunger and starvation. But the much longer description is of Lazarus, a poor man covered with sores. He is truly miserable and he lives longing for scraps, like a dog. But the dogs are better off than he is and he is so weak and helpless that even dogs lick his sores. And he lives at the rich man's gate, right under his nose, in full view. But this is not just a story about two men separated by a gulf in life. It is about economics, classes in society, and the far-reaching effects of this gap between rich and poor in the world. The notes in the *Christian Community Bible* locate this story in a universal context:

> This parable deals with the worldwide gap between the rich and the inhumanly poor. There is a deadly

law of money which makes the rich live separately: housing, transportation, recreation, medical care. The wall the rich man willingly built in this life becomes, after his death, an abyss which no one will be able to bridge. The one who accepts this separation will find himself on the other side forever....

The rich man did not see Lazarus at his door. The Lazarus of today is legion and is already at our door: he is known as third or fourth world. On a world scale it is the more advanced countries and the privileged minorities that have taken possession of the table to which all were invited: the real power, and the culture imposed by the media. The national industries and sources of employment have been destroyed by a free exchange unimpeded by any social or moral restraint. Hundreds of millions of "Lazarus" people are marginalized and rejected until they die in misery, or through violence arising from a dehumanized life.

Modern-day Lazarus is kept at a distance from the residential areas by police, dogs and barbed wires. He would like to get his fill of the crumbs which are left over from the feast, but there are few scraps falling back to the homeland, after everything is wasted on imported products or deposited in foreign banks. Lazarus lives among dogs and rubbish: he becomes a prostitute, or a pickpocket, until a premature death enables him to find someone who loves him.... (pp. 208-209)

In this context the parable has immediate and far-ranging implications for contemporary society, religion, and all organizations and institutions that continue to co-exist with the terrible gap that separates rich and poor. The notes continue with the instruction and explanation of what the gospel asks us to do: "The Gospel, in its desire to save the rich as well as the poor, asks us to work with a view to removing the abyss which separates them. The time for breaking down the barrier is in this life" (p. 209).

The story now moves to the after-life and becomes theological in expression. Abraham, the father of Israel, of many nations, and of faith, now becomes the teacher and spokesperson for heaven and earth.

> He called out: "Father Abraham, have pity on me and send Lazarus with the tip of his finger dipped in water to cool my tongue, for I suffer so much in this fire."
> Abraham replied: "My son, remember that in your lifetime you were well-off while the lot of Lazarus was misfortune. Now he is in comfort and you are in agony. But that is not all. Between your place and ours a great chasm has been fixed, so that no one can cross over from here to you or from your side to us." (Luke 16:24-26)

The reversal is described in terms of the blessings and woes of Jesus: now the rich man knows suffering, pain, and thirst and Lazarus knows comfort. In his lifetime the rich man has material possessions and pleasures and his fill of comfort in every regard. Now there is thirst that never ends and mourning and weeping, while Lazarus knows blessedness and comfort at long last. And the reversal is final and irrevocable. It is judgment and execution of the verdict. There is no bridge between the two characters. It is interesting that while the rich man now sees Lazarus, he does not speak to him but asks Abraham to send Lazarus to bring comfort, as though Lazarus were a servant to take care of his needs. He has not changed much. He tries again:

> The rich man implored once more: "Then I beg you, Father Abraham, to send Lazarus to my father's house where my five brothers live. Let him warn them so that they may not end up in this place of torment." Abraham replied: "They have Moses and the prophets. Let them listen to them." But the rich man said: "No, Father Abraham. But if someone from the dead goes to them, they will repent."

Abraham said: "If they will not listen to Moses and the prophets, they will not be convinced even if someone rises from the grave." (Luke 16:27-31)

The relationship between Abraham and the rich man is evident in the terms of address, "father" and "my son." These are all children of Abraham, children of the covenant. Now the rich man, who did not honor the demands and privileges of the covenant in life, pleads for his own family members. Although he has lost forever the opportunity of befriending those at his gate, maybe they will fare better. But Abraham refuses to even consider this as an option: sending the poor man to beg the rich man's brothers to repent to save themselves from justice and punishment. The reason is directed toward the living, to those who are hearing the parable: they have Moses, the prophets, and the rich tradition of the Law. It is their history and the source of their liberation from bondage in Egypt. They have the covenant, the feasts, and the teachings of those who have gone before them in faith. It is sufficient. They have only to heed and take to heart the words that were enjoined on their ancestors and on them. Even then, the rich man argues and refuses to see. It is Abraham, the father of faith, who tells his errant children that they are so hardhearted and blind and their faith is so lifeless that even someone rising from the grave would be ignored by them. Their lifestyles, their excesses, and the company they keep would all mitigate against their being open to this radical intrusion of the Holy into the world.

The story is told and it is clearly implied that here is where the judgment is made. Heaven and earth are intimately tied together. Once past the boundary of death, the gap opens up and becomes impassable. The poor man at our gate, on our doorstep, on our street, and in our neighborhoods and nations is crucial and vital to our life, our life of faith lived here and our life forever. Jon Sobrino writes about our need for the poor:

Oppressed persons are the mediation of God because first of all, they break down the normal self-interest with which human beings approach other human beings. Merely by being there, the oppressed call into question those who approach, challenging their "being human"; and this radical questioning of what it means to be a human being serves as the historical mediation of our questioning of what "being God" means. That is why those who do approach the oppressed get the real feeling that it is they who are being evangelized and converted rather than those to whom they seek to render service. (*Christology at the Crossroads*, Maryknoll, N.Y.: Orbis Books, 1978, p. 223)

Lazarus and all the billions of poor humans who live on our doorsteps are God on our doorstep, at our gates. If we do not learn compassion at the sight of them then we will never learn anything about the revelation of God who became flesh to dwell among us. The depth and riches of our religious traditions will remain dried up and useless wells, because we will be as blind and as closed to them as we are to the poor of the earth. To put it in a remarkable way in words from an Asian culture:

Compassion has nothing to do with achievement at all. It is spacious, and very generous. When a person develops compassion, he is uncertain whether he is being generous to others or to himself, because compassion is environmental generosity.... We could say compassion is the ultimate attitude of wealth: an antipoverty attitude, a war on want. (Chogyam Trungpa, quoted in *The Sun*, June 1997, p. 40)

Compassion: being with others in their pain, suffering, needs, and desires, being passionately concerned and in solidarity with others, knowing their pain as one's own and intolerant of allowing it to continue unabated or unrelieved. When we look at the major religious traditions we can say with certainty that without compassion there is no religion. The Sioux people have a saying: "First, you are to think always of God. Second, you are to use all of your powers to care for your people, and especially for the poor" (traditional wisdom of the elders to those coming of age in the tribe). Dogen, a master in the Buddhist tradition, was asked by a disciple: "What is your Way?" He answered: "My way is always and everywhere to set people free." On an individual and communal level, that task involves practicing the corporal works of mercy and being charitable whenever we can. On a world-wide environmental and developmental level, the task is gigantic.

The gap in our world today can be characterized by staggering statistics that reinforce the description of the two men in the parable. The following is quoted from an interview with Ismail Serageldin in the Spring 1997 issue of *Lapis*, a journal of arts, economics, religion, culture and politics.

> On the pragmatic side, environmentally sustainable development is about people-centered environmentalism, for we have an enormous environmental and developmental agenda ahead of us:
>
> 1.2 billion people live on less than a dollar a day;
>
> 800 million people suffer from hunger and malnutrition;
>
> 1 billion people do not have access to clean water;
>
> 1.7 billion people have no access to sanitation;
>
> 1.3 billion people, most in developing countries' cities, are breathing air below World Health Organization standards;
>
> 700 million people, mostly women and children, suffer from indoor air pollution from biomass-burning stoves equivalent to smoking three packs of cigarettes a day;
>
> hundreds of millions of poor farmers have difficulty maintaining the fertility of the soils from which they eke out a meager living. (p. 6)

Serageldin is interested in sustainable development and works for the World Bank. Yet he writes with the passion of a prophet critiquing our world and offering both declarations of the extent of our problems and visions of change. He describes our present world conditions:

...our times are marred by conflict, violence, debilitating economic uncertainties, and tragic poverty. A sense of insecurity seems to pervade even the most affluent societies. The richest fifth of humanity consumes more than four-fifths of the world's income, while the remaining four-fifths live off less than a fifth. And yet, so many of the rich want to turn their backs on the poor. Selfish concerns seem to displace enlightened self-interest. But we are all our brothers' keepers and we are all downwind or downstream of each other. This is more than ever a time for a united front of the caring. (p. 5)

More and more people are growing concerned about our future and the devastating conditions of the present, if only from an "enlightened self-interest" vantage point. We as Christians, as the Body of Christ, must care for one another's plight and love God with all our hearts and souls and minds and strength by loving our neighbors with equal passion. And so we, as the church, as human beings, are called to feats of imagination in charity, in justice, in ethics, and in work for social change. Walter Brueggemann writes:

Ethical thought must admittedly be an act of imagination.... Imagination must be critical and poetic, and then ethical. That is, the shaping of social reality is largely determined by the modes of discourse and the kinds of questions put in the act of imagination.

But for Brueggemann this act of imagination is collective, and requires undoing as much as doing:

Transformation is the slow process of inviting each other into a counterstory about God, world, neighbor and self. This slow, steady process has as counterpoint the subversive process of unlearning and disengaging from a story we find no longer to be credible or adequate. (Brueggemann's comments on the thought of Richard Kearney in *The Wake of Imagination*, in *Texts*

Under Negotiation: The Bible and Postmodern Imagination,
Minneapolis: Fortress Press, 1993, pp. 16 and 25)

What are some of those stories we are invited to disengage from, stories we need to unlearn? Aurora Camacho de Schmidt wrote in February 1997:

> To disengage from a story that is no longer credible
> . . . the story of national security and exporting democracy; the story of the need for economic hegemony; the old but still alive story of white supremacy; the story of "taking care of our own first"; the story of "compassion fatigue"; the story of a limited pie and a zero-sum economy or society; the story of NAFTA as a solution to Mexico's economic problems; the story of overpopulation as a master explanation for all ills; the story that says some immigrants are "legal" and some are "illegal." (From a paper, "Salt and Fire: The Church in the Newest Immigration Debate," given at the National Asylum Conference in Menlo Park, California)

Jesus' parables and stories are primers in this task of unlearning, of disengaging, of being converted, of "bending the knees of our hearts" (as the Irish say). The counterstories of Jesus are radical and subversive, but also life-generating, sustaining, and hopeful. One such story, even though it ends badly, is the account of a rich ruler's encounter with Jesus.

> A ruler asked Jesus, "Good master, what shall I do to inherit eternal life?" Jesus said to him, "Why do you call me good? No one is good but God alone. You know the commandments: Do not commit adultery, do not kill, do not steal, do not accuse falsely, honor your father and your mother." And the man said, "I have kept all these commandments from my youth."
> Then Jesus answered: "There is still one thing you lack. Sell all you have and give the money to the poor, and you will have riches in God. And then come and

follow me." When he heard these words, the man became sad for he was very rich. Jesus noticing this said, "How hard it is for people who have riches to enter the kingdom of God! It is easier for a camel to pass through the eye of a needle than for a rich person to enter the kingdom of God." The bystanders said, "Who then can be saved?" And Jesus replied: "What is impossible for humans is possible for God." (Luke 18:18-27)

The story is realistic in the sense that when the man receives the answer it is not the one that he is expecting. He is disappointed and saddened. He has obeyed the commandments from his youth and wants to inherit eternal life. Jesus offers him the kingdom now, here, and tells him there is still one thing he lacks: selling what he owns, giving it to the poor, and having riches in God. And it is the one thing he does not want to hear, precisely because he is very rich and very attached to all that being rich entails. Jesus is offering him what we now term "the preferential option for the poor" as the basic prerequisite for discipleship and for eternal life, salvation. And we have the distinct feeling that the man will turn it down and refuse Jesus' invitation. It is an invitation extended to every Christian, not just to the rich. The poor, as well as the rich, have to choose to live in favor of their brothers and sisters. The gospel imperatives are preached to all classes and people.

What is this preferential option for the poor? There are a number of ways to look at it. Albert Nolan of South Africa describes it most clearly:

The option for the poor then is an uncompromising and unequivocal taking of sides in a situation of structural conflict. It is not a matter of preaching to some people rather than to others. Or a matter of being generous to the "underprivileged," or a judgment about the personal guilt of the rich, or even, in the first instance, a matter of lifestyle. It is the assertion that Christian faith entails, for everyone and as part of its essence, the taking of sides in the structural conflict between the oppressor and the oppressed. Nothing could be more threatening to the cherished beliefs of so many of today's Christians. Nothing could be more threatening to so many of our Churches in the way they operate in the world today. Nothing could be more controversial and challenging for our theology and our practice as Christians.

Those who feel threatened will say that this is not the gospel, it is politics. The gospel, they will argue, is about peace and reconciliation and not about taking sides in a conflict. Yes, but surely the gospel does not require us to reconcile good and evil, injustice and peace? Does it not rather demand that we take sides against all sin and especially the all-pervasive sin of oppression? (From "The Option for the Poor: What Does It Actually Mean?" published in *Resistance and Hope,* ed. Charles Villa-Vicencio and John W. de Gruchy, David Philips, Claremont: South Africa)

That is the meaning of the preferential option for the poor within structures and theology, pastoral practice and preaching, but it goes deeper than this, into every culture and every individual's life. Carlos Mesters says:

There's a poverty in every human life.

When we're aware of our limits, we're more open to change and conversions. If our limits are at the individual level, like alcoholism or alienation, our awareness can provide a change so that we can grow beyond this.

Here in Brazil, our limits are very much at the social level—hunger, homelessness. We struggle to become aware and change these things. But sometimes after engaging in a long social struggle nothing grew inside of us. Maybe in the U.S. your limits are more at the personal level. But sometimes when you are struggling individually, you realize that you have to address the social dimension to arrive at the personal dimension.

Without integration of the personal and the social we won't be full persons. We may start at different points, but we arrive together. The struggle is one. (Quoted in Mev Puleo, *The Struggle Is One*, Albany, N.Y.: State University of New York Press, 1994, p. 119)

Mev Puleo, a photographer and writer, says in her book: "The option for the poor means that we struggle so that all the goods God gave the world are distributed so that all people can have life." Simply and succinctly put, it involves lifestyle, prayer commitments, solidarity, and work for justice. Jean Vanier, founder of L'Arche communities that provide community and living accommodations for severely handicapped and disabled adults, speaks of it in terms of separation: "Is it not one of our problems today that we have separated ourselves from the poor and the wounded and the suffering? We have too much time to discuss and theorize, and have lost the yearning for God that comes when we are faced with the sufferings of people."

The monk Thomas Merton puts it in terms of traditional spiritual language in his book, *No Man Is an Island* (New York: Harcourt Brace, 1978):

Take the antithesis between love of self and love of another. As long as there is a question of material things, the two loves are opposed. The more goods I keep for my own enjoyment, the less there are for others. My pleasures and comforts are, in a certain sense, taken from someone else. And when my pleasures and comforts are inordinate, they are not only taken from another, but they are stolen. I must learn to deprive myself of good things in order to give them to others who have a greater need of them than I. And so I must in a certain sense "hate" myself in order to love others. (pp. xvii-xviii)

This option for the poor, this answer that Jesus gave the rich ruler about what brings eternal life here and now, is descriptive of the very nature of God: it is the one thing still lacking in much of our religious practice. Martin Luther says it this way: "God is the God of the humble, the miserable, the oppressed, and the desperate, and of those who are brought even to nothing; and his nature is to give sight to the blind, to comfort the broken-hearted, to justify sinners, to save the very desperate and damned."

And finally Gustavo Gutiérrez, in his book *We Drink from Our Own Wells* (Maryknoll, N.Y.: Orbis Books, 1984), describes this spiritual poverty, this making ourselves poor for the sake of the kingdom in terms of spiritual childhood:

> ... entry into the world of the poor has always demanded a measure of humility. In fact, that entry can come only as a result of an experience of what the gospel calls childhood. Medellín approaches this matter in a way that is enlightening. It does not present spiritual poverty primarily under the aspect of detachment from material goods; in an approach that is both more profound and more evangelical, it identifies spiritual poverty with spiritual childhood. It is therefore defined as "the attitude of opening up to God, the ready disposition of one who hopes for everything from the Lord," and the Church is told that its task is to preach and live "spiritual poverty as an attitude of spiritual childhood and openness to the Lord" (Poverty, nos. 4-5).
>
> This point is central. Spiritual childhood is one of the most important concepts of the Gospel, for it describes the outlook of the person who accepts the gift of being a child of God and responds to it by building fellowship.
>
> This spiritual childhood has in Mary, the mother of the Lord, a permanent model. Daughter of a people that put all its trust in God, archetype of those who want to follow the path to the Father, she points out

the way. The Magnificat, which Luke places on her lips, gives profound expression to what the practice of Latin American Christians is bringing to light once again in our day. The canticle of Mary combines a trusting self-surrender to God with a will to commitment and close association with God's favorites: the lowly, the hungry. (pp. 126-27)

Those who, like Mary, rejoice in the favor of God's mercy extended toward those most in need are blessed and know the joy and comfort of God in the midst of their mourning and struggle. "Solidarity with the poor and the oppressed should be a source of joy, not of strain, just as gratitude to God will be pregnant with effective commitment here and now" (Gustavo Gutiérrez, *The God of Life*, Maryknoll, N.Y.: Orbis Books, 1991, p. 47). And Jesus assures us of this blessedness often in the gospels. Once when he is speaking a woman from the crowd cries out: "Blessed is the one who bore you and nursed you!" Jesus replies: "Surely blessed are those who hear the word of God and keep it as well." This blessing that Mary knew as she sang the glory of God is offered to all.

In the story of the rich ruler who refuses the invitation there is another assurance. Peter and the disciples have witnessed this scene and heard Jesus' words about how hard it is to enter the kingdom when you are rich, how hard it is to be saved. Peter is quick to look to his own self-interest in the afterlife:

Then Peter said: "We left everything we had and followed you." Jesus replied, "Truly, I tell you, whoever has left house or wife, or brothers or parents or children for the sake of the kingdom of God, will receive much more in this present time; and in the world to come he will have eternal life." (Luke 18:28-30)

Jesus' words hearten his followers, and they are part of the remedy to the problem of rich and poor. Whatever we leave behind in the following of Jesus is returned to us even here in blessing, because we will have riches in God that are enduring.

We read in Deuteronomy that we should have "no poor in [our] midst," no cause for weeping and mourning, if we but "listen to the voice of Yahweh," our God (Deut 15:4a, 5a). The place for lessening the gap, for reaching out to one another, is here.

There is a poignant story that brings all of this home, gathering all the pieces into one. It was printed in *Salt* Magazine (July 1997, p. 25) and is a story told by an old Bosnian Muslim, found in Ivo Andric's novel, *The Bridge on the River Drina* (translated by Lovett F. Edwards, University of Chicago Press, 1977). Its power is highlighted by the fact of the destruction of many of the ancient bridges during the conflict in Bosnia over these past years. I quote it as it appeared in those pages, since I have not told it yet anywhere.

*   When Allah the Merciful and Compassionate first created this world, the earth was smooth and even as a finely engraved plate.

That displeased the devil, who envied humanity this gift of God. And while the earth was still just as it had come from God's hands, damp and soft as unbaked clay, he stole up and scratched the face of God's earth with his nails as much and as deeply as he could.

Therefore deep rivers and ravines were formed which divided one district from another and kept the people apart, preventing them from traveling on the earth that God had given them as a garden for their food and support.

And Allah felt pity when he saw what the Accursed one had done, so he sent his angels to help the people and to make things easier for them.

When the angels saw how the unfortunate people could not pass those abysses and ravines to finish the work they had to do but tormented themselves and looked in vain and shouted from one side to the other, they spread their wings above these places and the people were able to cross. So the people learned from Angels of God how to build bridges, and therefore, after fountains, the greatest blessing is to build a bridge and the greatest sin is to interfere with it.

The bridges are not only those made of stone, steel, and wood. They are also those between those who are full and those who are hungry and empty now, between those who are content and take their ease, happy now, and those who weep and mourn in their desperate struggle to survive. And so the bridges must be built of compassion, tender regard, justice, and merciful sharing. The place for building bridges is here, and the best time is now. Jesus invites us to a counterstory, a story of favor from the Lord coming true. Alas for all the world that refuses to believe in this Good News.

8

Alas for You Who Are Well Spoken Of

"Alas for you when the people speak well of you, for that is how the fathers of these people treated the false prophets" (Lk 6:26). This is the last woe of the Sermon on the Plain but it is also intimately tied to what follows: the sermon itself. The very next line reads, "But I say to you who hear me: Love your enemies, do good to those who hate you. Bless those who curse you and pray for those who treat you badly" (Lk 6:27-28). And the remainder of the sermon seems even more daunting. However, the blessings and woes set the stage for the sermon and for the rest of Luke's gospel, which is a primer on being a disciple of Christ.

Jesus is the beloved servant of the Isaian text who suffers, first, because he tells the truth about society, and then, because he takes sides in the stand-off between truth and falsehood. The gospel is about reversal, not of fortune or fate, but of reality and conversion. Because of sin, lies, and evil, human history is out of sync with God's original dream and intention. What is called the history of salvation is really the history of those who struggle with the Spirit to reverse the slide into inhumanity and repair the world. We have long sabotaged God's hopes for us and for creation and we are incredibly astute at deceiving ourselves and one another about the real nature of life and the state of affairs we have been creating in opposition to God's design.

171

But there are those who are intent on truthfulness, on exposing us for what we are, on adding a word of hope to the declaration of denunciation. A familiar image is G. K. Chesterton's description of St. Francis of Assisi standing on his head because that gave him a better perspective on the world.

The Talmud tells the story of a Rabbi Joseph who became desperately ill and fell into a coma that lasted for weeks. During all that time his father Rabbi Joshua ben Levi stayed faithfully by him, praying, chanting the psalms, and holding his hand while beseeching the mercy of the Holy One upon his beloved child. When Rabbi Joseph awoke from his coma, his father asked him: "What did you see as you hovered between this world and the next world?" Said Rabbi Joseph, "I saw a world turned upside down. I saw a topsy-turvy world." Rabbi Joshua listened, thought for a while, and said, "You saw a clear vision of how things really are. You saw the world as it is" (*Pesahim* 50a).

The fourth woe is about revelation, about seeing things as they really are, and about examining our world from God's vantage point. Conversion of heart, of structures, and of the sinful world order begins with telling the truth, and develops into a way of being that involves telling the truth to power and resisting evil as fiercely as one attempts to do good.

There is a story that tells of this process of learning to see what is most disconcerting about ourselves and coming to an initial conversion that then becomes a way of life. Its very title "Too Good," causes strong initial reactions. When asked how they would feel if someone were to describe them as "too good," most people respond by making faces of disgust or actually cringing, shrinking away from the very words. The phrase is an insult. It suggests hypocrisy, deceit, and falseness. Whether the comment is true or not is almost irrelevant. It stings and goes deep inside us and if the barb hits home it is doubly sharp and painful.

This story is Japanese; it is about a man who cares for a small local temple because he is a follower of the shrine's god.

✳   Once upon a time there was a businessman who retired and decided to look after the small shrine that he had often visited through the years. The tradition was that this shrine was a source of blessing, and if you went on pilgrimage there every day for forty days you would be sincerely blessed and genuinely changed. The shrine was in a fairly remote place, a small and unassuming village, and most people who went there stayed only a few days, but the brief visit was often enough and many left with peace, with a sense of hope and well-being. And, of course, they brought donations and gifts with them, in gratitude and respect for the god they sought and found there.

The buildings, gate and walls were made of stone that was hard to keep clean. The retired businessman spent much of his time washing the stone and polishing. He also had other tasks of sweeping and keeping the few objects of ritual like the water troughs and the great bell and the statues themselves in order. Gradually, however, he began to spend more and more time on the stone itself. He wanted those who came to visit to appreciate its beauty and the hard work that went into its care. His days passed in hard work.

Well, it happened that as he worked he came to know when visitors were approaching, for the birds in the trees would begin to sing out, fluttering around their nests and preparing for the crumbs and food that might soon be found in the area. On this particular morning, he had been working especially hard and feeling that no one really appreciated all the effort that went into making the stone shine. He waited for a few moments until he knew that the people would be approaching on the path. Then he positioned himself along the wall discreetly off to the side and began to polish furiously, intently, apparently oblivious to anyone or anything except his service. It was the custom to keep silence within the temple's grounds, and so he worked away while the visitors, a group of five or six people, went through the shrine and offered their prayers. And he heard them leave.

Immediately he raced down another path so that he would overhear their conversations as they came out of the temple grounds. He hid behind a tree to listen. One of the young men spoke immediately and admiringly: "Did you see that attendant? I've never seen anyone so devoted. He tends that shrine with such care, out here where there can't be many who come."

But another spoke in reaction, "Oh, I think it was all for show. He was working too hard. There's no way anyone could keep up that kind of pace for long. It looked too good."

The first man responded, "No, I don't think so. There was no way he could have known we would appear at just that moment. I'm impressed."

But the other retorted, "I'm not. I don't buy his act for a moment. He'd be too good." And many of the others agreed with him.

Well, the man was crushed and stung and angry. "Too good"—how terrible! They'd probably go into town still arguing and others would hear and be drawn into the discussion. He was ruined. How humiliating! And then he reacted: what do they know? They have no idea what a taxing and strenuous job it is to keep this shrine up. So few visitors and such paltry offerings. They certainly hadn't left much for their devotions. It wasn't fair. He had no help and now people would think poorly of him.

The days and weeks went by and he grew more and more agitated and angry. He thought about what had happened all day while he polished the stones. Ugly thoughts nagged at him all day and invaded his dreams at night. He tried forgetting the whole incident but it just wouldn't go away.

Then he remembered a local tradition. If you were troubled you could spend the whole night in devotion and reflection and with the dawn would come enlightenment and peace. So he did it and it was a very difficult night. With the dawn came a terrible insight: what the young man had said was true! He had been doing the work around the temple not as devotion to the god but to make himself look good, so that he'd be appreciated and admired for his service, so that he'd be praised and respected. It was true. How could he have been so blind

and conceited? Immediately he set about changing and
decided to do his own version of a forty-day pilgrimage.
For forty days he would work on the stone and work on
his own mind and heart, concentrating on doing the work
for no other reason that it should be done and done well,
without regard for what others thought of him. And he
set to this task.

The forty days passed and peace came to him. In fact,
he knew now that this was his way of life and that he had
to do this for the rest of his life as true devotion. And so
he devoted himself to his work and the service of his god
and his peace grew deeper and deeper.

Years later, as he was working, he was startled by a
voice calling "Master." He looked up to see a number of
young people regarding him with respect. The man who
had spoken was familiar. He had come off and on to the
temple to walk and pray. "Master, we have watched you
work and serve the temple, polishing the stone. You are
quiet and calm and so recollected. My cousin who is a
stonemason has told me that this type of stone is the most
difficult to keep shining and clean and that the work that
you do is remarkable. He couldn't believe that all this
stone was cared for so diligently by just one person. May
we be your disciples? Can you teach us to work with such
care and serenity? We would like to help you." And so the
man became a master with a number of disciples to help
him with the stone polishing.

The years continued and some left, others stayed.
One day the same young man came to him and spoke,
"Master, I do not understand. I am young and strong and
you are growing older and more frail. We both work on
the stone and you seem never to tire and the stone seems
to respond to you. I pace myself and work and yet I'm always so weary and worn out from the work. What am I
doing wrong?"

"Well," the old man responded, "I've been doing this
for years and am used to it now."

"But Master," he asked, "isn't there more to it than
that?"

The master stopped for a while and his eyes drifted away. He turned back to him and said, "Well, perhaps there is. It seems like a long time ago when I first started working here. I polished the wall, but for all the wrong reasons—mostly because I wanted to be respected and thought well of by others who came to the temple. And then one day I was caught by someone who saw that I was a fake, that I was lying even as I thought I was worshiping. I was described as being 'too good.' The only work I was really doing was trying to make myself look good, look better than what I was. I guess you could say I was worshiping myself and my reputation and what others thought of me. Now I try to remember why I'm here and what I must truly do."

The young man asked, "What do you think of me and my work, Master? Am I truly devoted?"

The master look at him and asked, "What do you think about when you work?"

The disciple answered, "Oh, I look at this large stone and concentrate on it. Then I gauge the length of the wall or height of the gate and figure out how long it will take to do this piece and that section and set my goal to finish a certain area as best as I can. But at least I know about how many days it will take to finish one wall or the gate or the bell shrine. I really try to polish each piece individually and that is my offering."

The master was silent for a while and then he looked at his young disciple. "That is good, but I can see why you get so tired. There is always more to do, and as soon as you finish, you start over again. That would tire you out."

"Can you tell me, Master, how do you do it? What do you think about as you polish a piece of stone?"

"Well," he answered, "in the beginning, after my seeing the truth of what I was doing and who I really was, I looked only at the piece of stone in front of me and thought only of polishing my heart. After a while I had the feeling that the god was polishing my heart. And then, and this is harder to explain, I began to think that it was the god polishing the wall, not me." And his eyes drifted off again, and his face was full of serenity.

"Is that all, Master? Is there anything else you can tell me?"

And the master spoke very softly and looked very young. "Yes. Sometimes—only sometimes—I see the god in the polished wall. And his face is shining!"

In the process of conversion it is hard initially to face the truth and be seen for what one really is. But the experience of humiliation often leads to deeper self-examination. It takes time to accept the truth, to internalize and change consciously in both intention and behavior. Then we must endure in the truth, living gracefully day after day without thought of others' appreciation or respect. And, as in the story, if others begin to model themselves on our lives or feel called to find out why we are the way we are, we must confess to our lacks and past dishonesty and share with them the truth with which we have been blessed as we obeyed our inner natures, as we learned to truly worship Another and to live with humility.

The movement from falsehood to truth is for all, but especially for those who are leaders in a community and for prophets, those who are entrusted with the truth for others and so are responsible for their own words and deeds and the effect of those words and deeds on others' lives and behavior. There is a long tradition in Israel and among Christians of true prophets who speak hard things in relation to the covenant and God's demands for true worship, not only in ritual but in reality. There is also a tradition of false prophets who tell people and leaders what they want to hear and so reap rewards for themselves here and now. They avoid anything unpleasant and allow injustice to continue, sometimes even encouraging it among people who must change if anyone is to survive. Sometimes it's blatantly clear, as in Isaiah:

Now go, write it down as a record for them, inscribe it on a scroll, so it will be an everlasting accusation against them.

These are a rebellious people, their children deceitful. They do not listen to Yahweh's advice.

To the seers they say, "See not," and to the prophets, "Do not prophesy the truth. Just tell us pleasant things; see illusions and prophesy deceits. Stray from the path, turn from the way! Take away from us the Holy One of Israel!"

Therefore the Holy One of Israel says, "Because you despised this message and resorted instead to lies and abusive taxes, choosing to stay with it, therefore this guilt of yours will be like a breach on a high wall, cracked and bulging, ready to fall; the crash will come suddenly and instantly.... "

For thus said the Lord Yahweh, the Holy One of Israel: "Conversion and calmness would have been your salvation, quietness and trust your strength." (Isaiah 30:8-13, 15)

This passage is about the people demanding that the prophets tell them only what they want to hear, but God's words are just as blunt when he speaks about the prophets and leaders and their unfaithfulness to his covenant.

Woe to the rebellious, the defiled, the city that oppresses. She did not pay attention to the call nor accept the correction; she did not trust Yahweh nor did she approach her God. Her kings are like roaring lions, her rulers like evening wolves that do not leave even a bone for the next day. Her prophets are blabbermouths and treacherous people: her priests defile whatever is sacred with no respect for the Law.

However, Yahweh the Just one is in her midst; he never commits injustice. Every morning he says what must be done; but the unjust do not even feel ashamed. (Zephaniah 3:1-5)

It seems that there has always been a tension between king and prophet and between false and true prophets. The true speaker demands, exhorts, and threatens in hope of conversion, of a shift of priorities and restitution so that what is spoken will not come to pass. The false speaker is intent only on immediate acceptance, reward, or extension of personal power. Amos, the dresser of sycamore trees and breeder of sheep, runs afoul of the false prophets when he goes after the royal family with the Word of Yahweh:

> Amaziah, the priest of Bethel, then sent word to King Jeroboam of Israel, "Amos is conspiring against you in the very center of Israel; what he says goes too far. These are his very words: Jeroboam shall die by the sword and Israel shall be exiled from its land."
>
> Amaziah then said to Amos, "Off with you, seer, go back to the land of Judah. Earn your bread there by prophesying. But never again prophesy at Bethel for it is a king's sanctuary and a national shrine."
>
> Amos replied to Amaziah, "I am not a prophet or one of the fellow prophets. I am a breeder of sheep and a dresser of sycamore trees. But Yahweh took me from shepherding the flock and said to me: Go, and from me, tell my people Israel.
>
> Now hear the word of Yahweh, you who say: No more prophecy against Israel, no more insults against the family of Isaac! This is what Yahweh says:
>
> Your wife shall be made a harlot in the city, your sons and daughters shall fall by the sword, your land shall be divided up and given to others, and you yourself shall die in a foreign land, for Israel shall be driven far from its land." (Amos 7:10-16)

Amaziah, in his own words, convicts himself and the king whom he serves when he tells Amos to "earn his bread by prophesying" elsewhere. A price tag on the word of the Lord is a sure indicator that the word has been "doctored" to make it more amenable to those who hear it. Amaziah and King Jeroboam are in league together and not at all concerned about the honor of God or the care of the people. And when the message is so blatantly rejected by those who "hear" it, Amos (and God) ups the ante, making the message and the call to conversion more of a necessity than ever before.

Always the word comes first to denounce specific behaviors of certain groups of people, coupled with what will happen if they don't drastically alter their behavior and return to Yahweh. Micah, the prophet, is known best for his one line: "You have been told, O man, what is good and what Yahweh requires of you: to do justice, to love mercy, and to walk humbly with your God" (Mic 6:8). But Micah is one of the truth sayers and the other side of his message is succinct and clear too:

> Then I said, "You rulers of the house of Israel, is it not your duty to know what is right? Yet you hate good and love evil, you tear the skin from my people and the flesh from their bones.
>
> Those who eat my people's flesh and break their bones to pieces, who chop them up like meat for the pan and share them like flesh for the pot, when they cry, Yahweh will not answer. He will hide his face from them because of their evil deeds."
>
> This is what Yahweh says of the prophets who lead my people astray:
>
> You cry: "Peace" when you have something to eat, but to anyone with nothing for your mouths, it is "War" that you declare. So night will come to you without vision, and darkness without divination. Then sun will set for the prophets and the day will be dark for them.
>
> Then the seers will be disgraced and the diviners put to shame. They will all cover their faces because no answer will come from God. But as for me, I am filled with might, with the spirit of Yahweh, with justice and courage, to declare to Jacob his transgressions, to Israel his sins. (Micah 3:1-8)

There are so many passages where God decries those who assert that they speak with the mouth of Yahweh but all they prophesy about is plenty and pleasure, dreams and their own illusions, while the true prophet of God speaks plainly in words that call people to conversion. It is God who describes what the word out of his mouth is really like: "Isn't my word like fire, like the hammer that shatters a rock?" (Jer 23:29). All of chapter 23 of Ezekiel are rails against those who supposedly speak for God but in reality are "burdens" that God will shrug off and destroy. The prophet of Yahweh is intent on the large-scale conversion of all the people and the individual conversion of those in positions of authority, those who have power and influence, whether religious, economic, or political. Attached to these accusations is a prayer that Yahweh will come in judgment, with justice and with mercy, and come soon because of the great needs of the people and the land. Habakkuk prays:

> I have heard, Yahweh, of your renown;
> I stand in awe of your work, O Yahweh.
> In the middle of years make it known;
> in your wrath even, remember mercy. . . .
>
> You stride the earth in wrath,
> you trample the nations in rage.
>
> You came out to redeem your people,
> to save your anointed one—
> you crush the head of the wicked,
> you lay him bare from head to foot.
> You pierce with your shafts his warriors who came
>   like a whirlwind to scatter us in joy,
> to devour the wretched quietly. . . .
>
> Yet I wait confidently for the day of distress,
> when we face the people coming against us. . . .
>
> My Lord Yahweh is my stronghold;
> he makes my feet as fleeting as the hinds;
> he steadies my steps upon the heights.
>   (Habakkuk 3:2, 12-14, 16b, 19)

In more contemporary language from a monk-prophet of our own century we find echoes of older insights. Those who are holy in any century care for the poor, for justice, and for the kingdom of God more than for anything else. They see clearly through the false facades of those who often make it in this world on the backs of the poor.

> I believe that God is sick of the rich people and the powerful and wise men of the world and that He is going to look elsewhere and find the underprivileged, those who are poor and have things very hard; even those who find it most difficult to avoid sin; and God is going to come down and walk among the poor people of the earth, among those who are unhappy and sinful and distressed and raise them up and make them the greatest saints and send them walking all over the universe with the steps of angels and the voices of prophets to bring his light back into the world again. (Thomas Merton, in *The Road to Joy*, ed. Robert E. Daggy, New York: Farrar, Straus & Giroux, 1989, p. 317.)

Anyone who consistently, publicly, and unambiguously denounces the state of the world's affairs on behalf of those who stumble and fall through the cracks of society, anyone who stands against the existing systems of oppression and injustice knows a God of judgment, a God who does justice and then exhibits mercy to the victims of the world's greed and callousness. When the world thinks well of you it is wise to wonder why and to do some reflecting on how you got to that point. The fact is that the values and virtues of Christianity are often at direct odds with the values of contemporary dominant societies. Far too many people are chewed up and swallowed whole or spit out by the forces of civilization, nations, and world markets to glibly honor those who "make it" in our societies. There is all too often a god of the rich and powerful and triumphant and a god of those trampled upon and ground under heel. But there is only one true God.

Archbishop Anthony Bloom has written of the changing face of God in his book, *Beginning to Pray* (New York: Walker and Co., 1986).

> During the [Russian] Revolution we lost the Christ of the great cathedrals, the Christ of the splendidly architected liturgies: and we discovered the Christ who is vulnerable just as we were vulnerable, we discovered the Christ who was rejected just as we were rejected, and we discovered the Christ who had nothing at his moment of crisis, not even friends, and this was similar to our experience.
>
> God helps us when there is no one else to help. God is there at the point of greatest tension, at the breaking point, at the center of the storm. In a way despair is at the center of things—if only we are prepared to go through it. We must be prepared for a period when God is not there for us and we must be aware of not trying to substitute a false God. (p. xvii)

A false God—it is so easy to worship and pay homage to such a one, oftentimes alongside the true God, or to have a number of idols that we serve, just in case one of them doesn't respond as we had hoped or expected. The sin, indifference, evil, violence, suffering and human misery in the world attest to the service and offerings to many false gods and idols that must be kept alive and functioning with the blood sacrifices of human beings' lives. The truth about the world begins with a realistic and honest assessment of situations and structures that are damning for so many that we lump in the category of "the poor." In the words of Jon Sobrino:

> Finally, this world must be exposed for what it is, because like all sin it tries to pass for something it is not. We need to expose the way in which human creations such as democracy, security, Western Christendom— legitimate and potentially positive in themselves—are used to obscure the truth about how things are. We

need to unmask the fiction that the human race as a whole is moving forward towards reason, freedom and life—this is true, and then no more than partially so, only of a minority of the human race.

To become converted to the truth, to see things as they are in themselves and recognize their causes, to act on what we have seen, is the most important thing the world demands of us. Terrified though we may be at the sight of the world we have built with our hands, if we do not start here, we will not be able to hear the voice of God's anger: "The wrath of God will be revealed against those who imprison the truth with injustice" (Rom. 1:18). No matter how tragic, we must start from the truth about our world: define it as *poverty* which leads to death, denounce it as *sin* and unmask as a *lie* the mechanisms that try to hide its truth. (From "Jubilee: An Appeal to Conversion," in *The Millennium Jubilee*, London: CAFOD, 1996, pp. 68-69)

Oddly enough, this beginning, this looking at the world honestly and turning from it, is the birth of mercy and compassion. We are all made in the image and likeness of God. The over-riding characteristics of Jesus' God are compassion, kindness, holiness, and we are to be merciful just as our Father is (Lk 6:35b-36). In the conversation and storytelling dialogue with the lawyer who asks him about what he must do in order to have eternal life, Jesus questions him on what the scriptures have to say about it. The lawyer quotes the great commandment of love, often referred to in the Jewish community as the only commandment: "You shall love the Lord your God with all your heart, with all your soul, with all your strength and with all your mind. And you shall love your neighbor as yourself." Jesus responds with delight, "What a good answer! Do this and you shall live" (Lk 10:27-28). But the man wants to make it as easy on himself as possible. We are told that he "wanted to keep up appearances, so he replied, 'Who is my neighbor?' " (Lk 10:29). To ask the question is hypocritical and betrays a lack of integrity and faithful-

ness. The lawyer knows that he is to love his neighbor because in the Jewish tradition any true love of God is expressed
in loving one's neighbors, with special consideration for those
most in need of community assistance and support. Love of
God and love of neighbor are inseparable in the Law and the
prophets.

Throughout the centuries, the prophets describe God in
the same terms: compassion, truth, justice, mercy, understanding, righteousness, holiness, and love—abiding, sustained,
and tender love. And all that God requires of us is imitation:
do justice and love mercy and walk with God. The story Jesus
tells the lawyer says this over and over again with examples
of both failure and obedience to the commandment. First a
priest who fails in mercy; then a Levite who fails again; and finally a Samaritan who obeys, who stops and bends in compassion, in imitation of the God of the Exodus who bends to
the pain of his people in Egypt and saves them. The God of
Moses and the prophets, the God of Jesus loves especially
those of our neighbors who are in distress, abandoned by
other human beings, many of whom claim allegiance to the
God of compassion. A number of medieval Jewish mystics referred to God as a neighbor, or a relative in need and distress,
calling God "Gottenu," our little God, or "Tattenu"—our little
Father (Byron L. Sherwin, "Toward a Just and Compassionate
Society: A Jewish View," in *Cross Currents*, Summer 1995, p.
156).

When he has told the story of an outsider, hated and despised, who has acted the way God acts, Jesus simply asks the
lawyer: "Which of these three, do you think, made himself
neighbor to the man who fell into the hands of robbers?" And
the teacher of the Law answered, "The one who had mercy on
him." And Jesus said, "Go then and do the same" (Lk 10:36-
37). What is unwritten is the undercurrent: "Go then and you
will live, do this and you will have eternal life now!"

Byron L. Sherwin, a well-known Jewish scholar, discusses
the fact that God and all of us are neighbors to each other:

The Talmudic rabbis admonish us: "Be like unto God;
just as God is merciful and gracious, so be you merci-

ful and gracious." But an attitude is not sufficient;
specific deeds are also required. Commenting on
Deuteronomy 13:5—"After the Lord your God shall
you walk"—Rabbi Hama bar Hanina said:

> How can a man walk after God? Is God not a con-
> suming fire?
>
> What is meant is that man should walk after
> God's attributes.
>
> Just as God clothes the naked, attends the sick,
> comforts the mourners, and buries the dead, do you
> likewise. (Mechilta d'Rabbi Yishmael on Exodus 15:2,
> quoted in *Cross Currents*, Summer 1995, p. 156)

Along with the Samaritan called good, we live when we
imitate God and in justice and mercy and compassion, when
we attend to others' needs rather than to our own. There is a
saying, "God knows the goodness that some do." God does
know and justice is served best by such mercy, more than by
any acts for which we are publicly accredited and esteemed in
society. To be accounted good by God—now that is a blessing
indeed.

When Jesus overheard his own disciples arguing about
which of them was most important and knowing what was in
their hearts, "he took a little child and stood him by his side.
Then he said to them, 'Whoever welcomes this little child in
my name welcomes me; and whoever welcomes me, welcomes the one who sent me. And listen: He who is found to be
the least among you all, he is great indeed' " (Lk 9:46-48). Certainly this is spoken in light of the last beatitude and woe uttered publicly earlier, while Jesus was addressing the crowds
that needed him. And it is a just description of Jesus, kneeling
before people desperate for healing, forgiveness, and simple
attention. Jesus himself becomes the least among us and he is
great indeed:

> Though being divine in nature,
> he did not claim in fact equality with God,
> but emptied himself,
> taking on the nature of a servant, made in human likeness,

and in his appearance found as a man.
He humbled himself by being obedient to death,
death on the cross.
That is why God exalted him
and gave him the Name which outshines all names,
so that at the Name of Jesus all knees should bend
in heaven, on earth and among the dead,
and all tongues proclaim that Christ Jesus is the Lord
to the glory of God the Father.
     (Philippians 2:6-11)

The compassion to which we are called is first of all conversion from evil and sin, conversion to goodness, as echoed
in our second baptismal promises: to resist sin and refuse to
be mastered by evil. We begin first by responding to the needs
of others with corporal works of mercy, by tending to the victims of injustice and violence and those ignored by society.
Part of what sustains this kind of work for justice is the naming of evil and forthright resistance to structures, decisions,
laws, and groups that benefit from or turn a deaf ear to those
who are most affected by their inhumanity and injustice. To
speak out on behalf of others is to invite retaliation and anger
from those who oppress the poor and are intent only on their
own lifestyles and security.

And as Jon Sobrino says, "Compassion must be exercised
as reparation. Structurally speaking there can be no doubt
that the sufferings of the poor are inflicted on them by the
world of wealth and power. Turning to them in order to help
is not merely to give them something; it is to give them back
what is theirs. Jubilee is more than a proclamation of compassion: it is a recognition of the obligation to make amends"
(from "Jubilee: An Appeal to Conversion," in *The Millennium
Jubilee*, London: CAFOD, 1996, p. 71).

Always those who are thought well of in this world want
to defend their privileges, obscure the truth, shirk their responsibilities, and avoid being held accountable for their
wealth and power by others who would confront them with
the truth. It is far too easy for the powerful in society, even in
the church, to make alliances with those who will better their

position and conceal their injustices and personal sin. Jesus turned on Peter and his own followers, calling them "Satan"—an ancient name that means "Hinderer"—because their notions of how to do things and what needed to be done were tainted with self-interest, ego, selfishness, and pride and were far removed from Jesus' understanding of the kingdom of his Father.

What constitutes being "thought well of by others and God"? What does it really mean to be human? Someone gave me a photocopied version of a short exchange between Robert Schuller, a television evangelist, and Coretta Scott King. She was asked what sustained her in the face of tragedy and violence, of broken dreams and murder. She answered, "When I was at Antioch College I heard that Horace Mann when he spoke to the first graduating class in 1850 told them: 'Be ashamed to die until you've won some victory for humanity.'"

The essence of what makes us human and worthy of another's esteem crosses many traditions. In the Jewish Hasidic tradition there is a prayer by Rabbi Nahman of Bratzlav. It was given to me by an old woman.

> May it be Thy will, O God, to extend peace, great and wondrous, in the universe. Let all the peoples of the earth recognize and know the innermost truth: that we are not come into this world for quarrel and division, nor for hate and jealousy, contrariness and bloodshed; but we are come into this world to recognize and know Thee. Be Thou blessed forever.

Conversion leads to mercy that is extended to all areas of life and to all peoples, even to our enemies and those who have harmed us and would do so again. In the Sermon on the Plain the blessings and woes are followed by this:

> But I say to you who hear me: Love your enemies, do good to those who hate you. Bless those who curse you and pray for those who treat you badly. To the one who strikes you on the cheek, turn the other cheek; from the one who takes your coat, do not keep

back your shirt. Give to the one who asks and if anyone has taken something from you, do not demand it
back. (Luke 6:27-30)

Impossible, we instinctively retort! We are not God! But if
we have listened well to the blessings and woes, we begin to
see God's logic and way in the world and we know in our
hearts that we must follow suit. Why? In Jesus' words a few
lines later: "But love your enemies and do good to them, and
lend when there is nothing to expect in return. Then your reward will be great and you will be children of the Most High.
For he is kind towards the ungrateful and the wicked. Be merciful, just as your Father is merciful" (Lk 6:35-36). We have
known much more of the compassion of God than of the justice of God and this experience we must extend to others. We
have been rescued from sin, from isolation, from evil. We are
never left to our own devices for long, for God is a restless
pursuer of those he has created and so we must be about the
rescue of others, the tending of wounds, and the encouragement of those most despairing, regardless of whether others
speak well of us, or malign or insult us, or think we are stupid
and not particularly sophisticated in the ways of the world.
This attitude is not even unique to Christianity. Xiujing, a
master in ancient China, wrote, "Heaven sends rain and dew
without choosing between the thriving and the withering."
The practice of justice and mercy with impartiality is good
grounding for creating a society that is ethical and lives with
integrity toward all.

The blessings and woes are about judgment, about justice
that is merciful and mercy that is just and true. They are about
balancing the world, recreating it anew with the Spirit of
Truth that is Jesus' vision of God the Father let loose in the
world.

There was a movie a few years ago called "Tender Mercies." I have watched it a number of times, haunted by a few
lines. It is the story of a widow whose husband was killed in
Vietnam and her young son. They try to make a life for themselves by fixing up an abandoned gas station. One day they
are befriended by a stranger passing through who has lost his

wife and child because of his drinking. They fall in love, all three of them, and are bound together with care. The widow wants the man and her son to be baptized, though neither seems particularly interested. They finally do it because it will mean something to her. After they have been ritually baptized in the river and come up soaking wet, the man asks the boy: "You feel any different?"

"Nope. You?"

"Me neither."

They all stand there smiling, at peace, and she says: "I just thank God for all his tender mercies." They are soaked in mercy, not from the water, but from the conversion of relationships, from reconciliation and from some form of restitution in helping one another survive with grace.

This last woe is primarily about mercy: a hope that we will know the goodness of God let loose in our lives and respond with gratitude rather than living on the shifting sands of others' opinion and our reputation in the world. We are called first as humans to be just (not simply to do justice). Then, in being just, we turn our attention and energies to alleviating injustice and making sure there is no increase in others' suffering that is caused by the roots of sin among us. It is a lifestyle of fending off evil, healing the ills of society, and tending to peoples' needs. It is what makes us human, like God.

So often in the gospels, those in need, those who know their true position in society cry out: "Jesus, Son of David, have mercy on me" or "Lord, have mercy on me, a sinner." It is the truth, beyond justice. Obedience to the kingdom of God, to following in Jesus' footsteps and knowing Yahweh truly, means learning to stretch the practice of justice. It means moving out in depth and expression to those who cannot foster our own positions and egos, to those who refuse to acknowledge what we do, and even to those who stand against us and think poorly of us or make life difficult for us. In short, it extends to all those we despise, demean, ridicule, hate, fear and do not think of as neighbor, but enemy.

Society is rarely just. It hardly knows what mercy is, let alone practices it. It is justice not to kill in the name of society.

It is justice to sentence Timothy McVeigh to life imprisonment, rather than the death penalty. It is mercy to begin to understand that he was trained to kill, and to see what he did as a response to anger and frustration. It is mercy to look for goodness in him, to go beyond defining him by the one act that we find most despicable. It is justice not to encourage others to retaliate in kind and have him legally, though unjustly, murdered. It is mercy to work with the victims of anger, murder, hate, and rage and to help them arrive at forgiveness and peace, rather than to murder in their minds and hearts and so kill their own souls.

It is Jesus on his knees tending to the lost ones who tells us what justice is in the words of the blessings and woes: the justice of the kingdom of God. And it is Jesus who models mercy: God on his knees before us. As in the beginning of the blessings, so the end of the woes, it is conversion that is needed, the bending of our hearts and knees to God and each other and the transformation of lives, structures, and ideas to conform to the vision of Jesus.

There is no end to justice, or to mercy, unbelievable as that might sound. This is a prayer that was found scratched on a piece of paper in the Ravensbruck concentration camp:

Lord, remember not only the men and women of good will but all those of ill will. Do not remember only all the suffering they have subjected us to. Remember the fruits we brought forth thanks to this suffering—our comradeship, our loyalty, our humility, our courage and generosity, the greatness of heart that all of this inspired. And when they come to judgment, let all these fruits we have borne be *their reward and their forgiveness.*

The emphasis is mine. These anonymous people, victims of brutalization, murdered and reduced to a nightmare existence by others, learned and knew the justice and mercy that mirror God's own. Those who are thought well of and accorded respect in societies that spawn violence, racial and religious hate, nationalistic superiority, callous indifference to those who starve to death are to be lamented and thought of as dead. Their esteem is built on a foundation of injustice and inhumanity to others, of ignoring the plight of most others in the human family so that they may enjoy their own life unencumbered by responsibility.

Are we aware of who hinders us from the kingdom of God, of who hinders the kingdom of God from coming into the world? To whom do we look for admiration, compliments, respect? Do we look to those who have made it in this society and are intent on staying where they are, come what may, or to those who cry out in need, or on behalf of others, who are truly the voice of God seeking justice and human dignity and respect? To whom do we tune our hearing and our hearts?

A friend of mine, Paul, plays the oboe, an absolutely haunting instrument. When it is played well, it produces exquisite music. Within an orchestral piece its sound blends in and out of the larger music and has a quality that carries those listening to silence and contemplation, memory and a sense of humanness that is hard to express in words—sighing expresses it better.

But the instrument is not easy to master. It requires discipline, concentration, breath control, endurance and a feel for the music and its layers of tonality, spacing, and tenderness.

There is a story told among musicians in New York of a brilliant young oboist who had been asked to perform with a string ensemble in a cathedral. It was a benefit concert and her piece was to be the highlight of the evening's performance.

✳ That afternoon the musicians all gathered together to practice. They sounded awful. Over and over again they practiced and the piece with the oboe was especially bad. It grated, almost distorted the other instruments and bruised the music. After a couple of hours, the leader of the group was frustrated and angry, insisting that the oboe was out of tune, instructing the oboist to re-tune her instrument so it would match those of the others. The music sounded worse with each attempt.

They took a break and the lead musician declared that it probably would be better if the oboe piece was dropped from the program, because the string ensemble sounded much better without it. The oboist was distraught and went off to a deserted part of the cathedral to practice alone. Alone, it sounded lovely.

During the break, an old man who had been praying in the back of the cathedral and listening to the music came forward and spoke to the musician in charge. He apologized for interrupting but he said he thought he knew how to remedy the situation. "I believe," he said very gently and firmly, "that the entire orchestra always tunes itself to the oboe because with its perfect pitch it has the truest note." The other musicians were shocked. Without the oboe, they had forgotten one of the first principles of playing together; they had tuned their instruments to one another, and so were hopelessly out of tune. And then they had insisted that the oboe be tuned to them. No wonder the music sounded so awful. It was they who were out of tune, not the oboist.

The situation was corrected and the music was stunning and unsurpassed in gracefulness. The old man, it is said, was a conductor of a major symphony and could hear what others, less knowledgeable or experienced, could not.

Do we tune ourselves to one another in our small worlds, churches, nations, and society or are we tuned to the truest, purest note: the Word of God, the cry of the poor and those in distress, those silenced by injustice and despair, and those whose lives sing of compassion, hope and mercy, mercy, mercy? Who speaks well of us and thinks kindly of us? Is it cause for rejoicing and blessing or lamenting and weeping?

9

The Sermon on the Plain

The blessings and woes proclaimed by Jesus are so strong that we often see them as a separate entity rather than as a prelude to what follows: the Sermon on the Plain. This sermon is a collection of carefully selected sayings of Jesus that flesh out in a practical way what it means to grasp hold of the kingdom of God and dwell within it as well as hasten its coming among us. The sermon takes on greater meaning and depth when the blessings and woes go before it and prepare the listener for the single-hearted and passionate intensity of its demands, to its matter-of-fact exhortations to what often seems impossible and unrealistic. The blessings and woes and the sermon itself are central to Luke's perception of who Jesus is: the suffering servant of Yahweh, the beloved and obedient child of the Father, and the hope of the poor, the imprisoned, those who belong to no one and are lost and isolated within a hostile world. Jesus' reverential posture toward God and toward others is carefully expressed in the words of the sermon.

But before we look at it in more detail, perhaps a story will prepare us to better hear and see what Jesus is trying to do. The story is by Leo Tolstoy, a Russian novelist, philosopher, and political ethicist who also wrote morality tales and children's stories that taught nonviolence, compassion, generosity, and integrity in personal behavior and public morality. It is called "Three Troubling Questions or Three Marvelous Answers." Both a parable and a *koan*, it seeks to confront and draw in the listener, evoking an awareness that can radically alter both behavior and a sense of being in the world. Jesus would feel very much at home with many of Tolstoy's stories, and probably could have told them himself!

✳ Once upon a time there was a king. He was a good and righteous king who struggled to rule wisely but often found himself in moral dilemmas and stymied by a lack of principles on which to form his decisions. He decided after much experience and reflection that if he just knew the answers to three central questions then he would always know what was just and true in any situation.

He wrote the three questions down and often reflected upon them:

1. When is the right time to do something?

2. Who is the most important person to remember and work with?

3. What is the one thing I should do at all times?

After months of thinking about these issues, he sent out a decree announcing that anyone who could answer his questions would be handsomely rewarded. The line of those ready to try an answer was lengthy but none of the answers were new or gave any insight to the king. He grew discouraged in his search for wisdom and understanding.

One day he heard of a hermit who lived in his domain, at the top of a mountain. This hermit was thought to be wise and holy. He never came down from his place apart and would see and help only the poor. So the king decided to disguise himself as a peasant, climb the mountain, and ask his three questions. He traveled to the base of the mountain and left his retinue there, with instructions to wait for him. Then he climbed, hot and weary, thirsty, and a bit winded from the unusual exertion. He found the hermit working in a small garden plot near his hermitage. The hermit looked up, saw the king, bowed in silent greeting, and continued to work. He was laboring slowly and sweating hard. The work was obviously taking its toll on him, for he was an old man whose hair and beard were white.

The king felt awkward, but he had come to ask his questions and so began: "I have heard that you are wise and understanding. I have three questions that have bothered and concerned me for years and perhaps you can help me. When is the right time to do something? Who is the most important person to remember and work with? What is the one thing I should do at all times?"

The hermit leaned on his shovel and looked intently at him, but didn't answer. He went back to digging. The king watched him and then took the shovel from his hand with the words, "Let me do that a while. You are very tired and I'm strong." And the king started digging, turning over the earth and moving along the rows. He worked a couple of rows and then looked up at the old man and repeated his questions. Again the man didn't answer, but rose from where he was sitting and took the shovel back saying, "Here, give me that; I can work now and you can rest awhile. The sun is hot and the work is hard."

They both had their hands on the shovel. But the king prevailed and continued to work in the garden. A few hours passed and the sun began to set. Finally the king stopped, wiped the sweat from his brow, and spoke again, "I came here to see if you could answer my three questions. They mean a great deal to me and I struggle with them all the time. Can you help me? If not, I'll just be on my way home."

The hermit looked at him and then, startled by a noise, asked, "Did you hear that? Over there? I think it's someone running." They both turned in that direction and saw a man emerge from the woods, running hard and fast toward them, intent but erratic and angry. The man's hands were spread over a deep wound in his stomach. He staggered toward them, bleeding badly, and then fell before the king. When the king leaned over and moved the man's hands, the blood gushed forth. The king then ripped off his shirt and tried to staunch the flow of blood, but the wound was deep and the bleeding continued. Suddenly the king remembered a spring. He ran to it, washed out the shirt, and brought it back to press against the man's wound. He did this again, and then a third time. Finally, the man stopped bleeding and asked for water to drink. Once again the king went to the spring, and this time he brought back a jug of water.

It was dark now, and the old hermit and the king carried the wounded man to the hermit's hut and laid him down on the hermit's bed. The man fell asleep quickly. And the king, exhausted from his exertions all through the long day, slumped against the door frame and slid down to fall into a deep sleep against the wall.

The sun rose early and bright and the king awoke. He was a bit groggy, and for a moment he wondered where he was and what he was doing asleep in a hut. Then he remembered. He opened his eyes to see the wounded man awake, looking at him intently, and then he heard him say in a soft and confused voice, "Forgive me."

The king went to him and bent over him. "Why? Why should I forgive you?" asked the king. "I don't even know who you are."

"I am your sworn enemy," said the wounded man, "and I have long vowed that I would kill you. In your last war you killed my brother and took his property and I have hated you ever since, plotting how I could kill you. When I heard that you were coming up here alone to see the old hermit I determined that this was my chance. I waited for you in ambush most of yesterday. But when you didn't come back down the path, I came out of hiding and ran into your attendants at the bottom of the hill. One recognized me and wounded me. Luckily I escaped and was running from them when I ran into you and the old hermit. You saved my life! I—who had intended to kill you in rage—was saved by you. Please, forgive me. I am ashamed and grateful to you. From this day forth I bind my life to yours and promise to serve you. And my children and my children's children will do the same. We are in your debt."

The king was stunned. He had not initially recognized his enemy. Now he accepted the man's obedience and offered to return his property to him and to compensate him for his suffering. He explained that he did not want the man's service, only his friendship and his trust as an ally. And he promised that his own physician would tend to his wound and care for him and that his attendants would accompany him home. The king left immediately and had his retinue carry out his orders.

Then, once again, he climbed the mountain alone to find the hermit. This time he found the old man sowing seeds in the earth they had worked on the day before, which now seemed so long ago. The king wanted once more to ask his questions.

They stood facing each other. "Old man, tell me, if you know: When is the right time to do something? Who is the most important person to remember and work with? What is the one thing I should do at all times?"

The hermit looked at him and smiled. "But your questions have all been answered," he said. The king appeared puzzled. "Look," said the hermit, "yesterday when you came to ask your questions and I did not immediately answer, you took pity on me because I was old and frail. Instead of going back down the mountain—where you would have been killed by your enemy—you worked with me digging in my garden. So the right time was when you were digging with me, because you had pity on me, and I was the person you were supposed to remember and work with, and the one thing you should do at all times is have compassion. Then, later you took care of that wounded man and tended his wounds. He did not die and you were reconciled with an enemy and found a grateful friend. It was the right time to aid him and he was the one to attend to and what you did was have pity on him and help him."

The king still didn't seem to understand. Then it hit him. "Oh, the right time is now, for it's the only time I have any dominion over! The person is whoever is right here before me, and the one thing I should be doing all the time is tending to the needs of others and aiding them as I can."

The old hermit smiled and nodded. "Yes, attend to bending in appreciation toward whatever is before you and you will always know what to do."

This story is also told by Thich Nhat Hanh in his book *The Miracle of Mindfulness: A Manual on Meditation* (Boston: Beacon Press, 1987). The answer to the three questions seems so simple, so unassuming. We must live with an attitude of reverence before all and everything and be a blessing for others, all others. It is another way of saying the first words that follow upon Jesus' proclamation of the blessings and woes:

> But I say to you who hear me: Love your enemies, do good to those who hate you. Bless those who curse you and pray for those who treat you badly. To the one who strikes you on the cheek, turn the other cheek; from the one who takes your coat, do not keep back your shirt. Give to the one who asks and if anyone has taken something from you, do not demand it back. (Luke 6:27-30)

The words startle, shock, and take us by surprise. Can we hear Jesus? He asks us to know and see who our enemies are and not treat them the way they treat us, not imitate them by doing evil. He asks us to relate to them simply by being human, open to them and offering them a relationship. We must not allow anyone's behavior to change our own for the worse, but continue to bless, honor, and respect others and to endeavor to love one another, as Jesus has loved us. The examples begin on an interior level and remind us that behavior originates in our hearts and minds, in our emotions, in our mindsets toward others. Then the examples move outward to physical actions, to violence and force and thievery.

Jesus' words are not what we'd expect. We are told not to retaliate or resist aggressive behavior. Instead, we are to act in a different way, one that disarms others. When we are slapped hard in the face it is usually with the back of someone's hand and the force can literally throw us off balance and turn us away from them. We are to turn back to them, to offer the other cheek while we continue to look at them and face them as equals, not as adversaries in reaction, but in a response that is stilled and not violent. This response takes the force and holds it still, stops it from escalating. What it does is force the aggressor to stop for a fraction of a second, to look and perhaps see what they are doing, its effect on the other, and to see themselves in the eyes and gaze of the other. If that eye and gaze are not angry or violent or enraged but calming, they can stop someone cold or confuse them for an instant when something can be said or a shift made. But this kind of response comes from discipline, from long training in containing emotion and learning how to resist harming others. It comes from a way of life, an attitude toward others, and from deep within, in a heart and mind that tend to life and freedom and non-violence: in a word, to love. To love one's enemies is the end result of loving a long line of folks, many of whom are not easy to love.

To not resist when something is taken from us forcibly but instead to respond by offering what was not taken means letting go. This kind of response is the result of a practice of non-attachment, of freedom, of a poverty that will not resist or do violence or use force in relation to material possessions. Such a response reveals an underlying attitude much like that of the beatitudes themselves. "Blessed are the poor" takes us off-guard, almost paralyzing us until we can get a grip on our emotions and reactions. Blessed are those who do not clutch, grasp, and fight to hold onto what they've got. Blessed are those who don't slap back. Blessed are those who will not curse or slander or persecute or imitate evil or do unto others what is done to them. It is the foundation material for sayings like: blessed are you who are persecuted and who do not harbor thoughts of getting even, but bless those who curse you and harm you.

The theme of the sermon is a continuation of Jesus' blessings and woes, but now the language is that of exhortation and direct command. The issue of violence—physical, structural, psychological, and religious—is central to Jesus' teachings and understanding of the kingdom of God, the place where justice and mercy reside and all know the presence of the Holy One. Those who have to live with violence, those who have experienced its destruction and been overshadowed by the fear and inhumanity it breeds, know what Jesus is talking about. Violence dehumanizes, and those who are violent cannot enter the kingdom of God. Those who would incite others to violence or encourage others in the use of violence are evil and do more to resist the Good News than probably any others. Donald McQuade, a Maryknoll priest, wrote a column for *America* Magazine in 1996 entitled "*Anawim*—Beloved of God" and in it he tells a story that reveals the heart of this command to love one's enemies and to resist violence.

✳ During the course of a retreat for priests a couple of years ago, Bishop Gaudencio Rosales spoke very movingly about the *anawim*. At that time he was bishop of the diocese of Malaybalay in the mountains of Mindanao. His diocese was the scene of continuous fighting between the Philippine Army, Muslim separatists and the leftist New People's Army. As usual, whenever shooting and violence break out, it is the common people, poor farmers in this case, who suffer most—both as casualties caught in the cross-fire and victims of the economic after-effects of all the turmoil.

The bishop fortunately had the respect of all the warring groups and could act as a peacemaker among them. During the retreat he made a very telling point, repeating it twice. He said: "Woe to those who would lead the poor (*anawim*) to violence. They would rob them of the only possession they have, the kingdom of God." He was referring to those who would seek to arm the poor as "vigilantes," or to others who would incite the poor to violence against institutions. Both approaches would lead them to kill and thus revert to the old dispensation of "an eye for an eye and a tooth for a tooth" (Ex. 21:24) instead of Jesus' law of love, even of one's enemies (Mt. 5:44). Violence and vengeance have a very strong emotional appeal for people living amid gross injustice, but to opt to become a person of violence is, as the bishop warned, to lose the reign of God. (p. 19)

The blessings and woes are personal and communal and so have much to say about violence, whether that violence is emotional, physical, psychological, or structural. Any form of violence is a direct antithesis to the kingdom of God, which is born of mercy, of God's faithful covenant and abiding love. In God's kingdom, loving one's enemies and practicing nonviolent resistance to evil and injustice and acting virtuously in the face of sin are perfectly rational and understandable, as well as necessary. Any form of violence is evil and works against the kingdom of God and the possibility of the Good News coming true in the world. Jesus' followers, children with him of the Father of Mercy, born of the Spirit of truth and reconciliation, must not do violence and must train themselves not to react thoughtlessly or emotionally to the violence of others.

Obedience to the command of loving one's neighbor— who is now everyone and anyone, especially those who do not love us back—begins with resistance to evil as well as practice with those people who perhaps are a bit easier to accommodate. The old adage "Practice makes perfect" fits in well here. Jesus' words give us a direction:

Do to others as you would have others do to you. If you love only those who love you, what kind of graciousness is yours? Even sinners love those who love them. If you do favors to those who are good to you, what kind of graciousness is yours? Even sinners do the same. If you lend only when you expect to receive, what kind of graciousness is yours? For sinners also lend to sinners, expecting to receive something in return.

But love your enemies and do good to them, and lend when there is nothing to expect in return. Then will your reward be great and you will be children of the Most High. For he is kind towards the ungrateful and the wicked. Be merciful, just as your Father is merciful. (Luke 6:31-36)

In all cases and in every circumstance, we are to do to others as we would have others do to us. Jesus is clear. We are not to do to others what they do to us, but what we would want them to do to us. More to the point, we are to do to them what Jesus would do to us. Do we respond like sinners, like the wicked and the ungrateful, or do we respond like the children of the Most High, like Jesus, with graciousness, with a blessing rather than a curse? Where do we stand? Where are our feet planted? In the kingdom or in the world? Or with one foot in each, depending on whom we are dealing with? Jesus' words, of course, are as consistent as God's mercy and graciousness to all—even to us, who in many instances fall into that category of enemies rather than friends of God, when we resist the Word and the coming of the kingdom in our midst.

Luke's rendering of the blessings and woes is more basic than the more personal and spiritual version in Matthew. Luke's account seems much closer to the economic and political realities of Jesus and those of his time: being dominated and taxed excessively, being occupied by foreign troops, being enslaved, controlled, and oppressed by the deliberate collusion between the structures of religion and those of the state. Jesus himself would die violently. His public torture would warn others about the danger of following in his footsteps, of believing in and practicing the freedom and the liberation, the conversion and the transformation that his message of the kingdom of God entailed. To be a disciple requires that we know evil, that we know our enemies and practice loving them in pragmatic ways. It requires that we learn to be wise in the ways of evil, so that we do not get caught in its web of violence and inhumanity. Aleksandr Solzhenitsyn wrote: "Violence does not always, not necessarily, take people by the throat and strangle them. Usually it demands no more than an oath of allegiance from its subjects. They are required merely to become accomplices in its lies."

Jesus is warning us to see, to look beyond the surface of reality and to become astute in the ways of the world. The rest of the sermon deals with economics and violence, with seeing, with generosity in responding to our neighbors, and with being formed in the image of our master. It is about single-heartedness and single-mindedness, about purity of heart and the desire to belong to and serve only one master: God. In the kingdom of mercy and justice all are the children of God and all can know in our meeting with them a touch of the graciousness that we have known from our God.

It is a matter of attitude, intention, intensity of focus. Are we about being converted, diverted from what is evil and destructive of the kingdom of God? Or are we intent on blame, on judging others and seeing ourselves as victims rather than as those who contribute to the sin of the world and resist parts of the Good News steadfastly, blindly, and self-righteously? Are we blind?

> And Jesus offered this example, "Can a blind person lead another blind person? Surely both will fall into a ditch. No disciple is above his master; if he lets himself be formed, he will be like his master. So why do you pay attention to the speck in your brother's eye while you have a log in your eye and are not conscious of it? How can you say to your brother: 'Brother, let me take this speck out of your eye,' when you can't remove the log in your own? You hypocrite! First remove the log from your own eye and then you will see clearly enough to remove the speck from your brother's eye." (Luke 6:39-42)

The image is glaring and blunt. It seems exaggerated, but Jesus is dealing with those of us who think of ourselves as good Christians and followers of Jesus but who are often unconscious of our own collusion with evil and our own sin, even if it is glaringly apparent to everyone else. And this is true of us, not just as individuals, but as communities and church. It is perhaps most glaringly apparent in the areas of collusion with economic structures, with unjust laws and violent systems that foster more individual and personal aspects of violence. The results of being poor are usually associated with violence of one form or another: drugs, guns, gangs, alcoholism, abuse, abortion, suicide. We must be careful to look deep within our own souls, to examine our lifestyles and ask the hard questions about why things continue as they are and what part we play in these ugly realities that are inhuman, violent, and evil. The gospel, and especially segments such as this sermon, provide a perspective that cannot be easily ignored or brushed aside by Christians.

In *Economic Justice for All* the American bishops wrote:

> Such perspectives provide a basis for what is called the "preferential option for the poor." Though in the Gospels and in the New Testament as a whole the offer of salvation is extended to all peoples, Jesus takes the side of those most in need, physically and spiritually. The example of Jesus poses a number of challenges to the contemporary Church. It imposes a prophetic mandate to speak for those who have no one to speak for them, to be a defender of the defenseless, who in biblical terms are the poor. It also demands a compassionate vision which enables the Church to see things from the side of the poor and powerless, and to assess lifestyles, policies, and social institutions in terms of their impact on the poor. It summons the Church also to be an instrument in assisting people to experience the liberating power of God in their own lives so that they may respond to the Gospel in freedom and dignity. Finally, and most radically, it calls for an emptying of self, both individually and corporately, that allows the Church to experience the power of God in the midst of poverty and powerlessness. (#52)

The imperative of the gospel to preach and be Good News for the poor is not just an admonition for the practice of personal virtue. It is an economic principle for institutions and for the corporate structure of the church, its parishes, its religious communities and its organizations. We are to be about crossing the lines of class, neighborhood, and nation and all barriers that separate people into those who have and those who need, into rich and poor, into those who hate and those victims who are tempted to hate and retaliate. We are to learn to be peacemakers, forgivers, reconcilers. We must be those who see clearly and can intervene on the side of those most at risk, befriending them and visiting them as "our God from on high has visited us" (Lk 1:68ff).

Jesus is clear about the practical aspects:

> Don't be a judge of others and you will not be judged; do not condemn and you will not be condemned; forgive and you will be forgiven; give and it will be given to you, and you will receive in your sack good measure, pressed down, full and running over. For the measure you give will be the measure you receive back. (Luke 6:37-38)

This is about social systems and not just about one-on-one relationships. It is about economics and politics, communities and corporate structures. It is about the Body of Christ in our midst and the practice of the corporal works of mercy. It is about incorporation and taxes, about debt and aid to dependent countries as well as about how we do ministry and how we set our priorities in allocating personnel, money, time, and service. To whom are we giving? Do those in most dire need, those most despairing and most forgotten, know that the kingdom of God is among us and is home for them? We talk in terms of economics and politics, trade and aid, debt and the World Bank, free markets and business ethics. And while Jesus does not speak in the specifics of our vocabulary, he uses prophet language to make us look at ourselves in light of the prophets' age-old cries on behalf of the poor and God's own command for the year of favor from the Lord. The jubilee year is the theological image of these last few years before the year of the Lord in 2000. In religious and economic terms, what does this image mean? In 1996 Julian Filochowski of CAFOD (a Catholic aid agency based in London) in an address to the European Congress of Jesuit Alumni in Leeds put it so clearly, so succinctly, and in both theological and fiscal terms.

The debt crisis compounds all the problems of the poor. Every year in interest payments alone 200 billion dollars are due from the Third World; that is 30 billion dollars more than all the aid and all the investment that flows from North to South. Much of the loans have never been seen. It is unpaid interest rolled over and added to the principal. In the final analysis it has to be paid. During the African crises of the 1980s more finance was flowing out of Africa than was going in because of debt repayments. At the end of the day we look back to the origins of these loans in the 1970s at the time of the glut of petrodollars. And we find on the whole they were stupid loans made by stupid bankers for stupid projects with stupid governments—and it is the poor who are paying. Some 40 severely indebted low-income countries owe huge sums to the World Bank and the International Monetary Fund. The payment of the debt is strangling economies and precluding growth. The structural adjustment policies that have been imposed upon them in order to find some way out of this unpayable debt involve the slashing of subsidies on food, the disappearance of medicines from so many hospitals and clinics, the cutting of education budgets and the firing of teachers. For people living on the knife-edge between survival and death these cuts push them over. The United Nations Children's Fund has estimated that every year 500,000 children die because of measures imposed to pay the debt. The President of CELAM [Latin American Bishops' Conference], Archbishop Oscar Rodriguez, has said that he has come to the conclusion that many of the international financial institutions have injustice in their genetic code. Pope John Paul II has described structures of sin in our world today. These are surely structures of sin—they bring not life but death.

Aid, concessionary aid, is being reduced across the world. We are further than ever before from reaching that tantalizing target set in the 1970s of 0.7% of our gross national product in aid flowing from North to South. Aid is being recycled to pay the debts. Aid, whilst falling in volume, is being increasingly used to finance the emergencies and calamities and less for investment in the future of the poor. Many are trying to say that foreign aid has had its day; it is passé, it is a 1960s idea. Last month in London Cardinal Etchegaray commenting on this phenomenon said the world community is being asked the age-old question "Am I my brother's keeper?" The answer being given is "No." It is the exit of solidarity, the drying out of solidarity. And that brings to the poor of this world not hope but despair.

This is the Sermon on the Plain. The blessings and woes of Luke are writ large and bold in contemporary economic language, addressed to the church and to corporations and communities of those who claim to be followers of Christ who startled his disciples with the words: "Blessed are the poor, for the kingdom of God is theirs now!" To whom do we lend? To whom do we give outright? How generous are we? Are we more conscious of the speck in the eye of the poor than of the logs protruding from our own eyes, our lifestyles and investments, our moral choices and laws and priorities? Are we more like the blind leading the blind, or are we learning to be led by the cries of the poor? Jesus continues and asks us today:

No healthy tree bears bad fruit; no poor tree bears good fruit. And each tree is known by the fruit it bears. Moreover, you don't gather figs from thorns, or grapes from brambles. Similarly a good person draws good things from the good in his heart, and an evil person draws evil things from the evil in his heart. For the mouth speaks from the fullness of the heart.

Why do you call me: "Lord! Lord!" and not do what I say? (Luke 6:43-46)

If we are trees, the orchard of the kingdom, what kind of fruit are we producing? Have we become thorns, thistles, brambles? Is our fruit soft, rotten, or too hard to eat? From where do we draw forth this fruit: from hearts that are poor, mourning, and hungry for justice or from divided hearts that put forth as much evil as good, or worse, more evil than good? Do we do what the Lord we call upon commands us to do?

There is a story from the early Fathers of the Church that brings this home on a more personal level. It can easily be transposed into the realm of the more institutional and corporate structure of church and groups as well.

✳ Once upon a time a holy man received some new recruits. When they presented themselves and asked to join him, they were welcomed and told they could stay as visitors as long as they wished, or stay permanently if they wanted to join more formally and commit themselves to this way of life. Then they were asked what kind of work they did to support themselves. At this, they were a bit confused and indignant. "We don't work," they said. "We pray and we've come to dedicate ourselves to prayer and to ministry within this church and community. We will pray 'continually' as the scriptures say (1 Thes 5:16-17)."

"Oh," the holy man responded. He looked at them and began to ask some questions. "Let me get this straight. You pray all the time and don't work?"

"Yes, that's what we have tried to do and want to do here."

"Hmm. Do you eat?"

"Of course," they said, "but we try to eat simply — only health foods."

"Hmm. Do you sleep?"

They were confused. "Of course we sleep. Otherwise we'd drift off and not concentrate on our prayer."

"Hmm. When you sleep and while you eat, who prays for you?" The young ones were reduced to silence. They had never thought of this and had no answer.

The holy man continued. "I find you very curious people. You say you want to pray always and that you don't want to work, but you take time out to eat and sleep and no one prays for you.

"Frankly. I don't understand. I work—in the fields, planting, harvesting, gathering, weeding, and I pray as I work and sweat, even if it's just short but fervent prayers, like 'Lord, Jesus Christ, have mercy on me, a sinner; have mercy on us all.' Or I just say over and over again the Our Father, though I drift a lot and have to start over again and again, sometimes only saying those two words: Our Father, Our Father. I find this always brings me back home to my heart. It reminds me that I am not alone and that all of us are before God always. So I pray and work as much as I can. And then when I've finished with my work, I give half of my harvest and what I sell to the poor. It is my delight and honor to share the work of my hands and my heart with them. And then they pray for me, so even when I sleep and eat they are praising God with gratitude for what I have been able to give and they have been able to receive. So I pray all the time. They know the fruit of my labor and I know the fruit of their gratefulness."

Those who had come to pray were silent and wondering to themselves, "Hmm, is this the way I want to live and pray?"

Hmm, is this the way we live? Is this the way we work and pray, sharing the fruit of our labors and sharing in the prayer of the poor who are bound to us in God and in a common struggle to eat, sleep, and live together in some sort of dignity and freedom with hope? If this is the way we live, God is remembered unceasingly, as are the poor, and all are blessed, for the kingdom is among us. Half of all our work, the fruits of our labor, are shared!

Julian Filochowski speaks about what Jubilee means:

Pope John Paul II completes the circle in *Tertio Millennio Adveniente* [The Coming of the Third Millennium] in paragraph 51 when he states "How can we fail to lay greater emphasis on the Church's preferential option for the poor and the outcast? Indeed in a world like ours marked by so many conflicts and intolerable social and economic inequalities, it has to be said that a commitment to justice and peace is a necessary condition for the preparation and celebration of the Jubilee." A necessary condition—that means that we may not celebrate it without it! He goes on, "Christians will have to raise their voice on behalf of all the poor of the world proposing the Jubilee as a time for reducing if not canceling outright the international debt which seriously threatens the future of many nations." It could not be said more plainly; it is not open to misinterpretation.

In light of Jesus' command "Give to the one who asks and if anyone has taken something from you, do not demand it back," the laying of intolerable burdens upon the poor cries out to heaven, summoning any prophet within range. This is a log jam that has been building for some time, even among Christian communities that are heavily invested in the dominant structures of corporate industry, technology, military, and national interests that generate profit and greed for a minority and suffering, deprivation, and death for the vast majority. As is made clear, Jesus has no tolerance for complacency in the face of the misery of millions who suffer starvation and shortened life expectancy in a world that has the resources and the ability not only to feed them but to help them feed themselves and create living conditions that are decent and human. Jesus abhors the kind of violence that breeds even more vicious violence and despair for those oppressed by injustice. Basic human rights begin with food, shelter and medicine, coupled with responsible use of resources that will provide the next generation of children with what they need in order to live with hope.

Jesus' sermon leads to root questions. From which place in our hearts do we act, goodness or evil, justice or injustice, solidarity and sharing with others or greed and selfishness? Have we committed ourselves to the kingdom of God and its coming among us or are we firmly committed to our own tiny kingdoms and domains carefully guarded and fortified against others? Or, in the words of the closing image of the sermon, have we built our house on the firm foundation of the rock of God's word or have we built it on the shifting sands of the world and our own whims? Jesus sums up all that he has said in his sermon with this image:

> I will show you what the one who comes to me and listens to my words and acts accordingly is like. He is like the builder who dug deep and laid the foundations of his house on rock. The river overflowed and the stream dashed against the house, but could not carry it off because the house had been well built.
>
> But if anyone listens and does not act, he is like a man who built his house on the ground without a foundation. The flood burst against it, and the house fell at once: and what a terrible disaster that was. (Luke 6:47-49)

Basically, the sermon ends with another set of blessings and woes. Blessed are those who build their lives on a firm foundation with stones and rock that is secure—the poor, the meek, the nonviolent, the hungry and mourning, the persecuted, and the truthtellers—for they can stand against anything and hold firm. And woe to those who build their house without a foundation on ground that shifts and is easily undercut. Woe to those who are happy, well-fed, content, thought well of, respected in this world, wealthy and full, self-satisfied and self-righteous.

Jesus' sermon, the heart of his message as the servant of Yahweh, the suffering and crucified one who heals and heartens the poor and those waiting for the promises of God to be fulfilled, ends with a choice: What are we building and where? What are we setting ourselves up for? Is our security in this world or in the kingdom of God? This is the same Jesus who in the very next chapter heals the servant of a non-Jew, an officer in an occupying army force, though he is described by the elders of Capernaum (Jesus' adopted hometown) as one who "loves our people and even built a synagogue for us" (Lk 7:5). This officer is described as a friend of the poor, the outcast, the oppressed. Even though he is a Roman, he is associated with the Jewish community. And Jesus heals the one that this man loves well, his servant. And a little later, Jesus is on the road again, and meets a funeral procession outside of the town of Naim. He takes pity on a widow who is burying her only son. This woman is the epitome of the *anawim* in the covenant history of the Jewish community. She is a widow, orphaned and isolated even within her own village. And Jesus raises her son from the dead and gives him back to her! He saves two lives, because he gives her back her only source of a future, someone to provide for her, since the law, the structures, and even the justice and the charity of her neighbors are lacking. He does this work of mercy with dignity and care. It is noted and the people react:

> A holy fear came over them all and they praised God saying, "A great prophet has appeared among us: God has visited his people." And throughout Judea and the surrounding country, people talked about Jesus' deeds. (Luke 7:16-17)

Here is the fullness of the reality of Jesus: a prophet appears among us and God visits his people. This is the kingdom of God. This is blessing. We are told that the people talked about Jesus' deeds, yet Jesus has been clear as a bell: "But if anyone listens and does not act. . . . " It is not enough to talk. If God has come to visit and this holy fear is to seep deep into our hearts, then we must be converted and our hearts must bend in reverence before all, and especially before those whom God reverences, in pity, in mercy, and with utmost graciousness. This means the poor, the outsider, the widow, the one left without resources. The true disciple is the one who loves the poor, who "comes to Jesus, and listens to his words and acts accordingly." It is time to act accordingly.

As always, a story can point us in the right direction. It can lay a foundation and remind us that what we are about is a process, a be-attitude, and the result of a relationship with the Master we follow. This is an "Ahimsa" story, from the Asian tradition on how to make pots, and how to put your own life on the wheel and become perfect, fired and glazed, something useful and a thing of beauty at the same time.

* Once upon a time one of the master's apprentices who was exceptionally good at making pots and had mastered all of Ahimsa's techniques went to the master and pleaded to be allowed to go out on his own, to teach in the master's name and to begin his own work that would culminate in his own singular style. He was refused without a reason and told to return to his duties.

Again he approached the master and was refused. This time he asked for a reason why, defending himself by saying, "Master, you know that I'm good. Why, some of my pots are even being mistaken for yours."

The master smiled and said, "Not yet. Go back to your work and, who knows, someday your pots won't be mistaken for mine." That puzzled him, but he obeyed.

Then one day, quite unexpectedly, the master approached him, smiling. "Time to go!" "What? Why? I don't understand," said the apprentice. The master picked up a pot from the rack before the student and said matter of factly, but with a glint in his eye, "I've found myself imitating your pots! Time to go!"

We are children of God, the Most High, followers of the Master, apprenticed to the kingdom of mercy, and justice for all. We work and obey and who knows, perhaps God is waiting for us to stumble upon a way to make earth a home for the poor, a way that even God would find worth imitating! But perhaps for now it's not time to go, but to stay and work at loving our enemies and being as gracious and merciful as our Father and building our houses on solid rock, and maybe throwing a pot or two with the leftover time and earth!

10

Other Blessings in Luke

Poor people bloom when they feel they count for something. (Ernestina Rivera)

While Luke has only four beatitudes in the Sermon on the Plain, the rest of the gospel is laced with blessings. A look at these "other" blessings will add depth and insight to our understanding of the four core beatitudes. Luke's blessings and woes are linchpins for understanding much of the rest of his material, especially the parables that are unique to this gospel.

The first and perhaps the most famous of Luke's blessings is found in the first chapter of the gospel, in the annunciation account. We have ritualized the words of Gabriel's greeting into the prayer of the Hail Mary: "Hail Mary, full of grace, the Lord is with you, blessed are you among women and blest is the fruit of your womb, Jesus." It is a greeting, an announcement, a proclamation of what God has done for her and is doing for her people, Israel, and for all believers. The greeting of Gabriel first to Zechariah in the temple and then to Mary in Nazareth ushers in a time of mercy. In the words of Elizabeth: "What is the Lord doing for me! This is his time for mercy and for taking away my public disgrace" (Lk 1:25). An apt description of blessing, certainly. And when Mary hears the angel's proclamation and the incarnation is set in motion, she moves too, to make sure that the words come true. She sets about making sure that what God has done for her will be extended into the world, that the words will bear fruit in reality, in history. The covenant will be honored, history will be fulfilled, and creation will be reconfigured with mercy, blessing, and the holiness of God. Grace will interfere again and again and again. Mary will bloom with the Word of God.

Mary sets out through the hill country of Judea. It is no easy trip and she arrives, wearied and exhausted after her silent, reflective pilgrimage, at the house of Elizabeth, who has been in seclusion since Zechariah became mute after his disbelieving encounter with Gabriel. And Mary's words of greeting to Elizabeth, traditionally the Jewish greeting of "Shalom," a blessing upon God, upon Israel, and upon the one greeted, startles and awakens both Elizabeth and John, the child in her womb. The sound of Mary's voice in Elizabeth's ears goes straight to her heart and the heart that sleeps beneath her own. John starts kicking in anticipation and delight as he recognizes the presence of hope in her voice. And Elizabeth responds clearly with a blessing that is immediately addressed to Mary, but is extended to all who act in accord with the word of God, as she has done. She cries out:

> You are most blessed among women and blessed is the fruit of your womb! How is it that the mother of my Lord comes to me? The moment your greeting sounded in my ears, the baby within me suddenly leapt for joy. Blessed are you who believed that the Lord's word would come true! (Luke 1:42-45)

This is a triple blessing, the blessing of a woman carrying hope within her. It is the recognition of a long-awaited child who will be the blessing of a nation and a universe, and of all who believe and stake their lives on making the Word of the Lord come true in them, on earth, now and for always. This sort of blessing gathers all pasts, offers them as gift in the present, and makes the future come truer to God's fervent hopes for all that has been set in motion toward wholeness and holiness. Mary's response is the song, the psalm of blessing God that is forerunner to her son's proclamation in the synagogue when he comes of age. It also anticipates the Spirit's proclamation after John's baptism when Jesus takes up his mantle of prophet, of servant, and of beloved child of his Father. She knows! She takes on the power of Gabriel singing her heart out to the very air and ground of Israel, announcing that its long pilgrimage of hope is over, that the time is at hand. The fulfillment of the promise lies sleeping and growing under her heart. Her presence is a blessing, and the blessing, like the power of God, is unstoppable. Mary describes God's long relationship with Israel: "He held out his hand to Israel, his servant, for he remembered his mercy, even as he promised..." (Lk 1:54-55). As always, every blessing is an acknowledgment of God's presence loose in the world and becoming clearer and more pronounced for those who have ears to hear and eyes to see and hearts to grasp hold of this new reality being thrust into our midst.

This blessing of Mary, this radical alteration of her person, her whole life and future to the word of the Lord is central to the gospel, the Good News to the poor of God. This blessing is the foundation stone upon which so much more will be laid. It is a rock of safety and stability. It is indestructible, reliable, everlasting and intimate as spirit and breath. God is true. God's word is true. And salvation is about this truth taking root and flesh in us, transfiguring us. Salvation is extended into the world by our presence. God blesses us and we become the blessing, repeating it, playing it out like jazz performers who take the same run of notes and tease them into individual creative "licks," sliding under and over those same notes in infinitely various ways. Luke's gospel is about blessing: the blessing of God and of those who, made in God's image, imitate and extend that blessing. Luke's Good News is about human beings coming true.

I discovered a marvelously enchanting story in a book called *The Heart Aroused* that I found in a bookstore in England last year. I took the book off the shelf and opened right to it. I even remember the page numbers—50-51. (I don't have the book, for I had no money with me, but I do remember the story.) It mesmerized me and I could see it right before my eyes. The words triggered photographic images for me.

* Once upon a time this young American (I think, or Eng-
lishman) was traveling in Asia, taking groups of tourists
high into the mountains of Nepal. He was equipped with
the latest trekking gear, business cards, guide books, and
a spirituality appropriate to such heights.

This time, however, he was alone, climbing the rocky
outcrops, carrying his pack. Suddenly he faced a bridge. It
was not just any bridge. In fact, it wasn't much of a bridge
at all. It was broken in many places, hanging precariously
over fast mountain streams far below. When he saw it, he
lost his nerve. His heart grew faint and an unease spread
throughout his body and soul as his mind retreated from
the crossing. He was good at mountain climbing and hik-
ing, but suddenly he just couldn't do it. Time to turn
around and go home.

As he turned he saw approaching him on the path a
small, bent-over woman. She was very old and she carried an enormous dung basket. Completely unaware of
him, she scrutinized the ground for any bit of yak dung,
twig, or scrap that was burnable. She was treasure hunt-
ing and what she was looking for was invaluable. When
she came within a few feet of him she spied his big feet—
a Westerner's feet—and she looked up, startled. She
straightened a bit, gazed up at him, and smiled. Her face
was wrinkled and weather-buffeted, toothy and childlike.
She greeted him with the customary word, "*Namaste*"
(loosely, "I greet the God in you"). It sounded like a song,
with the last syllable held. And she bowed, with her
hands raised in blessing! He bowed as well, bringing his
hands together and responding in the same manner. As
his head came up, she was past him and she sprang
across the rickety bridge, in a dance step or two, graceful
and free. She turned and looked at him mischievously,
laughing without a sound. Then she spun around and
disappeared with another few steps, dropping down to
another ledge of the cliff's outcrop.

He stood there, stunned, and then he sprang into motion and bounded across the swaying bridge as well,
landing firmly on the Himalayan ground, bound for a

new life, catapulted there by a total stranger's greeting, face, and action. She had invited him to dance, and he, entranced, had followed along behind her.

The memory has remained riveted within his mind and soul. Years later he writes about that encounter as a milestone, a turning point, a decision that set in motion much that followed.

This is a blessing, whether it is couched in traditional ritual words like *shalom* or *namaste*, accompanied or unaccompanied by a bow of reverence and respect and the raised hands gathering together the air and oneself, presenting them to the other with a smile of glee or a solemn face. It acknowledges the innate harmony of the universe and sets in motion magic and far deeper and truer things like salvation, mercy, and the next step that will release and free us all. As Mary remained with Elizabeth about three months and then went home, the blessings remain and then we take them home, to pass on to others. We extend the covenant, the promise, just by our presence as we go about our lives, regardless of whether we are aware of communion and the meaning that is moving and drawing us all together.

The realization of a blessing or the experience of a blessing invariably results in prayer, praise, and action. When Zechariah writes the name of his child, John, in obedience to Gabriel's command, his tongue is freed and he sings the bounty of God: "Blessed be the Lord God of Israel for he has come and redeemed his people" (Lk 1:68). He has visited his people, as it is sometimes translated, and redemption is set in motion. To speak of it is to contribute to its power and actualization. God's mercy in the mouth of the old prophets is coming true now (Lk 1:72). Zechariah's own child, John, will continue this tradition of salvation, "the work of the mercy of our God, who comes from on high as a rising sun shining on those who live in darkness and the shadow of death, and guiding our feet into the way of peace" (Lk 1:77-79). The blessing comes through angels and through little old ladies on high mountain passes, through bag folk, strangers and people who are familiar to us.

The account of the birth of Jesus is heralded by Gabriel and the choruses of angels that appear to shepherds in the fields. It is seen as God's glory in music to our ears: "Glory to God in the highest; peace on earth for God is blessing humankind" (Lk 2:14). And it is seen in a baby lying in a manger, wrapped in swaddling clothes.

When the time is at hand for obedience to the covenant, Joseph and Mary bring their first-born child to the temple as a blessing, an offering to God, and are met by Simeon, who blesses God at the very sight of them. For the sight of them is the sight of salvation, of mercy among us, of the word come true:

> Simeon took the child in his arms and blessed God,
>   saying,
> "Now, O Lord, you can dismiss your servant in peace,
> for you have fulfilled your word
> and my eyes have seen your salvation,
> which you display for all the people to see.
> Here is the light you will reveal to the nations and the
>   glory of your people Israel."
>   (Luke 2:28-32)

And then Simeon blesses Joseph and Mary and the blessing is disconcerting, for it speaks of power that divides, of contradiction, of revelations that will lead to persecution and suffering to those who honor the child who is the blessing of God:

> See him; he will be for the rise or fall of the multitudes of Israel. He shall stand as a sign of contradiction, while a sword will pierce your own soul. Then the secret thoughts of many may be brought to light. (Luke 2:34-35)

From the beginning there are blessings and woes. There are choices to be made, risks to embrace, secrets to be told. Once the blessing is uttered, its power moves and grows. It is like the Word made flesh, that grew "in stature, in strength and filled with wisdom: the grace of God was upon him" (Lk 2:40). That strength and wisdom, that grace of God seeps into everything it touches. It is either for blessing or for woe. It is always for conversion, for grasping hold of or rejecting, for laying bare or hiding from the gaze of others, for revealing the glory of God or scarring the face of God among us in the poor, in those who mourn and are hungry and are persecuted. These are the blessings at the beginning, the prelude to the blessing that walks among us teaching, healing, and announcing the Word of God making the dreams and blessings of old come true in ways quite unexpected and unimagined.

When Jesus begins to bless it is in his words of the beatitudes that introduce the Sermon on the Plain (Lk 6:17-26). The sermon can be summed up simply: "Be merciful, just as your Father is merciful." Jesus himself lives out that message as he sets off to do the works of mercy—healing, forgiving, telling the truth and calling to conversion, bringing the dead back to life. After John has been imprisoned, Jesus speaks with John's disciples and describes himself in greater detail by quoting from Isaiah the prophet:

> Go back and tell John what you have seen and heard: the blind see again, the lame walk, lepers are made clean, the deaf hear, the dead are raised to life, and the poor are given good news. Now listen: Fortunate are those who encounter me, but not for their downfall. (Luke 7:22-23)

The die is cast, the gauntlet thrown down. Jesus has just done all the deeds of blessing found in Isaiah. He is making the word of God in Isaiah's mouth come true. And everyone who encounters him, meets him, is greeted by him, will find him either a blessing or a woe, good news or downfall. His person, the very blessing of God in human flesh, causes all who find themselves in his presence to define who they are and with whom they stand—among those already blessed in the sight of God or those whom God laments and seeks to reconcile, redeem and turn toward blessing. The words that Jesus uses go back to Isaiah 61. Earlier, in Isaiah 35, we find

the same thoughts expressed in even more fluid and passionate language:

> Give vigor to weary hands
> and strength to enfeebled knees.
> Say to those who are afraid:
> "Have courage, do not fear.
> See, your God comes, demanding justice.
> He is the God who rewards
> the God who comes to save you."
>
> Then will the eyes of the blind be opened
> and the ears of the deaf unsealed.
> Then will the lame leap as a hart
> and the tongue of the dumb sing and shout.
> For water will break out in the wilderness
> and streams gush forth from the desert.
> The thirsty ground will become a pool,
> the arid land springs of water....
>
> There will be a highway
> which will be called The Way of Holiness;
> no one unclean will pass over it
> nor any wicked fool stray there.
> No lion will be found there
> nor any beast of prey.
> Only the redeemed will walk there.
> For the ransomed of Yahweh will return:
> with everlasting joy upon their heads,
> they will come to Zion singing,
> gladness and joy marching with them,
> while sorrow and sighing flee away.
>   (Isaiah 35:3-10)

The prophet of old, the prophet of Advent's coming and
Lent's turning, sings. He sings of reversals, of blessings and
woes, of conversion and ransom, of the mercy of God and the
justice that accompanies the presence of God's word in history. These reversals are described even more clearly earlier in

Isaiah when the prophet decries the hypocrisy of the priests and people and seeks to make them see:

> Because of this I will surprise them once more; the wisdom of the wise will be useless and the understanding of their prudent men will be at a loss.
> Woe to those who hide deep from Yahweh their plans,
> who work in the dark and say,
> "Who will know, and who will see us?"
> You turn things upside down,
> as though the potter were the clay,
> and of him it could say,
> "He did not make me; he knows nothing."
> In a very short time,
> Lebanon will become a fruitful field
> and the fruitful field will be as a forest.
> On that day
> the deaf will hear the words of the book,
> and out of the dark and obscurity the eyes of the
>   blind will see.
> The meek will find joy
> and the poor among men will rejoice
> in the Holy One of Israel.
>   (Isaiah 29:14-19)

The words of Jesus had many referents that were known to his listeners, certainly to the followers of the prophet John who baptized and announced that he merely went before the one who would come in fire, in spirit, and in power to save the people. This is what salvation looks like: besides healing the sick and raising the physically dead, it sinks deeply into the ears, eyes, and hearts of those languishing and dying, those who are determined not to see and hear the presence of God in their lives. It grasps hold of the poor, the ones burdened and bowed down. It sets them dancing with joy, embraced by the Spirit and crying out the praises of the Holy One of Israel. Jesus is this Holy One, the blessing of God, and blessed is anyone who hears and believes in him and follows him in the merciful work of blessing, of bringing justice and freedom to those who are crushed by the powers of the world.

And when Jesus' own mother and relatives can't get to him because of the crowds that surround him, he tells those gathered, "My mother and my brothers are those who hear the word of God and do it" (Lk 8:21). He is not excluding his own mother, for she is the first of the blessed for doing just this, hearing the Word spoken to her and making it come true by extending the blessing. Jesus is sharing the intimacy reserved in the past for blood relatives with those who are related and bound now by word and faith and practice. His disciples, followers, and friends are the new family of his Father, called now to live in the kingdom of God. This is the kingdom of justice and mercy described in such surprising terms in the blessings and woes of his preaching.

Halfway through the gospel, Jesus instructs his disciples and sends them out two by two to preach the good news, greeting those whom they encounter with the words of blessing, "Peace be with you," and either letting that blessing reside where it is accepted or allowing the blessings to return to them and moving on to others (Lk 10:5-6). The disciples go forth, as a blessing, to heal the sick and speak the word that the kingdom of God has drawn near to people. They return full of joy, exclaiming that even devils (hinderers) obey them. But Jesus corrects them:

> . . . don't rejoice because the evil spirits submit to you;
> rejoice rather that your names are written in heaven.
> (Luke 10:20)

And then Jesus prays in gratitude to his Father who gives to the children and hides from the learned and the clever. After praying publicly, Jesus turns and in private shares this thought with his disciples: "Fortunate are you to see what you see, for I tell you that many prophets and kings would have liked to see what you see but did not, and to hear what you hear and did not hear it" (Lk 10:24).

Jesus is saying much about himself. He is saying that he is the fulfillment of the promises of God, of the prophets' hopes and the kings' fervent desires. The disciples rejoice, but they have no real understanding of the depth and breadth of the blessing that is right before their eyes, within reach of their hands. Jesus continues to try to extend his disciples' perception of what is happening right before them and to them as well. In response to the clarity of his teaching and his forthright challenge to those who resist him, a woman cries out a blessing on him and upon his mother: "Blessed is the one who bore you and nursed you!" But Jesus is intent on making others see beyond family, beyond personal relationships that fit into easily acceptable and undemanding categories. He quickly retorts, "Surely blessed are those who hear the word of God and keep it as well" (Lk 11:27-28). He will not let the matter remain on the level of simple human connections. He is much more than the son of Mary and she, of course, would be the first to proclaim that in faith. He is nurtured by the Spirit of God as he has been fathered by God and is his beloved. Jesus is intent, single-heartedly and single-mindedly, to extend that blessing to all who will believe in his words and act on them.

Jesus' presence as blessing must be faced, and a decision must be made. When Jesus encounters resistance and rejection, he pronounces woes for those who refuse to believe and to be converted to the will and the word of God (Lk 11:37-54). He speaks that truth fearlessly and publicly, and warns those listening to him about hypocrisy: "Beware of the yeast of the Pharisees which is hypocrisy. Nothing is covered that will not be uncovered, or hidden that will not be made known. Whatever you have said in the darkness will be heard in daylight and what you have whispered in hidden places, will be proclaimed from the housetops" (Lk 12:1b-3). Jesus continues by telling his friends not to fear those who can put them to death, but to fear denying who he truly is, the Son of Man, the judgment and blessing of God for the world (Lk 12:4-12).

Jesus is concerned with a practical way of living. He exhorts his followers to practice belief in his word and obedience to his Father, to trust and to

Seek rather the Kingdom and these things [food, drink, clothing, etc.] will be given to you as well.

> Do not be afraid, little flock, for it has pleased
> your Father to give you the kingdom. Sell what you
> have and give alms. Get yourselves purses that do not
> wear out, and make safe investments with God,
> where no thief comes and no moth destroys. For
> where your investments are, there will your heart be
> also. (Luke 12:31-34)

In story, parable, and exhortation Jesus is repeating the
first of the beatitudes: Blessed are the poor for they have the
kingdom now. We are told that this kingdom is a blessing that
has been given to us as a gift already. It is the only possession
we have that is worth holding onto and all else has meaning
only within its context. And we are questioned. Where are our
hearts? Where are we heavily invested? Whose will are we intent on serving? Whom do we trust and care for? To whom do
we belong? Who lays claim to us and holds us?

What follows this exhortation and command is a short
parable that begins with a beatitude that people don't often
like, because it touches a nerve deep inside and scratches like
fingernails on a blackboard, as many of the beatitudes and
woes do. It describes a way of living, an attitude that we must
foster and practice and keep in mind.

> Be ready, dressed for service, and keep your lamps lit,
> like people waiting for their master to return from the
> wedding. As soon as he comes and knocks, they will
> open to him. Happy are those servants whom the
> master finds wide awake when he comes. Truly, I tell
> you, he will put on an apron and have them sit at
> table and he will wait on them. Happy are those ser-
> vants if he finds them awake when he comes at mid-
> night or daybreak! (Luke 12:35-38)

This parable serves as a link between the section of the
gospel that speaks of how to be a servant of God and the section that speaks of a time of justice and judgment, of bringing
fire on the earth to purify it and transform it. Jesus confronts
with additional woes the rich and those who resist the pro-

nouncement of God, those who are not ready because they are busy with their own affairs and investments. He tells stories about those who do evil, those who want the first places at table, those who refuse to change their ways. There is the three-fold story of the lost coin, the lost sheep, and the lost son; there is the story of the crafty steward who is intent on making sure he's accepted by others; and there is the story of the rich man and Lazarus. They are stories of money, of rich and poor, or choices made for good and for evil.

Then Jesus tells another story. This one is about servants and masters, and it is even more confrontational and clearly descriptive of the blessings and woes of his sermon.

> The apostles said to the Lord, "Increase our faith." And the Lord said, "If you have faith even the size of a mustard seed, you may say to this tree: 'Be uprooted and plant yourself in the sea,' and it will obey you.
>
> If you have a servant coming in from the fields after plowing or tending sheep, do you say to him: 'Come at once and sit down at table'? No, you tell him: 'Prepare my dinner. Put on your apron and wait on me while I eat and drink; you can eat and drink afterwards.' Do you thank this servant for doing what you commanded? So for you. When you have done all that you have been told to do, you must say: 'We are no more than servants; we have only done our duty.' " (Luke 17:5-10)

That image of the mustard seed calls to mind an earlier incident in the gospel, one in which Jesus tells those who are watching him in the synagogue that the mustard seed is a good symbol of the kingdom of God and how it comes and dwells in the world. He has just cured a woman bent double for eighteen years and has been castigated by the synagogue leader and those who would reject his compassionate interpretation of the word of the covenant. He responds by saying: "What is the kingdom of God like? What shall I compare it to? Imagine a person who has taken a mustard seed and planted it in his garden. The seed has grown and become like a small tree, so that the birds of the air shelter in its branches" (Lk 13:18-19).

This section of the Good News is about seeds and beginnings. It is about blessings planted that will bear fruit in justice. It is about a kingdom that grows and becomes a community, a place of shelter and refuge for those on one side of that far divide between poor and rich, between those in desperate need of God and those who are too insensitive and selfish to care, between sinners who cry out to God and those who refuse to admit that they too are sinners, between those who seek to obey the will of God and those who do evil and resist the Word of God. The kingdom is like a seed, inconspicuous but growing; like yeast, hidden but spreading and rising through the bread; like servants obeying their master, whether he is present or still yet to come.

To what degree have we internalized the blessings and woes, taken them to heart and put them into practice? How converted are we? How much do we believe? A mustard seed's worth? Are we good servants who are ready, attentive, watching, and listening for our master's return? How obedient to the word of God are we? How much do we keep back for ourselves, refusing to trust and obey, turning aside from those in need and not sharing what is given to us? How much of our duty do we do? Have we been plowing the fields and tending the sheep, or have we been about our own businesses and investments and self-worth? How much attention have we paid to the kingdom of God, the poor, the mourning and hungry, the persecuted and outcast? Are we blessed or is God lamenting the fact that we are so hardhearted, resistant, defiant, and careless of the Word that has been proclaimed to us?

Jesus tells two parables of a master and servant. In the first, the master dons an apron in delight when he finds his servants ready and he waits on them! In the second, the master demands that the servants do what servants are required to do: wait on the master, serve his dinner, and continue with their duties. Although the stories appear to contradict each other, the two are in fact saying something vital about the blessings and woes. Blessed are those who are the servants of the kingdom, of the poor, and of God, for God will wait on them! And those of us who think of ourselves as disciples of the Master must be ready, must be careful. Earth is for service, for plowing and tending the fields, and for worship. This is our duty as servants. We are not to expect anything different here on earth. We can expect to work hard. We can expect to have demands made of us. But we must not expect to be rewarded for doing what we are supposed to do. We must not expect God to wait on us because we are disciples, or even beloved children. God does wait on us, but only if we have learned to wait on the poor, on the kingdom of justice and mercy, and on those who are the presence of God most rejected in our midst. This paradox of servants and masters is central to Luke's gospel. Jesus is the suffering servant of God, the master who waits on us, and we are disciples who follow our master's ways, donning our aprons and bowing before those in need. It is an honor to serve those whom God serves and that is a blessing in itself. Poverty of spirit bends us before God and before the poorest children of God's family.

Jesus, the prophet and teacher of the Law of the Spirit, warns his listeners, and he warns us. We are told to be careful, not to cause scandal, to forgive even seven times in a day, even if it is the same person who keeps wronging us! We are asked: Have you done all that I have commanded, what you have been told to do? Have you waited on the tables, served the meals, put on aprons and waited on God, done your duty? Are you believers with faith the size of a mustard seed? As the sermon is told in stories, separations made, and those blessed are clearly distinguished from those unfortunates who will not listen, will not hear, and will not obey.

Jesus laments the lack of belief, the refusal of so many, and his whole being cries out. When he tells the parable of the mustard seed after the confrontation in the synagogue over healing the poor woman, he laments over Jerusalem:

O Jerusalem, Jerusalem, you slay the prophets and stone your apostles! How often have I tried to bring together your children, as a bird gathers her young under her wings, but you refused! From now on your

Temple will be left empty for you and you will no longer see me until the time when you will say: Blessed is he who comes in the name of the Lord. (Luke 13:34-35)

Soon after he refers once again to the mustard seed and tells the story of the servant and master, Jesus enters the city of Jerusalem, his face set toward the cross. He is welcomed with the greeting and blessing of the people: "Blessed is he who comes as king in the name of the Lord. Peace in heaven and Glory in the highest heavens" (Lk 19:38). Their song echoes the hymn of the angels in the field at his birth, but it is also shadowed by the cross that will soon loom over the people who will ultimately reject him. The blessings in their mouths will be short-lived, because they have no roots in the kingdom of God.

The last separation, the final distillation of blessings and woes, comes on the cross, with Jesus hung between two thieves. The story is familiar:

One of the criminals hanging with Jesus insulted him, "So you are the Messiah? Save yourself and us as well!" But the other rebuked him, saying, "Have you no fear of God, you who received the same sentence as he did? For us it is just: this is payment for what we have done. But this man has done nothing wrong." Turning to Jesus he said, "Jesus, remember me when you come into your kingdom." Jesus replied, "Truly you will be with me today in paradise." (Luke 23:39-43)

These are the last words of blessing before Jesus hands his life over to his Father, entrusting him now with his own body and the kingdom that has been planted, in the form of a mustard seed and in hard ground, but planted nonetheless. The word is spoken and the blessing is breathed out, sighed out upon the world and cried out in the death of Jesus, the Blessing of God that will not be stilled or broken or destroyed. The sign of the cross has become our blessing, our experience of mercy and the judgment of God's justice on the world. What remains is the blossoming, the emergence of the blessing in resurrection, in freedom, and in the kingdom of God firmly planted in all those who hear the Word of God and endeavor to put it into practice. The blessings are many and strong among those who remember the Word of God and bend before everyone on earth and say: "Blessed are you," "*Namaste*," "I greet the God in you." Blessed are you poor. Blessed are you who mourn and weep. Blessed are you who are hungry now. Blessed are you who are persecuted, rejected, ignored, and demeaned. Blessed are you who preach the Good News to the poor, who do the will of God and believe it with all your heart and soul and mind and strength. Blessed are you who have been brushed by the mercy of God in forgiveness, healing, and hope and pass on that blessing indiscriminately, kneading it into the hard bread of the world.

The blessing first rooted in the body of Mary cannot be held by the womb of the earth. It will push out from there too into the light and declare the goodness of God whose mercies are without end and must be sung of, danced with, and recognized especially in the poor and those cursed and cast off by the world. The ultimate blessing of God is Jesus' resurrection and our own. Blessed are those who believe that the Word of God that has come to us will come true.

Luke's gospel ends with the last instructions of Jesus to go and be witnesses to the kingdom of God, to the words of the prophets and psalms and the Law that were written about Jesus. "He opened their minds to understand the Scriptures" (Lk 24:45). The word, the blessing is found in the scriptures, in the memory of a community and in the minds and hearts of those who hear it, reflect upon it, take it to heart, and practice it. Luke ends with Jesus saying:

> And he went on, "You see what was written: the Messiah had to suffer and on the third day rise from the dead. Then repentance and forgiveness in his name would be proclaimed to all the nations, beginning from Jerusalem. Now you shall be witnesses to this. And this is why I will send you what my Father

promised. So remain in the city until you are invested
with power from above."

Jesus led them almost as far as Bethany; then he
lifted up his hands and blessed them. And as he
blessed them, he withdrew. (Luke 24:46-51)

The last blessing is just another form of the promise to
send the Spirit, the Blessing of God who breathes and lives
among us still. And he is blessing us still. He has only with-
drawn for a while; he will return. Are we ready, we who are
his servants, his faithful friends and close kin in the kingdom
of his Father? Will he find us waiting, our aprons on, the
fields plowed and the sheep tended? Will he find the kingdom of God among us as a shelter for all the poor who have
found blessing among us, as we have found blessing in the
heart of God? The kingdom of God blossoms first among the
poor, then in those who serve them, defend them, and hunger
for the justice of God to be a fuller reality in this world. The
poor count for something with God and when they count for
something with us then the blessing of God blossoms in us
and the kingdom grows strong, until it comes in fullness.

In the meantime, with Mary, we can only cry out, Bless
the Lord, my soul, and all that is within me, bless his Holy
Name. His mercy endures forever. We have heard his Word
and his Word is true. O God, may we be a blessing upon the
earth. Our Father, blessed be your Name. May your kingdom
come among us and be honored in those you seek out and
bend before: the poor and your faithful servants. You wait on
us and serve us. What can we do but turn in blessing, for so
much has been given. We bend before you and sign ourselves
in your power: in the name of the Father and of the Son and
of the Holy Spirit. Amen. Mercy visits us from on high and
seeks us out. Mercy blesses us all. Mercy sings in our midst
still.

Recommended Readings

Eberhard Arnold. *God's Revolution, Justice, Community, and the Coming Kingdom*. Farmington, Penn.: Plough Pub. Co., 1984, 1997.

_____. *Salt and Light: Talks and Writings on the Sermon on the Mount*. Rifton, N.Y.: Plough Publishing House, 1967.

William Barclay. *The Beatitudes and the Lord's Prayer for Everyman*. New York: Harper and Row, 1963.

Michael H. Crosby, OFMCap. *Spirituality of the Beatitudes: Matthew's Challenge for First World Christians*. Maryknoll, N.Y.: Orbis Books, 1980.

The Dalai Lama. *The Good Heart: A Buddhist Perspective on the Teachings of Jesus*. Boston, Mass.: Wisdom Publications, 1996.

Emmet Fox. *The Sermon on the Mount: The Key to Success in Life*. San Francisco: Harper, 1934.

Segundo Galilea. *The Beatitudes: To Evangelize as Jesus Did*. Maryknoll, N.Y.: Orbis Books, 1984.

Helen R. Graham, M.M. *There Shall Be No Poor Among You: Essays in Lukan Theology*. Quezon City, Philippines: JMC Press, Inc., 1978.

Dennis Hamm, S.J. *The Beatitudes in Context: What Luke and Matthew Meant*. Zacchaeus Studies: New Testament. Wilmington, Del.: Michael Glazier, 1990.

A. E. Harvey. *Strenuous Commands*. Xpress Reprints. London: SCM Press, Ltd, 1990.

Herman Hendrickx. *The Sermon on the Mount: Studies in the Synoptic Gospels*. London: Geoffrey Chapman, 1984.

Joachim Jeremias. *The Sermon on the Mount*. Facet Books. Philadelphia: Fortress Press, 1963.

John Paul II. *On the Coming of the Third Millennium: Tertio Millennio Adveniente*. Apostolic Letter, November 10, 1994. Washington, D.C.: USCC.

R. David Kaylor. *Jesus the Prophet: His Vision of the Kingdom on Earth.* Louisville, Ky.: Westminster/John Knox Press, 1994.

Thaddeé Matura. *Gospel Radicalism: The Hard Sayings of Jesus.* Maryknoll, N.Y.: Orbis Books, 1984.

The Millennium Jubilee. London, England: CAFOD, 1996.

Alan Robinson. *The Treasures of Jesus: A Meditation on the Sermon on the Mount.* Kildare, Ireland: St. Paul's, 1994.

Richard Rohr, with John Bookser Feister. *Jesus' Plan for a New World: The Sermon on the Mount.* Cincinnati, Ohio: St. Anthony Messenger Press, 1996.